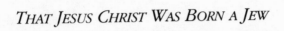

THAT JESUS CHRIST WAS BORN A JEW

Katherine Sonderegger

THAT JESUS CHRIST WAS BORN A JEW

Karl Barth's "Doctrine of Israel"

The Pennsylvania State University Press
University Park, Pennsylvania

Library of Congress Cataloging-in-Publication Data
Sonderegger, Katherine.
   That Jesus Christ was born a Jew : Karl Barth's "Doctrine of
Israel" / Katherine Sonderegger.
      p.   cm.
   Includes bibliographical references and index.
   ISBN 0-271-00818-0 (alk. paper)
   1. Barth, Karl, 1886–1968—Contributions in theology of Judaism.
2. Judaism (Christian theology)—History of doctrines—20th century.
I. Title.
BT93.S66   1992
231.7'6—dc20   91–25100
                                                                CIP

It is the policy of The Pennsylvania State University Press to use acid-free paper
for the first printing of all clothbound books. Publications on uncoated stock
satisfy the minimum requirements of American National Standard for
Information Sciences—Permanence of Paper for Printed Library Materials,
ANSI Z39.48–1984.

CONTENTS

To Sandy Vivian

PREFACE

Judaism and Christianity "have to do" with one another. That simple but profound fact guides the field now known as the "Jewish-Christian dialogue." It is a field that calls for passion and commitment, but demands restraint as well. The pioneers in this area, from Franz Rosenzweig and Martin Buber to the architects of *Nostra Aetate,* demonstrate the moral urgency and the theological deliberation that marks all genuine progress in this field. Their work makes possible a Judaic understanding of Christianity and a Christian reappraisal of Judaism that are at once tough-minded, secure in their traditions, and mutually respectful of the irreducible reality of one another. To this vibrant and expanding conversation, I hope to add the rich and often relentless voice of Karl Barth.

No easy companion in life, in theology Karl Barth was even more demanding. His is a fully *dogmatic* understanding of the people Israel, drawing Judaism into the compass of Christology and refashioning the doctrines of election and reprobation into the form of a covenant people "passing away" and rising to life in Christ. This stern anti-Judaism, however, does not stand alone. Barth was a lifelong opponent of anti-Semitism, a leader in the Confessing Church, and, at the end of his life, a strong supporter of the state of Israel. Indeed, his solidarity with Jews and his rejection of Judaism are of a piece. A theologian, Barth wrote, cannot proclaim Christ apart from the people to whom he came, by whom he was rejected, and to whom he belongs, properly and eternally. *How* this Christological redescription of

Judaism works is the subject of this book. To capture some of the power of Barth's massive project; to convey some of its vibrant life; to draw the reader into the complex beauty that real theological seriousness creates: these are the hopes of this book.

I am fortunate to have many people to thank. My warm thanks and gratitude for many hours of work and many gestures of support:

To my teachers at Brown University, who guided my graduate work; and especially to Wendell Dietrich, my dissertation director, who taught me by example the rigor and beauty of scholarship, and opened up for me the complex worlds of Christian and Judaic thought.

To my colleagues at Middlebury College, Robert Ferm, Robert Schine, and Larry Yarbrough, who read my revisions, commented on and corrected my text, and led me away from many pitfalls. They have taught me what collegiality really means.

To the librarians at Starr Library, Middlebury College, for their patient, reliable, and untiring search for the materials I needed for this book.

To two anonymous readers who offered insightful and thorough criticism of first drafts, and made this a better book.

To Fritz Rothschild of Jewish Theological Seminary and David Novak of the University of Virginia, two readers of subsequent drafts who commented on and graciously supported my work.

To Philip Winsor, my editor at Penn State Press, who guided me throughout a long, and—for a beginner—bewildering process and landed me safely on the other shore.

And to my friends and family, to Sandy Vivian to whom I gratefully dedicate this work and whose love and encouragement have made a difficult task possible, and turned a heavy load into a joyful commitment: Thanks to you all.

INTRODUCTION

In a collection of documents devoted to the "Jewish-Christian encounter," Frank Talmage introduces Karl Barth—a theologian he places "versus Israel"—with a stinging critique. In the preface to his selection from Barth's writings, Talmage draws a somber comparison:

> Selection 6 is taken from Barth's *Church Dogmatics*. Written during the Holocaust, it seems that—as in the past—the very misery and suffering of European Jewry is called upon as a witness to Christianity. Whether this can be ascribed to human frailty [as Michael Wyschogrod does, assigning at least some of Barth's "anti-semitism" to "human frailties"] is left to the reader to decide. The fact remains that on this topic the thinking of a Christian anti-nazi and that of a Christian nazi are not very far apart.[1]

These are words of uncompromised seriousness; but Talmage's brief against Barth could be stronger still. As Michael Wyschogrod has noted, Barth was "ambivalent" about Judaism and Jews as well,[2] and he demonstrated himself

---

1. Frank E.Talmage, ed., *Disputation and Dialogue: Readings in the Jewish-Christian Encounter* (New York: KTAV Publishing, 1975), 38.

2. Michael Wyschogrod, "Why Was and Is the Theology of Karl Barth of Interest to a Jewish Theologian," in *Footnotes to a Theology: The Karl Barth Colloquium of 1972,* ed. Hans-Martin Rumschiedt (The Corporation for the Publication of Academic Studies in Religion in Canada, 1974), 107.

more than capable of unrestrained debate over the *Judenfrage* and the "disobedience, arrogance and stubbornness" of the "Synagogue." His anti-Judaism is as tough-minded as any in the Christian tradition, and his well-known contempt for Liberalism honed his disdain for Christian "tolerance" of the "Jewish religion." Barth's ambivalence, however, was no mere "object of thought"; it had a personal dimension.

Like many German speakers of his generation, Barth was uncomfortable in the presence of Jews. Late in life, he wrote to his younger colleague and disciple, Friedrich Marquardt, that he suffered from a kind of "allergic reaction" to Jews, even "Jewish-Christians" [*Judenchristen*], an affliction Barth seemed genuinely to regret but was not surprised to find.[3] He wondered whether his condition "retarded" his doctrine, a charge Marquardt and others have leveled against Barth.[4] This is not, however, a charge of anti-Semitism; neither Barth nor his critics have gone so far. Though hardly a "philo-Semite,"[5] Barth was never tempted by Nazi ideology of any kind, and his active resistance to "German-Christianity," in fact, gave his theology a moral integrity from which a generation of Christians drew strength.[6] All the same, Barth's work may have been "retarded" by his superficial knowledge of Judaic thought.

Barth admired Marquardt's familiarity with "Baeck, Buber, Rosenzweig and so on" but found that his own thoughts were so taken up by "Israel" that he could not find time to study them.[7] And we should not be distracted from this point by Barth's knowledge of Hermann Cohen, the great Judaic thinker of the prewar years. In his student days, Barth came under the influence of the Marburg neo-Kantians; the technical vocabulary of Hermann Cohen's neo-Kantianism, and its respect for the share of ethics in Reason, pervades

3. Karl Barth, *Briefe, 1961–1968*, vol. 5 of *Gesamtausgabe*, ed. J. Fangmeier and H. Stoevesant, (Zurich: Theologischer Verlag, 1975), letter 260, p. 421.

4. Ibid. For reactions to Barth's positions on Judaism, see Friedrich Marquardt, *Die Entdeckung des Judentums für die christliche Theologie: Israel im Denken Karl Barths* (Munich: Christian Kaiser Verlag, 1967), particularly par. 5; and Wyschogrod, "Why Was and Is the Theology of Karl Barth of Interest to a Jewish Theologian"; and for an interpretation of Barth as a theologian "versus Israel," see Talmage, ed., *Disputation and Dialogue,* esp. his bibliographic essay, 361–91.

5. Barth's term, *Briefe, 1961–1968,* letter 260, p. 421.

6. Two recent publications offer sobering contrasts to Barth's conduct during the war years: Thomas Sheehan's comprehensive review of Heidegger's nazi period, "Heidegger and the Nazis," *New York Review of Books,* 16 June 1988, 38–47; and Paul de Man's anti-Semitic articles in his *Wartime Journalism, 1940–1942,* ed. Werner Hamacher, Neil Hertz, and Thomas Keenan (Lincoln: University of Nebraska Press, 1988).

7. Barth, *Briefe, 1961–1968,* letter 260, p. 420.

The Epistle to the Romans.[8] Cohen's explicitly religious works, like Kant's own, were reserved for the end of his life; *Religion der Vernunft aus den Quellen des Judentums* was published in 1919, long after Barth's student years.[9] But Barth could scarcely have read Cohen after that time. His reduction of Judaic monotheism to a false love of the number one betrays no acquaintance with Cohen's complex attempt to avoid just that delusion.[10] Cohen remained a philosophical, not a Judaic, thinker in Barth's world. But the scholarly study of Judaism did not occupy much room in the German university curriculum, and Barth was not alone in his ignorance of modern Judaism.[11] Franz Rosenzweig's own early work reveals deep and shrewd acquaintance with German Academic Theology; his celebrated "conversion" to Judaism prompted a similar study of Judaic sources.[12] Barth's harsh and unreconciled criticism of the Synagogue, then, does not reflect the scholar's rejection of Judaic systematic thought. Rather, Barth reveals in his own magisterial way the Christian obsession with Judaism, marked, as all obsessions are, by the controlling ambivalence of deep hostility and deep, unshakeable attachment. It would be a lifelong affair.

Years after the war, Barth was prepared to meet Jacob Petuchowski's sympathetic questioning with testy replies. "I have a question in my mind," Petuchowski begins. "St. Paul, speaking in Athens, said to the Athenians who worshiped the unknown God, that that unknown God whom they worshiped

8. For a summary of Marburg neo-Kantianism and its influence on Barth's early work, see Simon Fisher, *Revelatory Positivism? Barth's Earliest Theology and the Marburg School* (New York: Oxford University Press, 1988), particularly chaps. 1 and 4.

9. *Religion der Vernunft aus den Quellen des Judentums,* 2d ed. (Frankfurt am Main: J. Kauffmann, 1929); *Religion of Reason out of the Sources of Judaism,* trans. and ed. S. Kaplan (New York: Frederick Ungar, 1972).

10. Barth uses this criticism frequently; see "God's Threeness in Oneness," in *The Church Dogmatics,* ed. G. W. Bromily and T. F. Torrance (Edinburgh: T. and T. Clark, 1936–69), vol. 1, part 1, par. 9.2, pp. 406–23 [*Kirchliche Dogmatik* (Zurich: Evangelischer Verlag Zöllikon, 1932–70), vol. 1, part 1, par. 9.2, pp. 373–88]. For Cohen, see "God's Uniqueness," in *Religion of Reason,* sec. 1.

11. A notable exception to this rule is G. L. B. Sloan's "Das Problem der Judenmission und die dialektische Theologie," in E. Wolf and A. Lempp, eds., *Theologische Aufsätze* (Munich: Christian Kaiser Verlag, 1936), 514–23, in which Sloan seeks, in the style of Franz Delitzsch, to strengthen the Christian mission to the Jews through a more careful study of Judaic tradition and thought. Sloan contrasts such contemporaries as Martin Buber and Hans-Joachim Schoeps—with the "Barthian" Schoeps the clear victor—and buttresses his argument with a polemical discussion of Judaic thought from Mendelssohn to Cohen.

12. For his interpretation of the German Protestant tradition, see "On the Possibility of Experiencing Miracles," in *The Star of Redemption,* trans. W. Hallo (Notre Dame: University of Notre Dame Press, 1985), 93–111. For his "return to Judaism," see Nahum Glatzer, *Franz Rosenzweig: His Life and Thought* (New York: Schocken Books, 1961).

was the very one whom he, Paul, was preaching to them. It seems to me that Paul made some kind of identification there, and it would be rather strange if he would now be guilty of the kind of idolatry of mixing up Baal with Yahweh, of which we have just heard." "I wonder," Barth retorted, "that a Jewish theologian should say such a thing to me." Jaroslav Pelikan, the panel moderator, appeared to mediate: "You quoted his Bible—now he can quote yours." "Yes, yes," Barth replied, and though his voice is silent, we can imagine the flash of impatience from his brief reply.[13] Never an easy companion in thought and I suspect in life, Barth's dogmatic interpretation of Judaism will not find ready acceptance in modern theological circles, nor will it be free from offense. Barth, of course, never shied at causing controversy or giving offense, but such polemics belong to Barth alone; we belong to another time, another generation, and our questions must receive new answers.

Talmage's preface poses a serious question. Should Barth, in our day and with our understanding, be given a voice in the current study and reappraisal of Judaism within Western religious thought? Should Barth, "hardly the philo-Semite," the Christian theologian "too busy with Israel" for Judaic thought, the polemical and unyielding anti-Judaic dogmatician—should this Barth be offered a platform and an attentive ear? Or should such a voice fall silent, or remain instructive perhaps, even challenging, but, as an "ambivalent opponent to Israel," be heard only as speaking from the remove of an honored but irretrievable past?

I raise this question this way to close off a possible avenue of escape: the route of the disinterested or objective scholar. This ideal, pressed on us by the heirs of Enlightenment liberalism, has come under attack recently, but the criticism is not new. Indeed, by the close of the nineteenth century, the anguished pursuit of historicism by the great European modernists had made this ideal all but unattainable. Much has been written on this topic, and I could not pretend to do it justice here. But I am far from urging contempt for this model of detached objectivity; it remains for me a genuine ideal. Nevertheless, Barth's interpretation—and rejection—of Judaism should not be studied simply because his writings intrinsically merit attention as objects of academic study. The history of our troubled century has closed the door on such self-justifying arguments.

The decision to study Barth, and study him on this particular, neuralgic

13. All these exchanges are recorded in "Introduction to Theology," *Criterion,* no. 1 (Winter 1963): 3–11, 18–24, a transcript of Barth's reply to questions following his lectures at the University of Chicago in 1962 during his only visit to the United States.

point, must justify itself on other grounds. Barth himself preferred what we might call "engaged objectivity." In a celebrated and controverted remark, Barth urged the work of dogmatics to continue through the war "as if nothing had happened"; yet he remained deeply committed to the ideas and struggles of his day. Like his teachers, the generation of the great Protestant Liberals, Barth was a socialist, and, for brief periods, a party member. He was an early opponent of Nazism—he seemed to recognize early on its menace and power—and gave direction and theological precision to the Confessing Church in its opposition to Aryan Christianity. Late in life, Barth vigorously supported the state of Israel, defending both politically and theologically its "right to existence." Yet this political activity found scant mention in the *Church Dogmatics,* the major work of his mature years. He denied a place within the inner courts of theology to such commitments; they were for him a form of "natural theology"—hardly a compliment coming from Barth! This combination of character and work—this engaged partisanship in worldly matters and principled rejection of worldly matters as the substance of theology—this dialectic of "engaged objectivity" gives Barth's life and thought particular value for religious studies, an example of the complex tie between theory and practice. A study of Barth's "doctrine of Israel" finds its justification here.

This relationship between theory and practice, or, more polemically, between knowledge and power, is a troubled one, and like any partnership of long standing I suppose, imperfectly understood. The ambiguities, significance, and complexity of this relationship richly deserve the attention they have received, and no simple answer will do them justice. Barth's dogmatic "doctrine of Israel," placed within the knowledge and powers of his day, is the concrete material for this debate, and offers a picture of real complexity for the Christian encounter with and reappraisal of Judaism. It is too easy to assume that Christian claims for final revelation in Christ, for example, are a "problem" that demands resolution or removal, because such claims lead sooner or later to anti-Semitism. This is boldly stated. Few theologians make such bald and direct connections between theory and practice. But many reformulations of systematic doctrine within the Jewish-Christian dialogue draw a moral urgency from unstated convictions of this kind.

The enormity of the destruction of European Jewry cannot be questioned nor can the implications of it be exhausted; such a recognition is mandated of any Christian. But the study of Barth's *Israellehre* opens two paths for theological reflection: Must Christian anti-Judaism be considered and extirpated as an early stage of anti-Semitism? More somberly, should Christians be allowed to "make use" of the Holocaust, if only as a lever in the machinery of reform? The life and thought of even so complex and masterful a figure as Karl Barth holds no answer to these questions; indeed, they seem unanswerable at our present stage. Barth's life and work, however, can raise these questions for modern scholars in an acutely discomforting way. As Barth might say, they can *only* do this, but they *can* do it.

But Barth's dogmatic interpretation of Judaism offers more than a particularly compelling object lesson in the relation of theory to practice. Though Barth is not, strictly speaking, the "last, great Christian supersessionist," he nevertheless rehearses, with a theological precision and passion that are his own, the interior language and logic of the classic Christian description of Israel and the Jews. The medieval inheritance of the Christian West—the language and world view of the ghetto and the blindfolded Synagogue—find their place in Barth's thought, and are put to work. So too are the great themes of the Christian exegesis of the people Israel: its election and covenant, its Word of Law and Prophet, its mission and light to the nations, and, more starkly, its rejection, disobedience, and sinful history from the days of Exile to the destruction of the Temple. Barth represents the broadest tradition of Christian anti-Judaism, preserving, sharpening, and elaborating the controversial theology that has been standard in Christian apologetics since Justin Martyr. In this area if no other, Barth merited the title others gave him, and he so reluctantly received, the defender of "neo-orthodoxy." To give close attention to Barth's dogmatic description of Judaism is to hear, in clear, precise, and often dissonant tones, the complex judgment Christianity has passed on its origin and rival. Christian theology has been "ambivalent" about Judaism, a scriptural and dogmatic ambivalence marked by conflict and contradiction, and by the love and fear that drive all obsessions. To read Barth's work carefully and to examine his political life are to discover this thought-world of obsession, spread before us in its power, its weakness, and its stark elegance. To study Barth is to come face to face with the Christian past.

As an ambivalent tradition, Christian anti-Judaism does not remain one-sided; it honors and praises Judaism as Christianity's origin, but rebukes Jewish disbelief. Barth's doctrine of Israel displays this ambivalence with unique power. His is a theology of filial love and rejection, underscoring the grace as well as the judgment that Christians ascribe to the fact that, as Luther wrote, "Jesus Christ was born a Jew." In fact, some students of Barth—Friedrich Marquardt is the most prominent—consider him an advocate and ally of Israel for "discovering Judaism," as Marquardt puts it, "for Christian theology."[14] That Barth's anti-Judaism is actually a type of "pro-Judaism" in its

14. From the title to Marquardt's dissertation, *Die Entdeckung des Judentums für die christliche Theologie.*

Christian form may seem like an odd piece of reasoning, a dialectical position of some daring, but readers of Barth will recognize the form of this argument immediately. From the period of *The Epistle to the Romans* through the years of the *Church Dogmatics,* Barth was inclined to find theological riches in dialectical positions and then deepen and sharpen these contradictions until they turn over into dogmatic strengths.

Consider to what advantage Barth turns the corrosive work of higher criticism. Biblical criticism cannot find the Jesus of history? Well! Barth would say, it is worse than that. The study of history cannot find us anything absolute or secure. All human history is relative, hidden, and passing away. Studying history is like searching the empty tomb: it can only say, He is not here. Such a sorry state is a theological strength; when all human powers fail, we turn to revelation, the gracious act of the God who has already turned toward us. Such dialectical argument was very nearly a frame of mind for Barth, a congenial and stable vision of Christian reality. We might expect Barth's anti-Judaism to proceed in just this familiar and unsettling way, but it does not.

Rather, Barth's doctrine may be called a "discovery of Judaism for theology" for reasons within and without Christian dogmatics. It places "Israel" at the center of the Christian proclamation of grace and presents it as the ground of Christian response to the world. Within dogmatic expression, Barth's anti-Judaism is taken up into the language of justification by grace alone. Though Judaism, in its forms as "Israel" and as "Synagogue," is an archetype of disobedience and rejection, it does no more than exemplify the sinful, fallen nature of all creatures. Jews are sinners; in the *Epistle to Romans,* the highest example of the religious sin of self-achievement. But it is to sinners of just this kind, Barth writes, that God turns in Christ. God's gracious act of reconciliation—the election of the creature in Christ—is a work of condescension. The Creator bends down to the creature, taking its part, standing in its place: the Judge is judged in its place. From the beginning of his break with Liberalism to the end of his career, Barth found this central movement of grace—from the Just to the unjust, from the Humble and Obedient to the proud and disobedient—described the nature, goal, and Christological identity of the One who loves in freedom. That the Jews are sinful and proud, that they reject their Messiah, that they persist in rejecting this End of their Law, that they will go their own way and make their own path, that Judaism represents these people and these acts merely confirms their eternal election as the flesh that Christ will bear, and the sins that Christ will bear away. Barth's anti-Judaism "discovers" Judaism within dogmatics because it defines the people Israel as the witness to creaturely sin and as the living reminder of the Messiah who will graciously reconcile the creature apart from merit.

As an expression of Christian address to those beyond the Church, critics find in Barth's doctrine of Israel a new openness toward Judaism because it redirects Christian doctrine towards its source and biblical type. There is an irony here, as Barth would be quick to point out. A theological position, both traditional and conservative, has been discovered—by some—to be more radical and progressive than its Liberal opponent. Such an argument certainly works "against the stream." The urbane concepts of Protestant Liberalism, those refined ideals of "religious consciousness" and the "spiritual world view" appeared to offer Judaism a new freedom within the Christian West. Christians could be called to extend tolerance, indeed sympathy to it, as a distinct and distant religious form, an utterance of the one experience of piety in a different speech. Barth, however, would find little to treasure in such sentiments. To treat Judaism as a religion, or even as a particular form of world religion, to which Christian theology owes toleration and deference is, to Barth's mind, error and insult. In a way characteristic of him, Barth reached behind the Enlightenment to revive doctrines that critique and correct modern thought. Like many cultural critics, Barth treated the elegant ideals of Liberalism with distrust. Not too far beneath the husk of toleration, he taught, lay the kernel of quiet contempt and preening self-satisfaction. Indeed, Liberals like Friedrich Schleiermacher and Adolf Harnack looked to the common property of the nineteenth century, the theme of development, to free the spirit of Christianity from the letter of "Jewish legalism" and "externality." Judaism was a lower form of religious piety and order from which the Christian consciousness, nurtured in faith and its own "inestimable worth," had emerged and must now separate. Barth took delight in stinging bourgeois piety. He would have appreciated, I think, the left's dismissal of *tolerance* as the consolation Liberals offer those they consider inferior, those they would prefer to forget. Barth's own position was both more radical and conservative than the theological liberals who defined for him the bourgeois world he would honor *and* reject.

Judaism cannot be a religion, Barth claimed, separate from, inferior to, or, under its own terms, equal with Christianity. In Barth's eyes, it cannot—strictly speaking—be considered a religion at all. It has no independent existence or reality, no separate identity before which Christians should feel the respect that belongs to something truly foreign. "Israel" and the "Church," Barth writes, belong together in the "one community of God." They are two forms of that one body, distinct and distinguishable, but not divisible. Together, as one people, one "environment" of Christ, the two forms represent the history, the promise, and the gracious atonement made complete and concrete in Christ. The God the Bible speaks of is the God of Israel; there is no other. It is to this people of the covenant, in their history and in their flesh, that God elects to come. Christians who imagine they worship another God, that they belong to another covenant, that they possess another identity have betrayed and lost claim to the Jew, Jesus, the Messiah of the house of Israel. The Church that has welcomed or permitted anti-Semitism, Barth warned, has called upon itself its own judgment. Called from Jew and Gentile, the Church is a gracious engrafting of the nations of the earth onto the elected people of Israel. Conforming his doctrine to the classical interpretation of Romans 9 through 11, Barth repeats the great pauline themes: the "Synagogue," though disobedient, retains the promise and election of God; the "Church," though confounded by this disbelief, retains its gift of grace; the last days, though hidden with the mystery of God in Christ, will finally bring all Israel to its elected End. Until this time of consummation, the one body of Christ remains broken into pieces called Church and Synagogue, but no human category of religion or history can subsume or make relative this single community and its calling in Christ.

This final turn in Barth's argument, the unifying of Judaism and Christianity under one biblical category, the body of Christ, constitutes the "discovery of Judaism" in what I have called the form of "Christian address to the world." Barth's position, however, hardly seems a study in the new "Christian openness," or nondogmatic irenics. Barth's doctrine of Israel achieves its significance for the realm outside the Church not in spite of but because of its severity and unyielding rigor. It is a voice—uncompromising, sometimes harsh, and invaluable—that deserves a hearing in the arena Talmage describes as the "Jewish-Christian encounter." This movement toward reconciliation and dialogue between Christianity and Judaism is built on two supports. It cannot be understood apart from theological reflection on the Holocaust,[15] but drew fresh energy from the Second Vatican Council. In a brief, but remarkable document on the "relation of the Church to non-Christian religions," *Nostra Aetate* repudiated the "teachings of contempt" against Jews, and pressed the Catholic interpretation of Judaism onto new ground.[16] In the decades following the Council, Catholics have driven the developments in the "Jewish-Christian dialogue" forward into fresh theolog-

---

15. As might be expected, this impetus for reconsideration of Judaism within theology is felt most keenly by Europeans, and by Germans in particular. Pannenberg, Moltmann, Metz, Küng, and Schillebeeckx find their place here, as do many of Barth's disciples.

16. Vatican II, *Nostrae Aetate,* 28 October 1965; English text in Austin P. Flannery, ed., *Documents of Vatican II* (Grand Rapids, Mich.: William Eerdmans, 1984), 738.

ical debate and into the consciousness and conscience of American Protes-
tants as well. *Faith and Fratricide,* Rosemary Ruether's searing indictment of
Christian contempt for Judaism, staked out the territory on the left of this
debate, and laid out the charge with passion and scope that Christology
ignites the fire of Christian anti-Semitism.[17] The person and work of Jesus
Christ—the traditional focus of Christology—has dominated much recent
debate in the dialogue, and has directed fresh attention to the burden and
benefit of Christian claims about Christ.

In its classical form, the rich and highly technical language of Christology
creates remorseless and often contradictory sets of allegiances. The historical
setting of Jesus' life and teaching—that he was a first-century Palestinian
Jew—may reawaken Christian theology to its Judaic origins. Such historical
consciousness may entail a respectful turn toward Judaism, an honoring of a
common text and covenant. Some Christians within the Jewish-Christian
dialogue have insisted upon this concrete and often unwelcome fact—that
Jesus was born a Jew—casting off the colorless and wholly abstract Christology they see rising up from the axioms of philosophical reason.[18] They may,
in concert with Ruether, petition that this fact become the whole of the
Christian proclamation about Jesus: that he was a prophet from the house of
Israel. Indeed, this insistence upon the "historical particularity" of Jesus has
been seen as the tool to free Christianity from the confinement of "realized
eschatology," the claim of classical Christology that Jesus will not become the
Christ at the end of time, but is *now* and eternally the Christ. In Ruether's
judgment, such "realized Christology" defines the rift between Christianity
and Judaism. To see in this "historical Jesus" a Christian commitment to
Judaism is to form one Christological allegiance, a favored one among
Christians in the dialogue with Judaism.

On the other hand, the language of Christology may invite another, less
favored allegiance. Some theologians, considering the place of Christianity
within the world's religions, have shied away from such concrete, historical
particularity, laying claim to the broad, humanistic categories that Harnack
considered the Christian inheritance from hellenism.[19] While unexpected,
such unstated efforts to idealize Christology may in the end represent an

17. Rosemary Ruether, *Faith and Fratricide* (New York: Seabury Press, 1974).

18. This position dominates the Christology of most theologians within the Jewish-Christian
dialogue. For a summary of several positions in this line of argument, see John T. Pawlikowski,
Christ in the Light of the Christian-Jewish Dialogue (New York: Paulist Press, 1982), esp. chap. 3.

19. Consider, for example, Karl Rahner's "Transcendental Christology" and its relation to
"Non-Christian Religions," in *Foundations of Christian Faith,* trans. William V. Dych (New York:
Seabury Press, 1978), chap. 6.3 and 10.

instinct not altogether foreign to the dialogue itself. Consider the intractable anti-Judaism of Christian origins. Reaching back through the debates and trials of medieval Europe to the dialogues of the ancient Church, well into the New Testament itself, the Christian obsession with Judaism has returned, time and again, to this event—that Jesus came to his own, and his own received him not. Indeed, the themes of betrayal and rejection dominate the Christian interpretation of the lives of the prophets, bringing to a climax the canonical movement from promise to New Testament fulfillment. To emphasize the particular in the person and work of Jesus—that he was a Jewish prophet—is to bring Christology face to face with this theme of betrayal and rejection and its sharp condemnation of Israel. To "universalize" the life of Jesus, to expand—but not deny—his particularity is, in this line of argument, to break Christianity free of its obsession and let the cool air of "comparative religions" flow into closed quarters. If Christianity is not to disappear as a theological system, one could argue, if it is to lay claim to coherent doctrines, and advance its own self-understanding, Christology must endure and take its place in the public, pluralistic domain.[20] The hard work of theological debate and reconstruction—the material progress of the Jewish-Christian dialogue—begins here. I have only sketched the Christological allegiances that support their detailed work, and to which Barth's dogmatic claims may add background and a sharpened perspective.

Like the German academic theologians before him, Barth placed Christology at the center of his work; indeed, he inscribed the nature and history of Judaism with the mark of Christology. So massive an experiment in Christology exposes the deep reserves in such doctrinal concentration, opening up the complexity of this debate. In my judgment, the Christian encounter with Judaism can only be enriched by a study of such a "thoroughgoing Christology" as Barth's. I do not intend to offer Barth as a flawless exponent of Christian doctrine, nor even as a "Christian classic" who demands respectful attention. Indeed, though theology is, for me, a field of rare beauty and power, I do not assume that the Jewish-Christian dialogue is, above all, a theological encounter, nor do I wish it so. As Schleiermacher so wryly observed, religion could hardly be at heart a matter of knowledge, since the scholar would then be the best Christian—"and no one will admit this to be the case!" The political and moral forces that drive Christianity to reinterpret and encounter Judaism are inescapable and unsurpassable; I consider my

---

20. The proposals David Tracy advances in *The Analogical Imagination: Christian Theology and the Culture of Pluralism* (New York: Crossroad Publishing, 1981) show signs, I think, of this form of argument, particularly in Part I.

own religious history incomprehensible without them. I count theology as one of these, one force among others, but with a dignity and coherence all its own. "Theology has its own theme," Barth used to like to say. That methodology is appropriate here, too. The Jewish-Christian dialogue may find rich theological rewards in the study of Barth. He is anti-Judaic, yet not anti-Semitic; he makes full Christological claims, yet will not allow Christianity a life without Judaism; he denounced Nazism; he supported the state of Israel; he honored and extended the full compass of Christian doctrine, but from beginning to the end, Barth called for "Jewish-Christian solidarity, today!" These are reasons enough to study Barth, but he offers more.

That Barth took theology seriously is a commonplace, an understatement, perhaps, in the face of a life's work of over ten thousand pages of dogmatics. But Barth's seriousness should not be overlooked in the Christian reappraisal of Judaism. In Barth's hands, the Christian thought-world unfolds slowly and elaborately before us, each dogmatic segment opening up leisurely for our inspection and our reflection. The rhythm of the loving detail of Christian speech imitated what Barth called "God's time for the creature." The theologian has time in which to work, to "hasten and to wait," because God gives it, freely and abundantly. Nothing will be lost, but all will be preserved, enriched, enjoyed. I believe this to be Barth's true gift to theology: the great freedom in his dogmatic work; its open expanse that stretches out on all sides, in method, in historical criticism, in history of doctrine; its patient, confident and complex description of Christian reality. When encountering the world, Christian thinkers are too ready to give ground, too quick to pare Christian claims to their "essence." I hardly mean to dismiss flexibility or good will in theological work; indeed, I hope to encourage it. In theology, genuine progress can be achieved only by paying out the scope it deserves. For that reason alone, I believe that Barth offers a theological "way of life" to those within the Christian-Jewish dialogue, a way marked by full theological seriousness and the deliberate leisure that makes Christian systematics inexhaustible and joyful. Barth's doctrine of Israel deserves such a careful, critical, and patient hearing.

Such a hearing has unexpected benefits. The reappraisal of Barth's life and thought, now twenty years after his death, has shown itself to be slow work all its own. Each piece of Barth's theology must be carefully tested. Each must find its proper place. Barth's interpretation of Judaism, another piece, provides a site to review his central doctrines—election, the "analogy of faith," Nothingness, and reconciliation—that give depth and definition to his Christology. His exposition of God's predestinating act in Christ begins with the calling, gathering, and establishing of the people Israel, the realization in creaturely time and space of the God who wills to be with the creature. Barth's affirmation of the ineradicable election of the Jews—an election given witness, he thought, in the founding of the state of Israel—provides fresh material for the interpretation of his doctrine of the divine Being in Act, and the relationship between time and eternity.

Barth's systematic thought, in its very strengths and achievements, contains critical weaknesses that perpetually threaten theology. Consider the claim, so effortlessly endorsed before, that "theology has its own theme." From the period Hans Frei calls the "second break with Liberalism" forward, Barth considered the "best apologetics to be a good dogmatics." Christian theology must take up the language and events of biblical revelation, describe and animate them, enter them fully so that their inner life and logic may come to dominate the believer's own. No "propositions borrowed" from fields outside revelation can determine theology: it must listen to One voice alone. This is a daunting task for theology, and Barth showed sign of the strain. His doctrine of Israel both obeys and betrays his dictum by being more dogmatic and more apologetic than appears at first. In his anti-Judaism Barth takes up the language and imagery of medieval controversy and assumes these caricatures into the interior structure of his dogmatics. Nor was Barth immune to the idiom of the New Romanticism and its volkist ideology, idiom riddled by a self-satisfied and vulgar ignorance of Judaic life and thought. Barth's interpretation of Judaism was constructed from sources within Christianity's resources and received opinions, well outside Jewish self-understanding and analysis. Barth's caricatures of Judaism can serve Christian theology as an object lesson here, as well.

In a celebrated passage, tinged with the sweet melancholy Barth reserved for his deepest passions, he wrote:

> Of all [disciplines] theology is the fairest, the one that moves the head and heart most fully, the one that comes closest to human reality, the one that gives the clearest perspective on the truth which every disciple seeks. It is a landscape like those of Umbria and Tuscany with views which are distant and yet clear, a work of art which is as well planned and as bizarre as the cathedrals of Cologne or Milan. . . . But of all disciplines theology is also the most difficult and the most dangerous, the one in which a man is most likely to end in despair, or—and this is almost worse—in arrogance.[21]

21. The complete English text can be found in *God in Action* (Manhasset, N.Y.: Round Table Press, 1963), 39. This translation is from Eberhard Busch, *Karl Barth: His Life from Letters and Autobiographical Texts,* trans. J. Bowden (Philadelphia: Fortress Press, 1976), 244. I have substituted the more common "discipline" for Bowden's "disciple."

Barth's dogmatic interpretation of Judaism—his confirmation, incorporation, and stark condemnation of the people Israel—captures in one clear, brilliant light this beauty and this danger.

THE
EPISTLE TO THE ROMANS

1

Karl Barth's *Epistle to the Romans* works an odd effect on its readers. From across their great divide, opponents and allies of Barth agree that *Romans* is no work of history. Among the opponents, we may count the historian, Adolf Harnack, and the higher critic, Adolf Jülicher, both great teachers of Barth's Liberal days. Though Barth must have been a prize student—at the University of Berlin, he sat "chained to Harnack"—Barth became a puzzling disappointment after his break with Liberalism. Harnack and Jülicher considered the Dialectical Barth a "despiser of historical criticism," and a modern day "Gnostic." In a well-known review of the first edition of Barth's commentary, Jülicher moved through a list of rather loose synonyms, calling Barth an amateur in text criticism; a "practical exegete" far from the higher realm of "strictly scientific exegesis"; a *Pneumatiker;* a Marcionite; and, in the dismissive kindliness of the *Ordinarius,* a "model for further progress in this field of edifying exegesis."[1] For his part, Harnack does not seem to have read *Romans;* he had, however, read Jülicher.[2] Like Jülicher, Harnack heard in Barth the voice of Marcion preaching the word of the "alien God." Barth's starkly dialectical lecture at Aarau—"Biblical Questions, Insights, and Vis-

1. Adolf Jülicher, "A Modern Interpreter of Paul," in *The Beginnings of Dialectical Theology*, ed. James Robinson, trans. K. Crim and L. DeGrazia (Richmond, Va.: John Knox Press, 1968), 1:73, 78, 79, 74.
2. Hans-Martin Rumschiedt, ed. and trans., *Revelation and Theology* (Cambridge: Cambridge University Press, 1972), 15.

tas"—unsettled Harnack; the open exchange between them in the journal *Christliche Welt* testified to the painful rift that had opened up between teacher and student. Harnack found Barth "unscientific"; incomprehensible; reactionary; and—for Harnack, the deepest cut—unhistorical.[3] To Eberhard Vischer, Harnack confided:

> I saw the sincerity of Barth's speech, but its theology frightened me. . . . The severity of the charges made in that address is still very vivid in my mind. Instead of losing any of its force, it appears to me more and more hazardous, yes, in a way even scandalous. This impression is in no way softened by the consideration that this sort of religion is incapable of being translated into real life, so that it must soar above life as a meteor rushing toward its disintegration.[4]

This affliction of the comfortable delighted Barth in his early days. His letters to Eduard Thurneysen bristle with the enthusiasm of the Young Turk who has skirmished with his elders and captured their high ground.[5] These victories came at some cost. Barth owed much of his breadth and seriousness as a theologian to Harnack and to Wilhelm Herrmann, two descendants of Albrecht Ritschl.[6] As members of a school of thought, Ritschlians were not so much bounded by method or program, as by what we might call an ethos. They sought value in the particulars of history; they drew back from speculation or "metaphysics"; they were marked by a deep earnestness in life and thought, with a conservative strain running throughout. While Barth devoted much of his early career to breaking with neo-Protestants of just this kind, he never lost his family resemblance. Frank admiration dominates his lecture on Herrmann's theological principles,[7] even as his respect for Schleiermacher— another gift from Herrmann—deepened throughout his career. We might say

3. Ibid., 29–31 ("Fifteen Questions to the Despisers of Scientific Theology"), 35–39 ("Open Letter to Karl Barth"), and 52–54 ("A Postscript to My Open Letter to Professor Karl Barth").

4. Agnes Zahn-Harnack, *Adolf von Harnack*, cited in Rumschiedt, *Revelation and Theology*, 15.

5. Barth's correspondence with Thurneysen can be found in James Smart, ed., *Revolutionary Theology in the Making* (Richmond, Va.: John Knox Press, 1963).

6. The comparison should not be pressed too hard. Herrmann had his quarrels with Ritschl's system, and his alliances with Schleiermacher and the Marburgers; Harnack was more the historian than systematic theologian. But Ritschl was a clear, perhaps the dominant, influence on both.

7. Karl Barth, "Die dogmatische Prinzipienlehre bei Wilhelm Herrmann," in *Die Theologie und die Kirche*, vol. 2 of *Gesammelte Vorträge* (Zurich: Evangelischer Verlag Zöllikon, 1957), 240–84.

that Barth's piety, his *Tendenz,* was conservative, though his politics certainly were not. To a scholar of such complex and abiding loyalties, the break with the Liberals of his youth must have been bittersweet. "Nevertheless [*Trotzdem*] yours," Herrmann wrote to Barth after the break; and Barth could have signed his name in just this way to his teachers throughout his career. To be considered a traitor to scientific theology, an amateur, an unhistorically minded enthusiast: these are stinging rebukes to a young scholar like Barth. From his assailants, these are serious charges, and Barth takes them as such. In the prefaces to his editions of *Romans,* he returns to them, repeats them, underscores and denies them. "Historical-critical method of Biblical investigation has its rightful place"; "I have nothing whatever to say against historical criticism, I recognize it and once more state quite definitely that it is both necessary and justified." "From the friendly reception by Bultmann I conclude to my very great satisfaction that the original outcry against the book as being an incitement to a Diocletian persecution of historical critical theology was not necessary."[8] His steps were dogged by historically minded critics long after Jülicher and Harnack had quit the trail, from Rudolf Bultmann to Paul Tillich to philosophers of history like Van Harvey. *The Epistle to the Romans* may be a powerful, stirring, perhaps revolutionary work; but a piece of history, these critics agree, it is not.

Barth's allies are hardly kinder. If we group such a loose collection as T.H.L. Parker, H. R. Mackintosh, Thomas Torrance, and Eberhard Busch together as allies, we can search in vain for an interpretation that presents *Romans* as a historical commentary. It is a piece of "theology"—Parker cites Barth here—an address "directed against the neo-Judaism [!] of religion itself, specifically of Protestantism under the sway of Schleiermacher and Ritschl";[9] it is not history that "can be vouched for by scholarly research, working on universally accepted scientific rules . . . [nor] apprehensible by a neutral observer, devoid of faith."[10] *Romans,* to these commentators, is a kind of code: for the pauline term Law, read Religion; for the term Israel, read the Church; for Gospel, read Revelation. Indeed, Torrance's chapter in his work devoted to the early Barth, "From Dialectical to Dogmatic Thinking," portrays *Romans,* after a few cursory glances elsewhere, exclusively in its guise as destroyer; Barth calls up forces from Kierkegaard, Dostoevski, and the Blumhardts, binds them into a company called up to meet, disrupt, and

8. *The Epistle to the Romans*, trans. Edwyn Hoskyns, (London: Oxford University Press, 1933), 1, 6, 16; *Der Römerbrief, 1922* (Zurich: Theologischer Verlag, 1940), v, x, xix.

9. T. H. L. Parker, *Karl Barth* (Grand Rapids, Mich.: William Eerdmans, 1970), 32.

10. H. R. Mackintosh, *Types of Modern Theology* (New York: Charles Scribner's Sons, 1937), 305.

overthrow Protestant Liberalism.[11] Like Barth's critics, his advocates hear
Romans addressing a modern audience, and more, addressing the past as
though it were subsumed and dissolved into the present.

For allies of Barth, such a "flat" interpretation of *Romans* may be fitting: a
battle was on, and these figures were partisans—some more engaged, of
course, than others—and *Romans* was relied upon to supply that day's need.
But this "unhistorical" or "coded" reading of *Romans* appears in those
interpreters at some remove, as well. Hans Frei's dissertation on Barth, *The
Doctrine of Revelation in the Thought of Karl Barth, 1909 to 1922,* describes
Barth's "break with Liberalism" as a movement in two parts, turning away
from "relational theology," in its first part, up through the second edition of
Romans, then turning away from Schleiermacher himself, up through the
first volume of the *Church Dogmatics.* Frei's discussion of the technical vigor
of Barth's thought, of its immersion in Idealism and Liberal method, its
repeated attempts to "overcome" the sophisticated and complex synthesis of
the *Glaubenslehre*—this extended discussion on the development of German
Academic Theology has become a kind of underground source of authority
for students of Barth. Frei's dissertation has been acknowledged in several
recent studies,[12] and a more thorough discussion of the problem of "faith
and history" in Barth's early work could scarcely be imagined. Despite Frei's
careful dissection of Barth's historical understanding of the moments of faith,
both before and after *Romans,* not a single line in the dissertation is devoted
to *Romans* as a commentary—on Paul; on first-century Judaism; on the early
Church; on the interpretation of the Law and Prophets; in short, on the
human and religious past. Like Barth's critics and supporters, Frei tacitly
confirms that *Romans,* for all its attention to the dialectics of history and
revelation, can speak no word about a past that does not address or collapse
into the present. *Romans* is not a commentary, but a work of theological
method, turned out in pauline dress.

All of this is the more remarkable in light of Barth's professed intentions.
Over and over in his prefaces, Barth underlines his commitment to "let Paul
speak":

> The question is whether or no [the interpreter] is to place himself in
> a relation to his author of utter loyalty. Is he to read him, determined

---

11. Thomas Torrance, *Karl Barth: An Introduction to His Early Theology, 1910–1931*
(London: S. C. M. Press, 1962), 48–95.

12. See, for example, Fisher, *Revelatory Positivism?*; George Hunsinger, ed. and trans., *Karl
Barth and Radical Politics* (Philadelphia: Westminster Press, 1976); Rumschiedt, ed., *Revelation
and Theology.*

to follow him to the very last word, wholly aware of what he is doing? . . . Anything short of utter loyalty means a commentary *on* Paul's Epistle to the Romans, not a commentary so far as is possible *with* him—even to his last word. . . . I cannot, for my part, think it possible for an interpreter honestly to reproduce the meaning of any author unless he dares to accept the condition of utter loyalty. To make an oration over a man means to speak over his body, and that is to bury him finally, deeper and without hope, in his grave. No doubt despair leaves no other course open. Indeed there are many historical personages whom it is possible only to speak *about*. Even so, it is still open to question whether the riddle they propound is really due to their obscurity or to our lack of apprehension. . . . Is there any way of penetrating the heart of a document—of any document!—except on the assumption that its spirit will speak to our spirit through the actual written words?[13]

Though Barth's understanding of interpretation varies, we can let this exclamation from the third preface of *Romans* stand—for the moment at least— for the whole. From preface to preface, Barth refuses to waiver: his focus is *Paul;* with Paul and through him, he contemplates the object, the *Sache* of Paul's letter, the "Spirit of Christ." Barth, at least, does not consider *Romans* a book about method in theology, or neo-Protestantism, or cultural criticism after the war; speaking strictly, we might say that Barth does not consider it a book *about* anything, but only a commentary that speaks with and through Paul. With a sly irony, Barth might contemplate the work of his interpreters: their verdict on *Romans* has overruled the author. "Look here for Barth's dialectic of time and eternity," the critics might say, "or for his interpretation of the *krisis* of all things human, but for Paul's view of the Law; for Barth's understanding of Judaism; for the place of the Church in the Graeco-Roman empire, we can only say: Why seek ye the living among the dead?" The past cannot hold its own, they would claim, against this voracious appetite of the present; everything must serve its desires, and be consumed in its ends. That, Barth's interpreters rule, is the force of *Romans*. It is an Idealism of a higher order that raises history from its alien and sovereign past into the design and will of the present. Chained to Harnack, Barth may have been taught the "awe in the presence of history" that was the inheritance of Liberalism,[14] but he seems to have forgotten his lessons. Barth may let Paul speak, but only with the words Barth alone supplies.

13. *Romans*, 17, 18 [*Römerbrief*, xx, xxi, xxii].
14. So Barth cuttingly summarizes his theological education (*Romans*, 9 [*Römerbrief*, xiii]).

Such has been the odd effect of *Romans* on its readers. This agreement between all schools of thought about Barth raises a pressing question about the topic of this chapter. In a book on Barth's understanding of Judaism, is a chapter on *Romans* advisable, or even possible? Can we really learn anything about Barth's interpretation of the Law, the Prophets, the Synagogue, or the Jews and Gentiles of the Empire by reading this commentary on Romans? Might a chapter of this kind be only a form of scholarly deference to the reputation of *Romans* for its power and startling freshness, and to the significance of Romans as the origin of Christian speech about Judaism? Paul's letter, after all, is the *locus classicus* of Christian polemic. Here lies the raw material that was fashioned into the structure of Christian anti-Judaism. The dialectic of letter and spirit; of law and gospel; of hardening and election; of disbelief and the "mystery of the Jews": these abiding categories of Christian judgment and belief concerning the people Israel take their life from Paul's letter to the Romans. We need not assume that Paul intended his letter for this use; indeed, the recent scholarship on Paul suggests that this particular polemic was far from view.[15] But the *use* of Paul's letter can scarcely be disputed: the history of the Christian "doctrine of Israel" is unimaginable without Romans.

So too we might say that Barth's entire work, even the magisterial *Dogmatics,* is inconceivable without his *Epistle to the Romans.* The stark sovereignty and freedom of God; the explosive irruption of election and judgment; the menacing line of death and the "end of all our ways"; the sole majesty of the Word of God; in short, the "joyful sense of discovery" that marks the *Epistle to the Romans* makes this work an obligation and delight to his critics. Far from losing its power as Barth moved on his path, *Romans* secured its hold as the place, the first firm and acknowledged place where everything began. To place these two formative powers together—to read Barth's reading of Paul—especially to those who interpret Christian views of Judaism, appears irresistible and contradictory at once.

A commentary on *Romans* that is "unhistorical" and an "enemy of higher criticism" does not present what Barth might call a "possible possibility" for the study of his understanding of Judaism. We might, after all, concur with Harnack and Jülicher, and see in Barth the Marcionite,[16] unwelcome in the

---

15. The now classic essay, Krister Stendahl, "The Apostle Paul and the Introspective Conscience of the West," *Harvard Theological Review* 56 (1963): 199–215, offers such a reconsideration; the works of W. D. Davies and E. P. Sanders are standards as well.

16. Marcion (d. 160) saw in the God of Israel a kind of primitive demigod, cruel and vacillating, whose dominion over the earth was not given over to the true God, the God of Jesus Christ, gracious and just. Marcion showed affinities with certain Gnostic sects and, like them,

early Church, a heretic, but welcomed as a liberator in the modern.[17] Barth himself felt the attraction of Marcion, and his marked emphasis upon the "moment," the unimaginable newness of revelation made Marcion a sympathetic and tempting companion. But Barth weathered that temptation—the Law is not sin, nor the revelation to Israel of no use—and did so increasingly in his later work. To those aware of Barth's verdict passed on all "religion," "religious experience and history," this is no small victory. Barth's attitude toward Marcion, in fact—a mixture of respect and rejection—can stand for more than Barth's acceptance of the Law; it may serve as our guide along the whole course through *Romans*.

Consider that Barth took the charge of *Pneumatiker* seriously; that he repeatedly denied his opposition to higher criticism; that he meant to study history in earnest and to let Paul speak from his age to ours; and that Marcion approached but finally could not stand in Barth's place. In all, these confessions and denials lead us to consider one final question. Might these controversies, these charges and countercharges, reflect Barth's own questions? Might he, too, be seeking to make theological use of the past, the particular, complex, and human past? Might Barth intend—at least, we can say that—intend to take pharisaic Judaism seriously; to follow Paul the pharisee in his movement toward and away from the Law; to see in Israel, in the prophets and teachers of the Law the ground and source of the Church? Might Barth, in short, seek to make his critics' questions his own; to attempt a commentary, a genuine commentary on Romans? In the preface to the English translation of *Romans,* Barth claims just this:

> It may not be irrelevant if I now make it quite clear both to my future friends and to my future opponents in England that, in writing this book, I set out neither to compose a free fantasia upon the theme of religion, nor to evolve a philosophy of it. My sole aim was to interpret Scripture. I beg my readers not to assume from the outset—as many in Germany have assumed—that I am not interpreting Scripture at all,

wielded great power in the early Church. Like "gnosticism" itself, "marcionism" has come to represent a tendency—or temptation—in Christian thought that repeats itself in times of crisis and is never fully overcome.

17. Thus, Harnack argued in his *Marcion: Das Evangelium vom fremden Gott, eine Monographie zur Geschichte der Grundlegung der Katholischen Kirche* (Leipzig: J. C. Hinrichs, 1921) that the early Church was correct to reject Marcion's repudiation of the Old Testament and Judaism, but the modern Church should not feel itself bound to that decision. The time had come, Harnack announced, to break free of Judaism. *Marcion: The Gospel of the Alien God,* trans. John E. Steely and Lyle D. Bierma (Durham, N.C.: Labyrinth Press, 1990), is a translation of the second (1924) edition.

> or rather, that I am interpreting it "spiritually." . . . I should be
> altogether misunderstood if my readers refused to credit me with the
> honesty of, at any rate, *intending* to *ex*-plain the text. I assure them
> that, in writing this book, I felt myself bound to the actual words of
> the text, and did not in any way propose to engage myself in free
> theologizing. It goes without saying that my interpretation is open to
> criticism; and I hope to hear as soon as possible of important and
> proper criticism of it at the hands of my English-speaking theological
> colleagues. . . . I shall not be impressed in the least by general
> propositions concerning the value or lack of value of my "spiritual
> outlook," or of my "religious position," or of my "general view of
> life." My book deals with one issue, and with one issue only. Did Paul
> think and speak in general and in detail in the manner in which I
> have interpreted him as thinking and speaking? Or did he think and
> speak altogether differently?[18]

Perhaps we may not be able to follow Barth with "utter loyalty," perhaps not
"to the last word." But we may be able to follow the path he points out, the
direction he intends to take. We will ask—*with* Barth, we might say—is this a
commentary on Paul's letter to the Romans, or a "free fantasia" on the theme
of culture-Protestantism?

In our answer, several topics crowd in for attention. Barth's discussion of
Abraham and the promise of election; his treatment of the Law and the
prophets; the engrafting of the Gentiles and the covenant with Israel: each
one demands attention. We might broaden our scope. The influence of the
Marburg neo-Kantians, Hermann Cohen in particular, on the young Barth;
the ethical task that drove the Protestant commitment to culture; the debate
over the prophets that defined Liberal religion, Judaic and Christian; the
category "ethical monotheism" itself—all deserve a hearing. But we will let
these wait their turn. We begin with the theme that Barth placed at the center
of his commentary, the theme that opens up the *diastasis* between heaven
and earth: God's free justification of the ungodly.

"But now apart from the Law the righteousness of God hath been mani-
fested." Barth scans this famous verse, the "Reformation verse," emphasizing
its opening words: " 'But now.' We stand here before an irresistible and all-
embracing dissolution [*Aufhebung*] of the world of time and things and men,
before a penetrating and ultimate *krisis*, before the supremacy of a negation
[*Nicht-Sein*] by which all existence is rolled up. The world is the world; and

18. *Romans, ix, x.*

we now know what that means."[19] Barth hears, in Paul's voice, the decisive word passed over the earth, the judgment and mercy that points to the freedom of God. Throughout the 1920s Barth fought to preserve the sovereignty of God over the claims of religious faith, to free the divine act from the suppositions of human experience. These methodological worries clearly occupy Barth here, but he considers himself taught to worry over just these things by Paul, and by the shattering of Paul by God's act in Christ. The divine grace to the ungodly is the axis upon which the entire letter turns; it is in this act, Barth claims, that "we are broken upon the Godness of God." *Romans* bristles with these evocative and suggestive phrases, and one often wishes Barth could relinquish some power in favor of some clarity. But he is attempting to utter what he considered unutterable—the Word of God—and his prose darkens and breaks in the task. In part, Barth believes that Romans is a letter about election, the election of Jew and Gentile in Christ. The doctrine of election will preoccupy Barth throughout the second volume of the *Dogmatics*—a masterful and creative preoccupation—but even here the theme of election dominates Barth's exegesis.

We might say that "election" is Barth's name for the distinction, the dialectic that separates creature from Creator. Human beings, Barth argued, acted and willed in their own creaturely freedom, but always under the dominion of sin and death. God, however, elects. God is free from human claims of priority and preference; and God is free over the creation, to judge and order it, to call and to choose, to kill and to make alive. Later, Barth will make much of this twofold form of election; indeed, we might say that in the *Dogmatics* it is the sum of the Law and the Prophets. But in *Romans,* Barth is intent on showing that while God is the *Ursprung,*[20] the unimagined Origin of all life and thought, the final Unity of reality and truth, humanity must live and speak only indirectly, in dialectics and disunity.

Barth's dialectics are often treated as a kind of *via negativa*—unsuccessful, of course, in its predications—in which all affirmations of God must be followed by denials, all positive attributes by negative. This interpretation has

19. Ibid., 91 [Römerbrief, 66].
20. This is a term Barth inherited from the Marburg neo-Kantians. Fisher, in *Revelatory Positivism?*, sheds much light on the technical tangles of Cohen and Natorp's Kantianism, and shows clearly, I think, that Barth borrowed freely from its vocabulary. But Fisher, as I understand it, doubts that Barth wishes to use these terms technically, and it seems to me that these doubts are justified. Barth appears to me much more the disciple of Herrmann than of Cohen, and follows Herrmann's freedom in use of philosophical terms. That Barth considered God the unobjective origin and unity of thought and being is plain throughout *Romans*; and perhaps his fondness for mathematical images in the second edition stems from Cohen, but to press the allegiance much beyond this seems unwarranted.

much in its favor. God is mercy *and* judgment; *Yes* and *No;* life and death; election and rejection. In *The Word of God and the Word of Man,* Barth describes the tireless motion of the dialectician, running along a mountain ridge, looking first on one side then the other, pointing to this cliff then the next. Theologians cannot speak directly of God; that can only be done, as Kierkegaard wrote, of idols. In part, Frei too follows this interpretation: "The purpose of 'dialectical' theology is to posit affirmation and negation against each other, so that men may see that God is 'immediate' only in himself, 'identical' only with himself, that all knowledge of God waits upon God himself"; "To a dialectic of objects, magnitudes or realities ('history and experience', 'religion and life', 'life and Bible') Barth now added a dialectic of concepts or judgments. Each affirmative judgment is balanced by a negative judgment with regard to the same object or relation between two objects."[21] We exhaust thought, we submit it to a "self-irony," by holding in tension contradictions without sublation or resolution. In such an exhausted state, thought points away from itself to the unity and freedom of God.

Such a severe, dialectical method of contradiction certainly makes its appearance in Barth's early work; and Barth took too much schooling from German Idealism for its method not to leave its mark. But if Barth's commentary in the second edition of *Romans* is read as a whole, and as an exegesis on Paul, it is striking, I think, how little of this kind of dialectics we actually encounter. "God is in heaven; and thou on the earth" Barth intoned in those years, and it is *this* dialectic—the distinction between Creator and creature— that pulses through *Romans.* Barth rarely understands Paul to teach that God must be addressed in contradiction: God is good and evil; light and dark; being and nonbeing. Rather, Paul teaches that God and creature must not be uttered in one human breath:

> God affirms Himself by denying us as we are and the world as it is. In Christ God offers Himself to be known as God beyond our trespass, beyond time and things and men; to be known as the Redeemer of the prisoners, and consequently, as the meaning of all that is—in fact, as the Creator. He acknowledges Himself to be our God by creating and maintaining the distance by which we are separated from Him; He displays His mercy by inaugurating His *krisis* and bringing us under judgment. He guarantees our salvation by willing to be God and to be known as God—in Christ; He justifies us by justifying Himself.[22]

21. Hans Frei, "The Doctrine of Revelation," dissertation, Yale University, 1956, 3, 132.
22. *Romans*, 40, 41 [*Römerbrief*, 16].

That, Barth writes, is the "Theme", the *"Sache"* of "the Epistle."

With the taste for the concrete that animated all his work, Barth described this *diastasis* between heaven and earth in his early lecture in Aarau:

> We all know the curiosity that comes over us when from a window we see the people in the street suddenly stop and look up—shade their eyes with their hands and look straight up into the sky toward something which is hidden from us by the roof. Our curiosity is superfluous, for what they see is doubtless an aeroplane. But as to the sudden stopping, looking up, and tense attention characteristic of the people of the Bible, our wonder will not be so lightly dismissed. To me personally it came first with Paul: this man evidently sees and hears something which is above everything, and which is absolutely beyond the range of my observation and the measure of my thought. . . .
>
> And if ever I come to fear lest mine is a case of self-hallucination, one glance at the secular events of those times, one glance at the widening circle of ripples in the pool of history, tells me of a certainty that a stone of unusual weight must have been dropped into deep water there somewhere—tells me that, among all the hundreds of peripatetic preachers and miracle-workers from the Near East who in that day must have gone along the same Appian Way into Imperial Rome, it was this one Paul, seeing and hearing what he did, who was the cause, if not of all, yet of the most important developments in that city's future.[23]

A scent of apologetic hovers over this passage, and in the years ahead Barth would move away from it, and many other "relational" claims he makes in this essay. But this address that so startled Harnack, "Biblical Questions, Insights, and Vistas," records the motion in Barth's thought in the period between the two editions of *Romans*. Not only the figure of Paul—first, and perhaps the central—but also the prophets and people Israel stand on center stage: "There were once, a few centuries earlier or later, men who lived by faith like Abraham, who were strangers in the promised land like Isaac and Jacob, who declared plainly that they were seeking a country, who like Moses endured as seeing him who is invisible. There were once men who dared." That Barth had particular, living Jews in mind is unquestioned in this essay:

23. "Biblical Questions, Insights, and Vistas," in *The Word of God and the Word of Man*, trans. D. Horton (New York: Harper & Row, 1957), 62, 63.

People like others, surely, were the people of Israel and Judah, but they were people among whom lofty things were being seen and heard continually, a people among whom attention to a Wholly Other seems never wholly to have lapsed. Or are we suffering from an historical hallucination when we say this? One glance at those mysteriously moved and mobile people, the Jews and Jewish Christians, as they live in our midst today, may serve to teach us that their race must once, certainly, have seen the beginning of new and striking developments.[24]

Those familiar with Christian *Israellehre* recognize this spirit at once: it is the evidence offered to Frederick the Great as proof of God's existence—"Sire, the Jews!" Barth would make constant use of this apology throughout his career; indeed some critics have seen in it the last remnant of "natural theology" in Barth's dogmatic empire.[25] But we need not go that far to assure ourselves that Barth meant to address the historical actors in the Bible. The peoples of Israel and Judah, the Jews of the Second Temple, pharisees like Paul: these are the figures Barth catches sight of, their faces turned to the heavens; they point up, and beyond, and in *Romans* Barth hopes to follow their gaze.

Now, Barth does not attempt to deny that human reality, in itself and apart from the divine *krisis,* is dialectical or bound up in opposition. Throughout *Romans,* he acknowledges the tentative, conflicting, and "questionable" nature of human knowledge and action. In the creaturely realm, the term "dialectics" refers not so much to a hegelian "dwelling in contradiction" as to a world of relativity and gradation that Schleiermacher placed at the heart of human experience. Each experience of freedom over the world is balanced or graded against a dependency upon it; each act of mastery in knowledge is counterweighted with a passive reception of the object through our senses. So also in the realm of piety, sin is recognized by grace; doubt measured by faith; heresy by correct doctrine. This, in part, is what Schleiermacher meant by "mediation": human experience acts as a kind of third party that draws together the opposing forces of the world and mingles them to achieve the balance that makes up the aim of human life. Barth never doubted that this form of Idealism captured worldly experience; but he was quick to sense the relativism that lay just beyond its vision. Combined with his attraction to skepticism and the "anti-theologians," Barth saw these

24. Ibid., 64, 65.
25. Marquardt, "Paradoxien der Verwerfung," in *Die Entdeckung des Judentums,* chap. 5.3.

"dialectics" as the corrosive of certainty. Of the promise to Abraham in Romans 4:23–25, Barth writes:

> But Abraham cannot be our contemporary; he can say nothing to us which we are competent to hear, apart from the radiance of the non-historical. Unless, quite apart from the study of documentary sources, there exists a living perception of the one constant significance of all human occurrence, history becomes merely a sequence of epochs and a series of civilizations; it consists of a plurality of different and incommunicable elements, of separate individuals, ages, periods, relationships, and institutions; it teems with phenomena which charge about in all directions. This is non-sense. . . . A past, marked by a chaos of faces, is not an eloquent, understood, and apprehended past. If history can present no more than this, it is trivial. Be the material never so carefully and critically brought together; be the devotion in delving into the past never so great, and the accuracy of the scholar never so precise; be the understanding of an ancient culture and manner of life never so sensitive, and the sympathy with different point of view thrown up by the past never so delicate—yet this, for all its competence is not history; it is photographed and analysed chaos.[26]

Barth would never leave this view of history behind. Though the *Dogmatics* would quietly drop all talk of the "menacing line of death," this description of human life, caught up in the cycles of seed time and harvest, light and dark, the antinomies of freedom and fate, knowledge and doubt, will remain. The "radiance of the non-historical" or, later, the "grace of Jesus Christ," can alone bind up human life and create out of chaos a covenant, a world of unity and meaning. In *Romans,* the dialectics of experience encased human life in an airless cell. Often blissfully unaware, the prisoners chase about, building fortifications, pursuing projects, calling up volunteers. Or, they recognize their plight, and see all about them life hurtling toward death, good surrounded and corrupted by evil, knowledge and will swallowed up by the mystery and misery of individual life. Who are we? And what are we to do? These are the questions that haunted Barth in these years, questions that could find resolution only Beyond our time and space. As Barth would argue in his address, *"Schicksal und Idee,"* given at the close of the Dialectical period, true philosophy can bring us only to this point—to the antinomies and oppositions that border all human truth. Theology takes up its post at

---

26. *Romans*, 145–46 [*Römerbrief*, 122].

this border, raising the question of God, and posing a dialectic that no philosophical system can overcome.[27]

And it is *this* dialectic, this *krisis* between God and creature that Barth hears addressed in Romans. Critics have often found in the language of dialectics an easy means to attack Barth's position. They understand Barth to argue in *Romans* that God and the creature are *opposites,* that they are defined by their contradiction, and that human sin is sign of God's justice. Emil Brunner, Barth's early ally and later opponent, understood Barth in just this way, presenting a "negative point of contact" between the human *imago* destroyed by sin and restored in Christ. Barth acknowledged in his famous reply, "No!," that such a confusion was possible, likely perhaps, in places throughout *Romans,* but a confusion it remained all the same.[28] Barth intended, at least, to speak not of an external relationship—positive or negative—between God and the creature. That would be to remain on the field of Liberal method: to search for a contrast, an opposition, an immediacy in which God and the world are thought or experienced together. It may be that the common focus of Barth's critics—and at times Barth himself—on Dialectical Theology as a theological *method* invites such confusion. But as a *commentary, Romans* is quite clear. To speak of dialectics in the language of Romans is to speak of election.

Romans teaches Barth that the dialectical relationship between God and the creature is this: that God is revealed and justified through the divine election of the ungodly, apart from the Law. This point is worth stressing. Barth is often thought to teach, in this period, that God and creature have *no* relation, or connection, that God, as the Wholly Other, has broken free of the creature and dwells alone in measureless majesty. Like Brunner's "negative contact," this interpretation of Dialectical Theology places, once again, the emphasis upon human experience—its desolation and misery; its sin and isolation. The Wholly Other would have nothing but wrath for such a creature. Barth roars judgment in *Romans;* there is no doubt about that. But that *No,* in Barth's idiom, rests upon the *Yes.*

God and creature, Barth insisted, *are* related; they are drawn together; and human beings may experience, in faith, just this relation. Barth does not wish to deny this and, over and over, underscores the possibility of faith. But this entire relationship—the experience, the grace, the dwelling together—all

27. "Schicksal und Idee," in *Theologische Fragen und Antworten,* vol. 3 of *Gesammelte Vorträge,* 54–92.

28. Frei discusses just this point in "The Doctrine of Revelation," 179–85. For Barth and Brunner, see *Natural Theology,* trans. Peter Fraenkel (London: Geoffrey Bles, Centenary Press, 1946).

this depends upon what Barth here called the "impossible possibility," divine election. But even this description, "divine election," is too poor a thing for the Subject Barth invokes; it is too static, too "hardened and congealed," to convey the living freedom of this divine act. Better the active voice: God does and will elect. The creature does not possess election, does not carry a "potency" that is realized or "perfected" in grace. Rather, the creature stands *within* election; we are "inside and not outside the knowledge of God," Barth wrote elsewhere. Now, we might press Barth a bit here: just what can it mean to stand "within the knowledge of God"? On this rather enigmatic phrase, after all, turns the entire argument of *Romans,* and the revolution Barth led against Liberal theology.

God elects: if we begin here, and not with the language and presupposition of theological method, we may catch a glimpse of the motion of Barth's thought. God is the Subject of this act, the Origin and End of this decision. The creature is the object of this act; God alone knows human beings, knows them first and in knowing them determines and creates them. As we are known, we are thrown into relief by this light: we see because we are seen. Election depicts a relationship that cannot be reversed: only God elects. And more, the elect cannot be determined from the rejected—individual election, Barth insisted in *Romans,* is a "mythological" category—nor can those determined by election discern, by "a little introspection," their standing before God. To live "inside and not outside" the knowledge of God means that the creation is "bordered" or limited by God, enclosed by the electing will of its Creator. It was a commonplace of Idealism, after all, that the external object exists within the subject, through the mastery of thought. Far from being alienated or sealed off from the divine presence, the world and its human creatures are "hemmed in," encircled and defined by their being known by God. "It is a dangerous thing to fall into the hands of the living God," Barth would repeat throughout his career. We are not forgotten or abandoned by God, floating in the still and silent sea of space, but we are *judged:* known by a God who presses in upon us, an "attacker" who breaks in upon the creature and claims it, who elects to wrath and mercy, to kill and to quicken. The human relationship to *this* God follows the divine initiative. Because God knows and elects, the creature may repent and give thanks. In this way, Barth seeks to place the method of "relational theology" within, not without the circle traced by divine act. Election is the pauline name Barth gives to the divine possibility of faith in God.

But it remains a dialectical, not a direct, possibility. Or, to speak in biblical idiom, God elects the ungodly. Barth understands election as a twofold determination: that electing mercy reveals itself as wrath and that the religious occupy the main theater of this war. Both represent the "qualitative distinction" between God and creature; both carry the "crimson thread" Barth finds in Old and New Testaments, binding together the history of Israel and the Church, Jew and Gentile. They speak of the human condition, that all flesh is grass; and they speak of God, that God loved Jacob and hated Esau. The *krisis* God sets against the creature manifests itself in the overturning of the elder son, the attack upon the religious elite.

Scattered throughout the commentary, Barth focuses this interpretation on Romans 3:1–20, "The Law," and 7:1–25, "The Frontier, Meaning and Reality of Religion." Here Barth sharpens his polemic: that Law stands at the center of religion, from Israel forward; and against this "highest human possibility" God turns in wrath and in electing judgment. But Barth's celebrated and often cited critique of Law stems from Romans 2:14–16:

> The law is the revelation once given by God, given in its completeness. The law is the impression of divine revelation left behind in time, in history, and in the lives of men; it is a heap of clinkers marking a fiery miracle which has taken place, a burnt-out crater disclosing the place where God has spoken, a solemn reminder of the humiliation through which some men had been compelled to pass, a dry canal which in a past generation and under different conditions had been filled with the living water of faith and of clear perception [*vernünftiges Schauen*], a canal formed out of ideas and conceptions [*Begriffe, Anschauungen*] and commandments, all of which call to mind the behaviour of certain other men, and demand that their conduct should be maintained. The men who *have the law* are the men who inhabit this empty canal. They are stamped with the impress of the true and unknown God, because they possess the form of traditional and inherited religion, [*überlieferte oder übernommene Religion*] or even the form of an experience which once had been theirs. Consequently, they have in their midst the sign-post which points them to God, to the *krisis* of human existence, to the new world which is set at the barrier of this world.[29]

A touch of melancholy passes through these lines. Like much Barth wrote in these years, he seems to *wish* he could say more, and more directly than he can. Instead, he points to the outposts that though lost must be held, the intimacy once enjoyed now broken, and to the law that remains in the midst

---

29. *Romans*, 65 [*Römerbrief*, 40].

of human experience, a canal, at one time flowing and now dry, by which a few chosen religious must sit and wait. These religious are Jews—though not only they—who "possess the traditional and inherited religion," for whom piety consists of "conduct," "memory," "concepts," and "commandments." The Law, Barth reasons, is the center of "Israelite religion"; it defines the Jew, guides the religious life forward and back, upholding tradition and recalling God's mighty acts toward Israel. To be sure, this is a definition of the Law governed by pauline pairings—the Law as opposed to Gospel; the Law as guardian til Christ; the letter against the spirit—and reflects both the long tradition of Christian polemic against the Law and the Protestant indictment of "works-righteousness."[30] In short, Barth adopts, and certainly adapts, the pauline presentation of the Law and gives it its distinctive Christian cast. Not the wise and tender guide of rabbinic Judaism, this is the Christian Law of "reckoning" and "conviction of sin," of wrath and deprivation. A Christian interpretation, certainly; but grounded in the prophets and pharisees of higher criticism.

On one side of the Law, one element of "possible possibility" in religious history, lies the Law as the religion of the Pharisee. Here the Law speaks not of loss, not of the empty canal, but of possession, of righteousness as a human possibility. In its lowest form, it is "romantic unbelief," a "mist" of the religious erotic that envelops the no-God of this world, a "pharisaism" Barth savages:

> For the initial misunderstanding [of the fact that the goodness of God leadeth thee to repentance] causes every human thought and word and action, however, pure and delicate, to unite as elements in the composition of one hard and solid lump. There comes into being what is known as the "religious" life, which is regarded as something peculiar, which is contrasted with the life of the generality of men, and which, because it is nothing more than romantic unbelief, has no protections against the enmity of those who despise it. There emerges from the *righteousness of God* of the Prophets the human righteousness of the Pharisees, which is as such ungodliness and unrighteousness. Each concrete and tangible disposition of human affairs so that they may conform to the will of God marks the presence of the

30. For a survey and critique of Protestant exegesis of the Law and pharisaic Judaism as "works righteousness," see E. P. Sanders, *Paul and Palestinian Judaism* (Philadelphia: Fortress Press, 1977), 1–11 ("Paul and Judaism in New Testament Scholarship") and 33–59 ("The Persistence of the View of Rabbinic Religion as One of Legalistic Works-Righteousness").

prophet turned pharisee: he who engages in dispositions of this sort
stands under the authority of him who is No-God, and round him
gather the threatening clouds of the wrath of God. He has falsified his
accounts by failing to disclose how serious his position is. Though he
piles up higher and higher his divine claims, his divine assurance,
and his divine delights, he does but built a Tower of Babel. Behind
the screen of his daily disposing waits the eternal day of wrath and of
the just judgement of God.[31]

The religion of "prophet turned pharisee" stretches back—and forward,
too—through the history of Israel, through the restoration of the Temple,
through the outbreaks of idolatry, through the greatness and pettiness of the
patriarchs to the beginning of the nations, to the "Tower of Babel." For Barth,
the "summary of the Law" as a human story is grasped in this one transformation: the prophet turns pharisee. In the elevation of things human—
conduct, experience, commandment—to the divine realm, the "biblical
personality" communes only with idols, and fashions them out of its own
wealth. Against this personality, this "point of view," the Unknown God
breaks out in wrath. To be religious, to be pious in the house of Israel, is to
be relentlessly, constantly attacked, uprooted, made restless by God.

But Barth does not simply fill up the term "Pharisee" with any content,
like an empty jar put to many uses. From the research and controversy of the
higher critics, Barth borrows two images of the Pharisee that sharpen his
critique: the Pharisee as "reformer" and as "set apart."[32] These portraits hang

31. *Romans,* 60–61 [*Römerbrief,* 35, 36].
32. Barth often passed over in silence the sources of his critical ideas—a frustration to
scholars! For these more modern interpretations of the pharisees, several sources are possible.
Adolf Harnack appears most likely. In the *History of Dogma* (1900; New York: Dover Publications,
1961), 1:68, Harnack offers his own rather cryptic, and lofty footnote to the pharisees:

> It is asserted by well-informed investigators, and may be inferred from the Gospels . . . ,
> and perhaps also from the Jewish original of the Didache, that some representatives of
> Pharisaism, beside the pedantic treatments of the law, attempted to concentrate it on the
> fundamental moral commandments. Consequently, in Palestinian and Alexandrian Juda-
> ism at the time of Christ, in virtue of the prophetic word and the Torah, influenced also,
> perhaps, by the Greek spirit which everywhere gave the stimulus to inwardness, the path
> was indicated in which the future development of religion was to follow. . . . So far as a
> historical understanding of the activity of Jesus is at all possible, it is to be obtained from
> the soil of Pharisaism, as the Pharisees were those who cherished and developed the
> Messianic expectations, and because, along with their care for the Torah, they sought also
> to preserve, in their own way, the prophetic inheritance. If everything does not deceive
> us, there were already contained in the Pharisaic theology of the age, speculations which

together. The Pharisee, far from the well-used caricature of "wooden legalist" or "hypocrite," holds himself apart—to the standards of a "higher righteousness"—in order to restore the people Israel, to reform and renew it. In fact, Barth cheerfully admits that pharisaic Judaism, understood as a part of religious history, represents the essence not only of Judaism, but of early Christianity as well:

> It is . . . a quite sober statement that Paul is making when he asserts that the other Pharisees know and say and represent and possess all that he knows and says and represents and possesses of the Gospel. Nothing that *men* can say or know of the Gospel is "new"; for everything which they possess is identical with what Israel possessed of old. Historically, and when it is treated as the negation of divine revelation, the *New* Testament seems to be no more than a clearly drawn, carefully distilled epitome of the *Old* Testament. What is there is Primitive Christianity which has not its clear parallel in later Judaism [*Spätjudentum*]? What does Paul know which the Baptist did not? And what did the Baptist know which Isaiah did not? . . . Is there anything that we can possess more than the whole fullness of the Old Testament?[33]

---

were fitted to modify considerably the narrow view of history, and to prepare for universalism. The very men who tithed mint, anise, and cumin, who kept their cups and dishes outwardly clean, who, hedging around the Torah, attempted to hedge round the people, spoke also of the sum total of the law. They made room in their theology for new ideas which are partly to be described as advances, and on the other hand, they have already pondered the question even in relation to the law, whether submission to its main contents were not sufficient for being numbered among the people of the covenant.

This remarkable aside—itself an echo of Emil Schürer's position in *The History of the Jewish People in the Age of Jesus Christ*, ed. G. Vermes, F. Miller, and M. Black (*Geschichte des jüdischen Volkes im Zeitalter Jesus Christi*, 1885; Edinburgh: T. and T. Clark, 1979)—may have found its way into Harnack's lectures on dogma that Barth so admired. We also know that Barth had a copy of Hermann Cohen's later work, *Der Begriff der Religion im System der Philosophie* (Giessen: Alfred Töpelmann, 1915), in which the "religion of the Prophets" figures prominently. The English sources for the Christian reconstruction of pharisaic Judaism, though contemporary with *Romans*, are an unlikely influence, as Barth did not read readily in English in those years. Harnack and Cohen seem the most likely sources for Barth's notion of "reform"; but that remains conjecture. For Cohen's understanding of ethical monotheism in the prophets, see William Kluback, *Hermann Cohen: The Challenge of a Religion of Reason* (Chico, Calif.: Scholars Press, 1984); and on Cohen's debate with Troeltsch over the continuation of the "prophetic ethos" in rabbinic Judaism, see Wendell S. Dietrich, *Cohen and Troeltsch: Ethical Monotheistic Religion and Theory of Culture* (Chico, Calif.: Scholars Press, 1986), especially 32–36.

33. *Romans*, 338, 339 [*Römerbrief*, 322, 323].

The pharisees as heirs of the prophets, and of the "fullness of the Old Testament"—a claim worthy of defense by scholars like Geiger and Cohen— seems to be effortlessly surrendered by Barth. Indeed, we might say that, for Barth, the pharisees represent one pinnacle of "human possibility," the essence of "ethical monotheism." Like Schleiermacher, like Cohen, like "culture-Protestants" of the kind of the young Barth himself, the Pharisee sets out to reform and transform culture with the ethical spirit that is poured out on the followers of the One God. The ethical obligation and task, so prominent in *Romans,* belongs to Barth's training in Liberalism. German Academic Theology, Christian and Judaic, bound itself to the work of building culture, a moral kingdom infused with love and compassion. But to borrow a phrase from Hans Frei, we might say that the "flow of interpretation" of Liberalism should be reversed.[34] Not that pharisees are "culture-Protestants" or types of "religious socialists," but that "ethical monotheists" of all stripes are types, reenactments of the pharisees. The search for the religious foundation of ethical culture, after all, took its terms from the debate over the prophets: which may be called the rightful heir of these "religious geniuses of Israel"[35] rabbinic Judaism or Protestant Christianity? Hermann Cohen and Ernst Troeltsch, but also Adolf Harnack, Julius Wellhausen, and Abraham Geiger—all these advocates of Liberal religion defended and claimed the prophets for their own. The call to reform entailed a method and a world view; that cannot be disputed. But the ethical task of religion was a *biblical* call to arms; at the head of these forces stood the prophets and—for some—the pharisees.

On the opening of Romans 14, on the "vegetable eaters," Barth writes: "All reformers are Pharisees. They suffer from a lack of a sense of humor, [and cannot refrain from condemnation]. Deprive a Total Abstainer, a really religious Socialist, a Churchman, or a Pacifist, of the *pathos* of moral indignation, and you have broken his backbone."[36] This portrait of the pharisees as pious bourgeoisie will never leave Barth's collection of images of Judaism, though it will deepen and darken as it moves into the realm of the *Dogmatics.* It is an image that absorbs the scorn and bitter disappointment Barth experienced at that event he called the *"dies ater,"* the day the teachers of his youth put their names to the German war effort. Oh, they were Liberals, all right; earnest workers for good; socialists of the most pious

34. See Hans Frie, *The Eclipse of Biblical Narrative* (New Haven: Yale University Press, 1974).

35. A phrase of Abraham Geiger's. See "Revelation" in his *Judaism and Its History* (Lanham, Md.: University Press of America, 1985), third lecture.

36. *Romans,* 509 [*Römerbrief,* 493]. Translation altered.

order! Barth saw their easy collapse into collaboration as the "open secret" of all Liberals: they are pharisees who "have the Law" and will judge for themselves. In *Romans,* this diagnosis controls the entire treatment.

Pharisees withdraw and hold themselves apart from the Gentile, from the unclean, from what Barth calls the "generality of men." Not because they are arrogant or narrow-minded—Barth shows his historical sophistication here—but they set themselves apart because they are earnest and dedicated, the pious religious. They have to do with God, and their lives reflect the singular isolation of this task. Barth reserved a special irony, here and in the *Dogmatics,* for these self-appointed religious heroes; they were the Titans in their most clever and demure disguise. But Barth never indulged in simple denunciation; as a type the Pharisee both establishes and dissolves the religious quest for God.

Like religion itself, the Pharisee is as old as the human family. In the garden of Eden, this religious ideal makes its entrance. Commenting on Romans 7:11, "And the commandment, which was unto life, this I found to be unto death: for sin, taking occasion by the commandment, deceived me, and through it slew me," Barth draws the religious life into the Christian exegesis of Genesis as the Fall. Religion—the commandment—is a kind of "necessity"; it drives its sufferers to "stretch out towards the tree in our midst, the desire to know good and evil, life and death, God and man." The Law acts as the "lever or occasion of sin"; it satisfies the human hunger for God by "clothing time [*Mittelbarkeit*] with eternity [*Unmittelbarkeit*], by presenting "piety as a human achievement." It "evokes worship which knows not how to be silent before God, and names such worship 'religion' "; it compels the worshiper to "lift up hands in prayer, then lets them drop back wearily, and in their weariness spurs him unto prayer again." Again and again, restlessly and relentlessly, religion teaches an intimacy with God, a "visible relationship" on which the higher life is built, a knowledge of good and evil—"Ye shall be as gods!"—by which the tireless work of reform is guided. But this is a confidence bordered by despair: "Death is the meaning of religion; for when we are pressed to the boundary of religion, death pronounces the inner calm of simple and harmless relativity to be at an end. Religion is not at all to be 'in tune with the infinite' or to at 'peace with oneself.' It has no place for refined sensibility [*noble Gefühle*] or mature humanity [*edle Mensch-lichkeit*]. . . . Religion is an abyss: it is terror."[37]

With a motion he would repeat throughout the *Dogmatics,* Barth "turns over" the religion of the Pharisee, pressing its zeal and effortless spirit to its

37. Ibid., 252, 253 [235, 236].

limit, drawing out of its smooth piety the sting of loss and misery. The Law demands that its will be done—Barth follows the Lutheran reading of Paul closely here—but no one can do it, for sin has dominion over all things human. Only wretchedness and need, the "sickness unto death," can be recognized in the demands of the Law. The Pharisee reaches for the fruit of the tree of life and tastes death; he seeks holiness and learns of sin. The Law as the piety of Israel calls its followers together, to stand apart from humanity, to practice its tradition and keep its commandment, but this very call places the religious along the edge of the abyss, for "God justifies the ungodly."

In the "very centre and kernel of the Epistle," Romans 3:22–24, Barth drives this point home:

> *For there is no distinction.* The reality of the righteousness of God is attested to by its universality. It is not irrelevant that it is precisely Paul, who, daring, in Jesus, to put his trust boldly in grace alone, is able, in Jesus, also to perceive the divine breaking down of all human distinctions. . . . God can be known only when men of all ranks are grouped together upon one single step. . . . The Pharisee who prays can indeed become a missionary, but not a missionary of the Kingdom of God. The strange *union*—of men with one another—must assert and expose the strange, and yet saving, *separation*—between God and man. . . . Nothing must be retained of that illusion which permits a supposed religious or moral or intellectual experience to remove the only sure ground of salvation, which is the mercy of God. The illusion that some men have an advantage over others must be completely discarded. The words, *there is no distinction* needs to be repeated and listened to again and again.[38]

Although this may not yet be the "triumph of grace," there is no mistaking the pronounced Lutheran tone of Barth's voice here. Again and again, he hears Paul through Luther: the Law teaches us that we are bound to sin, that we may be reckoned righteous through grace alone. Jew and Gentile, Israel and the Church, stand united before this one frontier of grace. But the stiff rejection of that leveling grace, the proud refusal to hear the free election of God, belongs to the religious.

"Having undertaken this impossibility [of hearing and speaking the Word of God], the Church is weighed down as it can be weighed down by no other activity; and the proof of this is that it has—crucified Christ. The Church

38. Ibid., 99, 100 [74, 75].

seeketh after God; and when it meets Him, being unable to comprehend Him, it rejects Him."[39] So Barth comments on Romans 11:13–15. The systematic union of "Israel and Church" or "Synagogue and Church" in one community or "environment" of Christ belongs to the *Dogmatics,* but that masterful theme is foreshadowed here. The human possibility of religion, the Law as human achievement and experience, binds Jew and Christian together under judgment and reminds them of their loss.

All this the Pharisee may glimpse and at odd moments of restlessness, recognize, but the Prophet—the religious figure at the frontier of the Law—*knows.* The Prophet, in Barth's commentary, is the legitimate "religious genius," the fullness of the Law, and the true greatness of human possibility. The Prophet realizes that the creature has to do with God, and that the religious believer must be shattered on God. The Prophet knows that "all flesh is grass," that all religion leads to death, and that sin has dominion "so long as a man liveth." Following the broad scholarly consensus about the Prophets at that time, Barth finds in them the religious who, emerging from the Law, critique it and the cult that surrounds it, and announce the universality of the God of Israel:

> From the point of view of comparative religion, the evolution of religion reaches its highest and purest peak in the Law of Israel, that is, in the assault made upon men by the prophets. . . . Now the prophetic *krisis* means the bringing of the final observable human possibility of religion within the scope of that *krisis* under which all human endeavour is set. The prophets see what men in fact are: they see them, confronted by the ambiguity of the world, bringing forth the possibility of religion; they see them arrogantly and illegitimately daring the impossible and raising themselves to equality with God. . . . In light of the prophetic condemnation of this final achievement we perceive the condemnation also of all previous and lesser achievements. . . . If God encounters and confronts men in religion, He encounters and confronts them everywhere.[40]

Throughout the essays and addresses of these early years, Barth returns to the haunted and compelling figure of the Prophet stricken by God. Though Barth ranged over many topics in his break with Liberalism, the great prophets of Israel are the biblical type, the synthetic center, the living reality

39. Ibid., 405, 406 [390, 391].
40. Ibid., 243, 244 [225, 226].

at the heart of his theological purpose. By the "major prophets," however, Barth refers to an extended family. The ancient prophets, from Amos and Hosea through Isaiah and Jeremiah are the principal members, and the category belongs to them. But like the figure of the Pharisee, the Prophet can be extended, typified, forward and back. Barth treats the apostle Paul as both Pharisee and Prophet—*the* Pharisee turned Prophet—and even certain moderns like Kierkegaard, Dostoevski, and Overbeck stand at the periphery. And, as an exemplar, an enactment of the divine *krisis,* Jesus of Nazareth becomes the great, the final Prophet of lowliness. To understand this pattern—better, this reality—of the Prophet in Barth's thought is to catch sight of the unifying power of his theological work in its first, mature expression. The poverty of human identity, the burden of "religious experience," the inexpressible longing and incapacity for God, the troubling and gracious victory of Eternity over time: all these themes of Barth's early years, the confessions of Dialectical Theology, are brought together and brought to life in the prophets of Israel.

The genuine religious spirit, Barth argues, belonged to those "who dared"; it was hardly a voice of reason, an example of calm self-possession, a living demonstration of the "higher life" and its benefits. It belonged to the religious believer who stood on the frontier, who suffered, yearned, and was never refreshed in affliction, who sought God and lived the life of Job, surrounded by the pious, marked out by the line of death. Like Jeremiah, the believer is consumed by the fire of God, betrayed, assaulted, and commanded by the God of Israel. Like Isaiah's Messiah, they are "derided and rejected," filled with "sorrow and acquainted with grief." The prophets suffer the tribulation of God: they know the God of Israel is holy and that all flesh is sin. They know that this is the meaning, the end, and the glory of the Law.

But surely, we must ask, this is not all. To hold out hands that are empty, to witness that "God is not there" in religion, to point with unwearying arms to the Unknown that lies Beyond: can Barth mean that *this* is the sum of the Law, the *Sache* of Paul's letter to the Romans? Is the religious history of Israel, and beyond, nothing but death and loss and sin? Or, to borrow questions from the history of doctrine, Is Marcion right? Is the Law sin?

These questions, after all, are the ones that dogged Barth throughout the Dialectical period. His "contempt for history," his cavalier dismissal of higher criticism, his open "theological exegesis" of Romans: these charges, laid and never fully disarmed, can be summed up in Barth's interpretation of the Law. On the one hand, Harnack and Jülicher appear to hold the field; Barth's understanding of Israel, and religious history in general, seems to be little more than a death sentence. On the other, Brunner wins the day; Barth allows, at least, for one genuine religious response, the "negative *imago*" of repentance. Barth himself seems to have heard the call of this temptation:

> *The Law—sin?* It seems obvious that we are almost compelled to the judgment that the law is sin. Whenever we have been brought to understand the double position which the law occupies as the loftiest peak of human possibility, we have been on the brink of subscribing to this judgement. And why should we not surrender to the pressure and say roundly that religion is the supremacy of human arrogance stretching itself even to God? Why should we not say that rebellion against God, robbery of what is His, forms the mysterious background of our whole existence? Would not this bold statement represent the truth? And why, then, should we not embark on a war against religion? Would not such an engagement constitute a human possibility far outstripping the possibility of religion? Why should we not enroll ourselves as disciples of Marcion, and proclaim a new God, quite distinct from the old God of the law?[41]

I have argued that Barth resists just this temptation—indeed, he claims that for himself repeatedly—but the price of Barth's resistance, I think, is high. Once again, Barth's argument turns on the theme of election.

In what Barth would later call a "doublet," and later draw that twofold reality of life deep within Christology, here Barth describes the Law as at once judgment and grace, human and divine possibility, rejection and election. The Law takes up these oppositions—or better, God takes them up—and establishes them, dissolving and confirming one in the other. In the beginning, and beyond history, God elects the creature and dwells with humanity in grace and completeness. Borrowing the language of the Marburgers, Barth described this unity as the *Ursprung:* God is the unintuitable center, reality, and origin of being and thought. This harmony, this *Ineinandersetzung*—Barth does not shrink from these hallmarks of Liberalism—is the fullness and end of revelation, and is given "in its completeness" in the Law. Barth meant to give this harmony a reality beyond history by calling it a "memory"—a kind of platonic movement, I think—and to find in the Law the memorial of that loss, the imprint of God's presence that, in itself, is but its negative. To speak in Barth's translation of Paul, religion is not meaningless or aimless—the Law is holy, and righteous, and good—but in its emptiness, and in its possession, it "points beyond itself" to God. Religion speaks of

41. Ibid., 241 [223].

God, and though it does so in a wholly human way, testifying to the sway of sin over human having and being, it nevertheless speaks that word, and reminds humanity of that communion it has lost. That it may do so, in the midst of sin, is the free gift of God.

In the final, masterful reversal of *Romans,* this divine gift, this elected grace, poured out on the ungodly, is the "divine possibility" given in death. "Death is the meaning of religion," but more, "in Adam, all have died." Existentialism held great attraction for Barth in this period, in part because it pointed to this last, inescapable fact of death. Two elements converge: before death, the religious and secular stand as one—all must die; and because death is the "wages of sin," wrought through the commandment, the religious too are the ungodly. This twofold election to death and life stands behind Barth's understanding of Abraham, the "father of a peculiar race and of a particular historical brotherhood [*Abraham den Vater des historischen Brudervolkes*]," declared righteous by faith:

> *He believeth on him that justifieth the ungodly* . . . Abraham never "possessed God": God possessed him. . . . The occasion of this *possession* does not lie in Abraham, but in God that *justifieth* him. In Abraham it is the wrath of God which is established. Before God, Abraham's human righteousness and unrighteousness is merely *ungodliness.* That he awoke to his position and was aware of the *krisis,* that in this *krisis* he feared God, that he heard the "No" of God and understood it as His "Yes"—this is Abraham's faith. . . . Through the classic figure of Abraham we learn the truth that we can boast only in the righteousness which has been manifested by *the blood of Jesus* and which is *reckoned* unto men. . . . When it is affirmed in the book of Genesis that Abraham has a righteousness of which he can boast, it must be understood as the model which points to the life of Christ and directs attention to the preeminence and purity and earnestness of the "Moment," with which everything which was before and which shall be hereafter is contrasted—as that which is the signpost to the Resurrection.[42]

For Barth, this is the heart of the Gospel. In a motion he would repeat throughout the *Dogmatics,* cutting deeper furrows at each pass, Barth reads the Old Testament Christologically, through the death and resurrection of Christ. In *Romans,* Barth understands Paul to teach nothing more of Jesus of

---

42. Ibid., 123, 124 [99].

Nazareth than "his blood": we know Jesus after the flesh no more—a phrase Barth could scarcely repeat too often. By this he meant that the earthly Jesus, like Abraham, like the prophets, like the pharisees and religious of all ages, that this historical figure must die. His life, as summed up by Paul and presented in the Gospels, reaches its goal, its truth in death. A religious man, born to a religious people, Jesus will bear witness to the meaning of religion; he will follow it to its last, bitter destination. He will cry the words of dereliction and despair, and take his place among the ungodly.

But, "God will raise him up." Commentators have drawn attention to Barth's Christology as "prolegomena" in these years, but we might say even more forcefully that his doctrine of the Trinity is barely prolegomena. The resurrection, Barth writes in *Romans,* manifests the true and full relation of humanity to God, a vertical descent of revelation beyond history, like a tangent to a circle, leaving its sign on earth like a crater after the shell explodes. This miracle stands at the turning point of history; it is the "hinge," Barth writes, the closed door, and the exit. By all these metaphors, Barth intends to portray the "double position of the Law" before God. Though death has entered through the Law, and covers all human thought and act in cold relativity, through death, also, God has made all alive. "God kills in order to make alive," Barth repeated, and we see its force here, in the divine possibility of the Law.

All history, religious and secular, finds its meaning outside history. Its direction and promise are lit up from outside, where God elects all to "die in Adam" and "live in Christ." Christ is the End of the Law, because in him, death turns over into eternal life. So long as all mortal life is closed up in sin and unrighteousness, passing its way to death, then all may be raised up in Christ, the Object and End of divine election. So too the Law by which sin shows its dominion over the earth, may become the divine possibility of grace, the new life in Christ. This revolution, this drawing up into and turning from death to life, is the event, the *Ereignis,* the shattering *Sache* of the Epistle to the Romans.

I have attempted to let Barth speak, even as he hoped to let Paul speak. I have underscored his attention to the figures and realities of Israel, and of the use made of them in early Christianity. I have emphasized the Law, and its advocates, the prophets and pharisees. In short, I have treated Barth's *Romans* as a commentary on Paul, an exploration and translation of the ideas and deeds of the past. But have I, or has Barth, succeeded? Just what kind of history, what expression of the human past does Barth actually capture and put to work?

I think, in fairness to Barth and with an irony he might have enjoyed, we can only say that our answer must be two-sided, and never fully at rest. We can say that Barth does not discard history, empty it, or make it of no use or value. To speak theologically, we might say that the world remains creation, elected in grace and toward an End. The figures of Prophet and Pharisee, far from being a code stripped of meaning and particularity, work instead as genuine examples from the history of Israel—biblical history, to be sure— that expand and become transparent to the conflicts of the present. They do not function as yet, I think, as true historical types, but they anticipate this great, creative revival of typology in the *Dogmatics*. The Law, too, takes on more of the texture of historical reality that its translation, Religion, suggests. While Barth clearly has questions of method, and more, the method of "neo-Protestantism" in view throughout *Romans,* he sees them in the light of Paul's preaching, in the "joyful discovery" of the divine act of *krisis* and election.

But on the other hand, and when thrown up against the vast expanse of the *Dogmatics, Romans* casts a pale shadow. It is not just the constriction of method, the pressure of dialectic on the work and theme of theology. It is more that Barth here cannot make history—particularly the history of Israel—expand, develop, define itself, and change as all human history must. This is a history that is compressed, "rolled up" into a few, singular peaks that must stand for the whole. There arise out of the plain of history a few figures, the Prophet, the Pharisee, Paul, and Jesus of Nazareth; they stand out and are recognizable, but they must all utter the same theme: that the meaning of religion is death. Of course, Barth wished to follow Paul's letter closely, and, following Paul, to focus on the resurrection, his head turned upward to the novelty of God. But Barth, in these years, cannot find a place for this electing God to enter history, not as a tangent to a circle, but to fully enter it and take it up—enhypostatically assume it—into the divine life. Barth seems to catch a vision of this land, the motion of the Son of Man into the Far Country, but he remains, in *Romans,* on its border. In the *Church Dogmatics,* Barth will finally find this place where Israel and the "Synagogue" can be brought fully into Christian dogmatics, the place where, in Luther's words, Jesus Christ was born a Jew.

THE
CHURCH DOGMATICS

The Philosophical and Theological Roots of the Election of Israel

2

Bertold Klappert has written that "Karl Barth's theology is inconceivable and incomprehensible without Barth's exegesis and doctrine of Israel."[1] A strong statement, one that appears—as does so much having to do with Barth—to be both true and false, if not also somewhat exaggerated: It sounds like the enthusiasm generated by long hours devoted to Barth's doctrine of Israel. While the doctrine of Israel is not every critic's favorite, Klappert is not alone in his search for the sole interpretive key to Barth's theology. As the vast Barth scholarship testifies, *The Church Dogmatics,* the massive and masterly work of Barth's maturity, can be understood through countless idioms. But Klappert makes more than the enthusiast's claim. He makes the stronger assertion: without the doctrine of Israel, Barth's work is *inconceivable.* Israel is the sole, exclusive, and necessary key to the *Dogmatics.* And this threatens to undo the Christological concentration of Barth's work.

Apart from Christ, Barth's work has no irreducible doctrine without which his theological mechanism breaks down. If a key were required for entry into the *Dogmatics,* the doctrine of Israel appears to be an unlikely prospect. While biblical exegesis can be found throughout the *Dogmatics,* a discrete doctrine of Israel or the "Synagogue" occupies only a small part of volumes 2, 3, and 4.[2] Barth turned to the *Judenfrage,* as he called the topic even then,

---

1. Bertolt Klappert, *Israel und die Kirche: Erwägungen zur Israellehre Karl Barths* (Munich: Christian Kaiser Verlag, 1980), 11.

2. The principal sections in the *Dogmatics* for Barth's *Israellehre* are: vol. 2, part 2, pars. 34 and 35; vol. 3, part 3, par. 49; and vol. 4, part 3, par. 72.

in his short postwar addresses,[3] but a cool eye I think will see that such topics were not prominent on Barth's horizon. Perhaps, Klappert has gone too far.

But on the other hand, the critical line may have been drawn too fine; Klappert appears to be right, too. The Christian reappraisal of Judaism, and of the people Israel, commands attention today. Since the Vatican II document, *Nostra Aetate,* and the German confession "in the face of Auschwitz,"[4] theologians have been forced to attend to Christian anti-Judaism.[5] The reinterpretation of major theological systems on the basis of new interests, knowledge, and commitments is the task of a living "theological imagination."[6] It may be, as Marquardt claims, that Barth "discovered" Israel for Christian theology, and that Klappert's interpretation of Barth reveals a foundation of the *Dogmatics* scarcely acknowledged by its author.[7]

3. See his "Die Judenfrage und ihre christliche Beantwortung," in *Der Götze Wackelt,* ed. K. Kupisch (Berlin: Käthe Vogt Verlag, 1961); and its English translation in *Against the Stream* (New York: Philosophical Library, 1954), discussed further in Chapter 5.

4. J. B. Metz, a former disciple of Karl Rahner, has used this phrase to describe the task of theology today, especially when it is a part of the wide-ranging "Jewish Christian Dialogue," prompted to a great extent by German self-interrogation about its Nazi past. Prominent among Protestant voices in the dialogue have been Helmut Gollwitzer and Friedrich Marquardt, both pupils of Barth; among Catholics, Clemens Thoma and Johannes Oesterreicher. This by no means exhausts the list.

5. A theological condemnation of Judaism, based on Christian doctrines of revelation and salvation. This condemnation has been called by some the "teachings of contempt." See the classic work by Jules Isaac, *The Teachings of Contempt: Christian Roots of Anti-Semitism* (New York: Holt, Reinhardt, and Winston, 1964). For theological use of anti-Judaism, see Luther's late essay, "The Jews and Their Lies," and Eugen Rosenstock-Huessy's *Judaism Despite Christianity* (Tuscaloosa: University of Alabama Press, 1969). Anti-Judaism may be distinguished from anti-Semitism, a racial theory, in which Jews, as Emil Fackenheim has written, were despised and killed simply because they had Jewish ancestors. Such anti-Semitism may stem from anti-Judaism, as Rosemary Ruether in *Faith and Fratricide* has forcefully argued, or it may be considered a modern savagery quite separate from religious dispute. See, for this point of view, among others, Wyschogrod, "Why Was and Is the Theology of Karl Barth of Interest to a Jewish Theologian"; Viktor E. Frankl, *Man's Search for Meaning: An Introduction to Logotherapy,* trans. Ilse Lasche, preface by Gordon Allport (*Ein Psycholog erlebt das Konzentrationslager,* Vienna: Verlag für Jugend und Volk, 1946; Boston: Beacon Press, 1963), in which Nazism is understood as a virulent form of modern secularism; Uriel Tal, *Christians and Jews in Germany: Religion, Politics, and Ideology in the Second Reich, 1870–1914,* trans. Noah Jonathan Jacobs (Ithaca: Cornell University Press, 1975); Pawlikowski, *Christ in the Light of the Christian-Jewish Dialogue.*

6. I have borrowed a phrase here from R. Collingwood, whose influential essay on historical methodology, *The Idea of History* (London: Oxford University Press, 1956), argues, in part, that our interest and knowledge of the past arise from our current convictions, dilemmas, and "organic unity of [our] total experience." See part 5, "Epilogomena," particularly par. 5, "The Subject Matter of History."

7. Barth, for example, found Marquardt's reading of his *Israellehre* convincing and accurate though oddly unrecognizable. See *Briefe, 1961–1968,* letter 260, p. 420.

Klappert's claim does not rest simply on questions of authorial intent. Barth's mature work, with its Christological density, draws together its many disparate themes each time it encircles its one Object, each time reforming its picture of the world taken up in Christ. In hegelian fashion, the entire thought-world can be demonstrated from any starting point, and any theme, expressed in Christ, can justify its claim to a central and irrevocable place within Barth's work. The astonishing consistency of the *Dogmatics*—indeed of Barth's thought entirely—is one of Barth's great achievements, and Klappert's attention to the doctrine of Israel pays Barth the same compliment in different currency.

Klappert's strongest justification stems, I think, from the meaning Barth assigns to Israel and to Judaism. For Barth, to speak of the people Israel, past and present, is to speak of election. This equation, linking Jews and God's election, places Barth's *Israellehre* within his doctrine of God at the heart of his most powerful and innovative theological statement, the reformulation of God's predestinating act in Christ. Every major section of Barth's work has its advocates, of course. The doctrines of scripture, creation, and most prominently, I think, the doctrine of reconciliation have their champions, and Barth rewards his admirers at almost every turn. But the doctrine of election enjoys special privilege among Barth's achievements: it is genuinely new.[8] By itself, this is remarkable in a field as thoroughly rationalized as theology. But the

8. Some of the contemporary literature might make another critic more cautious about Barth's innovations. Consider the piece by Heinrich Vogel on "Praedestinatio gemina," in *Theologische Aufsätze,* 222–42, the festschrift for Barth's fiftieth birthday. He asserts that Christ must be taken as the true object of election, and that predestination so understood belongs within the doctrine of the Trinity. Collected in 1936, these essays must have been presented to Barth during his work on the crucial volume, 2.2, of the *Dogmatics.* While acknowledging and, more, extensively examining Peter Barth's essay "Die Erwählungslehre in Calvins Institutio von 1536" (*Theologische Aufsätze,* 432–42), Barth makes no mention of Vogel's work.

Barth is, however, aware of the "Christological meaning and basis of the doctrine of election . . . brought out afresh in our own time," generously pointing to Pierre Maury's address to the *Congrès international de théologie calviniste,* "Election et Foi"—the only discussion in the entire congress (including Peter Barth's address) that Barth seemed ready to tolerate (*Dogmatics,* 2.2:154, 188–94 [*Dogmatik,* 2.2:168, 207–14]).

From all this, we can conclude that Barth understood his own position to differ from any other he had studied and that Barth might have placed Vogel's work in the same honorable camp as Maury's: a trustworthy sign along the way. Barth's treatment is distinctive and new in the breadth and complexity of his discussion; in the rigor and innovation of his exegetical work; in the significance accorded to Christ as elector as well as elected; and, not least, in his thorough assimilation of the history of the people of Israel into the doctrine of election. Barth renewed nearly every doctrine he touched; even the disenchanted recognize this, but a special status can be reserved for the power and freshness Barth accords such a Calvinist workhorse as the doctrine of double predestination.

doctrine of election offers more than novelty. Barth's insistence that Christ, not the individual, forms the object of election at once takes up, enriches, and sets aside all the major themes of the scholastic doctrine of predestination. Barth's treatment is radical; it is deeply rooted in the past, yet sends up new growth altogether different from its seed. Central to this recast doctrine of election is the teaching about Israel, in its biblical and post-biblical forms. *This* theology of Barth's, sharpened in his treatment of the "Synagogue" and the "Passing and Coming Man," cannot be understood apart from his *Israellehre,* as Klappert correctly insists. At these crucial—and now, often painful—points, Barth presents, in a dreadful majesty Judaism as the object of God's electing wrath.

Barth's Doctrine of Election as the Basis of *Israellehre*

Since Augustine, the great architect of Christianity in the West, the doctrine of election has been tied to the doctrine of original sin. Interpreting Paul through the eyes of late antiquity, Augustine read the theme of election as a drama of the individual soul, condemned by sin but given faith through God's free and gracious act. No longer the record of a historical people, Israel, bound to God through times of wrath and of loving-kindness, the theme of election now revealed the divine judgment over all those closed up in death and sin with Adam. From all eternity, in secret counsel, God determines the recipients of grace, those souls brought to faith in Christ, to their eternal home after death, and consigns the rest to the punishment original sin deserves. In all things, God rules and is sovereign; it is on human beings that God's will is exercised. This Augustinian doctrine of election, triumphant over Pelagianism, gave to the Reformation its dominant themes and character.[9]

Though Luther proclaimed the doctrine a holy mystery and a comfort to the godly, it was Calvin who gave the doctrine of election its prominence and its elegant and ruthless consistency. In Calvin Augustinian themes recur, now heard however through the "introspective conscience" of late medieval piety.[10] Once again, the doctrine of election enacts the drama of human

9. This was the Reformers' understanding of their work, though how faithful they actually were to Augustine's theology is in dispute. See, for example, Barth's insightful comments on this point in *Natural Theology,* 99–105.

10. The phrase belongs to Krister Stendahl in his now classic essay, "The Apostle Paul and the Introspective Conscience of the West," 199–215.

salvation, justified by grace alone. Though a modern in many respects, Calvin honored the hellenism preserved in humanistic learning. His theology exhibits the structural dignity and dilemmas that Greek thought bequeaths to theism. To protect God's sovereignty and his perfection, Calvin recognized that salvation must be predestined. The decision about individual salvation must be eternal, immutable, and justified by God's righteousness alone. The worth of moral agency, the course of human history, the sacramental life of the Church, though given significance in the *Institutes,* played no part in Calvin's understanding of God's decree. Indeed, the very notion of sovereignty implied that God, as monarch, did not receive but determined human destiny, from the life of nations to the fate of a single merchant, lost in the forest.[11] And such determination was double—*predestinatio gemina*—because God's destinating activity was complete, direct, and total. God predestined every life to salvation or damnation; the godly would find in this austere majesty a solemn comfort, the wicked an offense and a secret terror.[12]

The refinement, justification, and final repudiation of this doctrine of double predestination provides the outline for Reformed Protestantism through the early nineteenth century. Like Schleiermacher, Barth knew the Protestant scholastics well, and his attention gave vitality to theological debates Liberals politely called recondite, but, more honestly, considered cruel and denigrating. With his zeal for the lost cause, Barth took these scholastics seriously. He admired their effort to speak theologically, though their work looked increasingly like museum pieces preserving language long lost to the curators. Undaunted, Barth addressed their controversies, compared their efforts in detail, and rendered verdicts. His devotion to this kind of historical theology, lovingly recorded in the opening sections of the second part of volume 2, justifies Barth's preference for the term, *Church Dogmatics.* From *Romans* forward, Barth wished to give equal weight to the two poles of Reformed doctrine: that God was sovereign in his election; and that election was twofold in intention and act. He shows no sign of being offended at its ruthless consistency. More likely, its offense to modern ears delighted him. Barth was restive over two aspects of the scholastic treatment

11. "Let us imagine, for example, a merchant who, entering a wood with a company of faithful men, unwisely wanders away from his companions, and in his wanderings comes upon a robber's den, falls among thieves, and is slain. His death was not only foreseen by God's eye, but also determined by his decrees" (John Calvin, *Institutes of the Christian Religion,* ed. J. T. McNeil, trans. F. L. Battles [Philadelphia: Westminster Press, 1960], 1:208–9). Chapters 16 and 17 bristle with such tough-minded examples of divine providence, "applied for our benefit."

12. This is, of course, a *theological* understanding of Calvin's thought, one far removed from William Bouwsma's, as Edward Dowey observes in his review of *John Calvin,* in the *Journal of the American Academy of Religion* 57, no. 4 (Winter 1989): 845–48.

of election: Greek thought had given God's perfection an immutability that was brilliant but static. And, that perfect act of election was considered apart from Christ.

These are criticisms we would expect from Barth, and as we would also expect, they can be combined into a single argument. Eberhard Jüngel, a prominent student of Barth, has described this argument as the *kein Menschlosigkeits Gott*.[13] God cannot properly—theologically—be conceived or known apart from the incarnation; there is no "non-human God." Barth criticizes his customary targets, Thomism and Schleiermacher-inspired Liberalism, for their eagerness to investigate a doctrine of God isolated from a doctrine of the Trinity. That Schleiermacher relegated the Trinity to an appendix to the *Christian Faith,* discretely labeled "Conclusion," merely confirmed Barth's worst suspicions. To begin Christian dogmatics with "pious self-consciousness" is to invite the hollow conclusion that "as ecclesiastically framed, the doctrine is not an immediate utterance concerning the Christian self-consciousness."[14] But Barth found the *"menschlosigkeits Gott"* among his friends, not just among his traditional adversaries.

The Protestant scholastics, and even Calvin himself, began theological reflection about God apart from and before the doctrine of the Trinity. The stately opening of the *Institutes,* setting forth the "theater of creation" in which God's glory shines, evokes the Creator before the Triune. But Barth objects to a fault more serious than the order of doctrines within a dogmatics. Calvin's classical cast of mind allowed him to conceive—contradictorily and, perhaps, unwittingly—of an election of the Father apart and hidden from the Son:

> But what does Calvin mean when he says that on His side God begins *a se ipso* (in contradistinction to *a Christo*) when He elects us, i.e.,

13. See, for example, Eberhard Jüngel's *The Doctrine of the Trinity: God's Being Is in Becoming* (Grand Rapids, Mich.: William Eerdmans, 1976), 108, and passim. His phrase is an extension of Barth's late essay, *Die Menschlichkeit Gottes,* Theologische Studien 48 (Zurich: Evangelischer Verlag, 1956); *The Humanity of God,* trans. Thomas Wieser and John Newton Thomas (Atlanta: John Knox Press, 1960).

14. Friedrich Schleiermacher, *The Christian Faith,* 2d ed., trans. H. R. Mackintosh and J. S. Stewart (Philadelphia: Fortress Press, 1928), 738.

Barth's analysis, certainly, is not the final word on Schleiermacher's doctrine of the Trinity. His position could be interpreted as confirming the traditional teaching that the Trinity is a mystery above human reason and experience, available through revelation alone, though we might then ask just what kind of piety this self-consciousness represents. For a discussion of the Trinitarian debate between Schleiermacher and Barth, see Robert Streetman, "Some Questions Schleiermacher Might Ask about Barth's Trinitarian Criticisms," in J. O. Duke and R. R. Streetman, eds., *Barth and Schleiermacher: Beyond the Impasse?* (Philadelphia: Fortress Press, 1988), chap. 7.

when the Father gives us the Son, when He predestinates us members of the body of this Head and partakers of His inheritance? And what is this *gratuitum beneplacitum* which plainly here precedes and is superior to the being and work of Christ? The question of the election is really the question of this *gratuitum beneplacitum* as such. . . . But Calvin was not prepared to think of [Christ] in this way. . . . It was inevitable, then, that in spite of the Christological reference the main emphasis in Calvinistic doctrine should come to rest in effect upon this reference to the secret *electio Patris*. . . . It was inevitable that a secret dissatisfaction should lead to its supersession by the real truth to be found *in Deo incipiente a se ipso,* in the *beneplacitum gratuitum* which was before Christ and behind Him and above Him. It was inevitable, then, that little store should be set by the revelation when there was no need to adhere strictly to it. It was inevitable that even within the revelation the main concern should be, not with a relative truth, but quite unreservedly and unhesitatingly with this real and inward truth concerning God.[15]

The God who elects apart from Christ, the Father hidden and distinct from the Son, acts in sovereign and classical justice towards humanity. The twofold motion of God's decision toward the creature, now freed from its order in Christ, falls cleanly into separate halves. God, the *Pater,* elects and rejects, judges in wrath and mercy, preserves the hidden saints, and consigns the sinners to their inevitable and richly deserved damnation. God's foreknowledge is ordered to his determining will: "Since [God] foresees future events only by reason of the fact that he decreed that they take place, they [Calvin's opponents] vainly raise a quarrel over foreknowledge, when it is clear that all things take place rather by his determination and bidding."[16] The outline of classical theism now comes into view, its conflicts and convictions in sharp relief.

"Nearly all the wisdom we possess, that is to say, true and sound wisdom, consists of two parts: the knowledge of God and of ourselves."[17] Calvin's celebrated opening of the *Institutes,* joining the knowledge—we might better say, confession—of the Creator with the knowledge of—and repentence for—the self ties together the great themes of sixteenth-century predestination, Catholic and Reformed: the ability of the self and the freedom of God.

15. *Dogmatics,* 2.2:66–67 [*Dogmatik,* 2.2:71–72].
16. Calvin, *Institutes,* 3:954–55.
17. Ibid., 1:35.

Creator and creature belong together; Barth certainly agrees. But they are naked subjects here, stripped of their covering in Christ. In God, we encounter the faceless, inscrutable Judge. In the human person, we meet the indefinite mixture of experience, the individual, moral and immoral, capable of virtue, worthy of damnation: the individual, in short, who provides for both sides signs of depravity healed by grace alone, and the modest progress of believers who do the good that is in them. The protracted, bitter debates over grace and merit, inherited from Augustine, riddled the Catholic and Protestant Reformations, leaving traces in the Liberal repudiation of original sin and exclusive redemption through Christ. Barth argues that these two subjects, the sovereign God and the imperfect creature, remain faceless and undefined apart from Christ. We cannot recognize the divine Judge, unless he be the Judge judged in our place; we cannot define the moral worth of the person until the individual is taken up in Christ, the rejected man, elected. This "Copernican revolution" in the doctrine of election places Christ in the center, the true object of wrath and grace, the sole determination of divine reprobation and election. The doctrine of election, refashioned Christologically, moves out from under the governing doctrine of salvation. In Barth's hands, the doctrine of election finds its ground in the doctrine of God, the Creator who wills not to be without the creature.

The traditional foundation for the Reformed doctrine of predestination has been Ephesians 1:3–4:

> Blessed be the God and Father of our Lord Jesus Christ, who has blessed us in Christ with every spiritual blessing in the heavenly places, even as he chose us in him before the foundation of the world, that we should be holy and blameless before him.

Calvin cites the passage in the opening of chapter 22 of the *Institutes;* Markus Barth dedicates an entire part volume to the first three chapters of the letter.[18] The passage carries weight for Barth; there are signs of its influence throughout the *Dogmatics.* Surprisingly, however, Barth does not place it at the head of his doctrine. His exegetical base rests, first, upon John 1:1–2: "In the beginning was the Word, and the Word was with God; and the Word was God; He was in the beginning with God." Barth rests his doctrine of the election of the community on an exegesis of Romans 9–11, the election of the people Israel. Even in turning to the heart of Reformed doctrine, the

---

18. Ibid., 1:933; Markus Barth, *Ephesians,* vol. 34 in the Anchor Bible Series (New York: Doubleday Anchor, 1974).

election of the individual, Barth passes by the classical text. He takes up, in its place, the twofold form of the individual, elected and rejected, calling up the Christ-like doublets of scripture: Cain and Abel; David and Saul; the man of Judah and the prophet from Bethel. All are drawn with light and with shadow, the shadows deepening as the story unfolds until the individuating lines are lost, until Judas and Jesus stand side by side, seen together but in sharp contrast and, in the end, Jesus himself stands alone—all others having fallen away—and the doublets of election and rejection finally rest and are taken up in him alone. These are remarkable passages, unique I think in theology, and critics have not failed to notice them.[19] But they lend an entirely different tone to the doctrine of election. These exegetical passages, from Genesis to Romans, John, and the synoptics, all offer an image of election consonant with but distinct from that in Ephesians. As the sturdy support of Reformed doctrine, Ephesians recorded God's eternal decision about the individual soul. In Barth's selection of texts, the attention is focused on Christ, as the head of creation, the foundation of the covenant in its historical and communal forms. The Christological center of Barth's doctrine brings election into the living relationship of the Trinity, where the community, its history, and finally its individual flesh, rejected and assumed, find their meaning and source. No longer a doctrine of individual salvation, election now unfolds the eternal giving and receiving of the Son, through whom the covenant with creation is realized. The decision about the individual, and indeed, of the community and all creation, cannot stand alone. These decisions are secondary to the decision made in Christ, and are made real only in this primary, divine drama of self-giving and self-revelation.

"Jesus Christ, electing and elected": this formula stands at the beginning of Barth's treatment of election, and in its compressed and alliterative form, expresses the whole. At times, Barth tolerates the phrase, "God elects Christ,"[20] but, in exact terms, he finds it intolerable. It is just this separation reflected in this description of God apart from Christ that Barth repudiates. Election is not a *decretum absolutum,* but a living, eternal reality. Election is the decision made in Christ, first in the Son, and then in the flesh assumed: Christ must be the elector and the elected.

In fine hegelian fashion, Barth scorns an abstract truth. Determination, God's self-determination in the concrete, demonstrates divine freedom:

---

19. Those interested in hermeneutics have taken particular notice: Frei, "Election and Rejection" and on Jesus as the "Royal Man," in *Eclipse of Biblical Narrative,* viii and chap. 5; D. F. Ford, *Barth and God's Story* (Frankfurt am Main: Peter Lang, 1981); D. Kelsey, *The Uses of Scripture in Recent Theology* (Philadelphia: Fortress Press, 1975), 39–55.

20. See, for example, *Dogmatics,* 2.2:94–95 [*Dogmatik,* 2.2:101, 102].

In the beginning, before time and space as we know them, before creation, before there was any reality distinct from God which could be the object of the love of God or the setting for His acts of freedom, God anticipated and determined within Himself (in the power of His love and freedom, of His knowing and willing) that the goal and meaning of all His dealings with the as yet non-existent universe should be the fact that in His Son He would be gracious toward man, uniting Himself with him.[21]

This act of determination belongs, first, to the inner life of the Trinity:

In the beginning it was the choice of the Father Himself to establish this covenant with man by giving up His Son for him, that He Himself might become man in the fulfillment of His grace. In the beginning, it was the choice of the Son to be obedient to grace, and therefore to offer up Himself and to become man in order that this covenant might be made a reality. In the beginning it was the resolve of the Holy Spirit that the unity of God, of Father and Son should not be disturbed or rent by this covenant with man, but that it should be made the more glorious, the deity of God, the divinity of His love and freedom, being confirmed and demonstrated by this offering of the Father and this self-offering of the Son.[22]

No necessity governed this election; "God did not stand in need of any particular ways or works *ad extra.*"[23] The Trinitarian life, complete in its freedom and self-determination, might, in itself, have formed the object of election. That the Son elects humanity, elects union with the creature, is an act Barth, in his most lutheran voice, calls "grace, sovereign grace, a condescension inconceivably tender."[24] The doctrine of the Trinity does not arise from the incarnation, or the divine relation to creation. The diremption of the Father in the Son; the laying down and taking up from the Son to the Father; the sublating love of the Spirit: this divine drama, too, is election, complete and wholly determined in itself. But God does not will to be alone. By the Father, in the Spirit, the Son elects the creature. Jesus Christ is the name of that act of election. In Jesus, Christ elects the son of man for God's

21. Ibid., 101 [108, 109].
22. Ibid.
23. Ibid., 121 [130].
24. Ibid.

glory; in the Son of God, God elects human wrath and punishment. This exchange, graciously weighted in the creature's favor, brings the Creator into closest connection with that which is rejected. In election, Christ draws near to evil and wrath, the powers that exist through divine condemnation.

The relationship of the Creator to the creature comprises the heart of Barth's doctrine of creation—volume 3 of the *Dogmatics*—and assumes a central role in the doctrine of election. These are standard locations, ones we would expect, and Barth does not disappoint his readers. But the relation of divine to creaturely being finds an unexpected home in the doctrine of Israel. Israel, we might say, is the name Barth gives to the relationship between Creator and creature, a relationship of judgment and rejection. The proximity of the creature to evil, to the being that is not, prepares the way for Barth's construction of an Israel elected for condemnation. God's election *ad extra* is a divine determination for suffering: Christ elects sinful flesh, the human enmity with God, the being that exists as a "vessel of wrath." Christ elects—Barth's logic is ruthless—Jewish flesh. Jesus was a Jew; his story is a Jewish one. The covenant for which creation takes place is the bond between Israel and the God of Abraham, Isaac, and Jacob. The dominance of sin, though universal and original to all humanity, is a particularly Jewish affair.[25]

Barth's Doctrine of Creation and Nothingness as Basis of *Israellehre*

In the doctrine of election, Barth draws together the disparate strands of the doctrine of evil and the doctrine of Israel through the figure of Satan. Strictly speaking, Satan has no part in the biblical story of the Fall. The serpent, after all, was merely "more crafty than any of the other wild creatures the Lord God had made." Indeed, the entire interpretation of the second creation

25. Friedrich Marquardt underscores the significance of the divine election of Jewish flesh: "So steht auch die *Geschichte Israels*—wie wir in der Beziehung von Gottes Sein und Bund schon sahen—*in engster Korrelation zum Wesen Gottes,* der 'in seiner unbedingten und unangreifbaren Freiheit, sich durch sich selbst zu setzen und zu behaupten,' auch dazu frei und willens ist, sein Sein je auch als künftiges Sein, sein Erbarmen je auch als künftiges Erbarmen zu erneuern, bestätigen und zu beherrlichen (KD II/2, 240)" (*Die Entdeckung des Judentums,* 251–52). [Thus the *history of Israel*—as we have seen in the relationship of the Being of God to his covenant—stands *in closest correlation to the essence of God,* who 'in his unconditional and unassailable freedom to posit and assert himself through himself' is also free and willing to renew, to confirm, and to glorify his Being as future being, his mercy as future mercy.]

narrative as a Fall, from grace to original sin, belongs to the Christian exegesis of Genesis and the patristic emphasis on the cosmic dimension of Christ's atonement. The figure of Satan, however, plays a lively part in the thought of intertestamental Judaism, and has a leading role in the New Testament passion narratives. A dogmatic theologian, Barth effortlessly extends this dominant role for Satan back into the primal history of God's way with his creation.

> That the elected man Jesus had to suffer and die means no more and no less than in becoming man God makes Himself responsible for man who became His enemy, and that He takes upon Himself all the consequences of man's action—his rejection and his death. This is what is involved in the self-giving [*Selbsthingabe*] of God. . . . Against the aggression of the shadow-world of Satan which is negated by Him and which exits only in virtue of this negation, God must and will maintain the honour of His creation, the honour of man as created and ordained for Him, and His own honour. God cannot and will not acquiesce in the encroachment of this shadow-world upon the sphere of His positive will, an encroachment made with the fall of man. On the contrary, it must be His pleasure to see that Satan and all that has its source and origin in him are rejected. But this means that God must and will reject man as he is in himself. And He does so.[26]

The victory over Satan takes place in what Barth calls the "heavenly sphere"— a cosmic victory. The rejection of humanity, however, though Satan's captive, takes place in history. The foundation, course, and, in the end, the content of this rejection is found in the history of Israel, and in its head, Jesus of Nazareth. For this reason, to speak of election is to speak of Israel. More significantly in this place, however, to speak of Israel in light of Christ is to speak of rejection.

Barth considers creaturely being to have a special vulnerability to the demonic. This conclusion, after all, follows directly from Barth's exegesis of Genesis 2. But Barth does not simply assert this vulnerability as a biblical fact; he argues his claim. Satan holds sway over humanity because creaturely being is determined by its frailty and easy corruption. It is too strong to say, I think, that Barth employs an ontological hierarchy in his doctrine of evil. But, using Trinitarian language, it might be fair to say that Barth makes use of varying "modes of being." The divine mode of being consists in sovereign freedom. It alone can fully self-determine its existence, combining perfect

---

26. *Dogmatics,* 2.2:124 [*Dogmatik,* 2.2:133].

freedom with perfect will. The divine reality can be characterized as actuality, a mobile and discriminating will. Creation, then, receives its form from a divine act to create, not by a participation in an immutable Being: God wills to create beings other than himself. But this decision requires a "passing over," a separating of chaos from creation, a judgment that something "is not." This is the mode of being of evil.

The reality of evil, represented in Satan, exists in negation, in the *Schatten-welt*. Evil is "non-Being," "nothingness," *"Nichtige"*; it is not, however, mere privation. Nonbeing *is:* it exists in the mode appropriate to a being rejected by God. These statements are the kind Barth himself might term "dark sayings." They call forth Barth's most poetic voice: evil exists on the "left hand of God." It is fair, I think, to ask what all this might mean. We can discern traditional elements in the picture. The neo-Platonic emphasis upon the lack of being and goodness in sin and evil; the phenomenological exploration of the anxiety about nothingness; the patristic assertion of divine lordship over all rebellion: these elements give Barth's doctrine its character-istic resonance and complexity. So, too, does Barth's effort to steer a course between those who risk trivializing the reality of evil and those who honor but eviscerate the sovereignty of God. The elements and intentions of Barth's doctrine of evil, however, do not settle the question of the doctrine's meaning. For that, we look elsewhere.

Barth considers the reality and power of evil to be indisputable. For many, it is a fact of experience, and Barth, no stranger to such experience, could hardly disagree. But theologically, of course, this experience must be taken up in the biblical witness to evil, first in the history of Israel, and in the end, in the suffering death of the Messiah. Barth approaches the theodicy with the presence of evil as a theological fact; the enmity of creation to the Creator will not allow an optimistic solution.[27] The doctrinal question must not be, Does evil exist, but, How and why does such evil exist?

The mode of being of evil belongs to the realm of creation. In the beginning, when the divine life existed *a se,* there was a time when evil was not. It entered the cosmos in God's decision to elect *ad extra,* to create beings that are not divine. Barth often terms this act the freedom of God to allow space and time for the creature. I think we must draw the inference from Barth's description: creation involves the negation of the divine mode

27. Such an optimism, linked to the rationalist solutions of Leibnitz, Spinoza, and some Deists, would be termed "pessimistic" in commonsense usage. Technically, however, the world in its present state is optimistic; for however miserable it may be, it nevertheless represents God's will, and is thus the "best possible."

of being from the cosmos, so that the other might exist. This is not precisely an hegelian idea—the divine and creaturely realities will never be sublated in a higher term—but the establishment of the other involves an act that alienation mimics and corrupts. As God dirempts his being for the sake of creation, evil enters as alienation, the severing of the connection between God and his world. This state of enmity Barth terms *"Gottlosigkeit,"* utter Godlessness.

God, however, did not create nothingness, though he is its master. Nor did he discover it, a being of discrete identity alongside the divine life. Nothingness, Barth insists, has no "autonomous existence independent of God"; indeed, "only the divine non-willing can be accepted as the ground of its existence."[28] Why—we still must ask the question—does God's "non-willing" provide the ground of evil? Why does the divine *No,* the judgment, the rejection, the actions Barth terms the "eternal passing-over," why do these acts of will demarcate the chaotic existence and reality of evil? In the end, does it not make much better sense to insist that what God rejects does not exist, that God's "non-willing" leaves no remainder?

We could assume that these are the sort of questions Barth would find distasteful. They give off the aroma of speculation, Barth might say, and they seek rationalized answers to questions not posed in revelation. But Barth offers a more serious response than this to our questions, and we need not be frightened off by a threatening exterior. Barth might be only "making a report," as he often insists in the *Dogmatics,* but it is an intelligible report. The questions raised about God's agency in the existence of evil concern the internal coherence of Barth's report.

Though hardly explicit in his doctrine, Barth I think assumes the following argument. The dualisms that inhabit our world—the light and dark; life and death; subject and object—far from representing only our shadow realm of becoming, belong in another form to the divine reality as well. Human agency requires a kind of dualism: to choose an object we must reject the alternatives. We act toward specific ends; we pass over the alternatives. We recognize and define objects of thought because they are "not-self" and "not-another." We create and order and, if the laws of thermodynamics have their way, we engender chaos as well. These are commonplaces, to be sure, but in Barth's thought they are also much more. The duality of the world and of human experience belongs to the divine ordering of creation. In withdrawing his being from the world, God creates an independent mode of being, a creature of light and shadow. This twofold world, however, is willed through

28. *Dogmatics,* 3.2:353 [*Dogmatik,* 3.2:407].

Christ, the "principle" and agent of creation. For Barth, this dogmatic assertion can lead to only one conclusion: the creation mirrors the duality of its Creator. Viewed as creation, the world, illuminated by its many little lights and shadows, reflects its one Light, who shines in and delimits the darkness.

Put briefly, duality belongs to God's inner life and agency as well. That is the significance, after all, of placing Christ, elector and elected, within the doctrine of God. Every divine act must be a division, a separation of the desired end from the surd.[29] Even creation involves a parting of the light from the dark, an ordering by which chaos is excluded. This chaos, the nothingness at the boundary of creation, recedes but is not annihilated. God's acts exhibit a kind of correspondence. Divine willing implies a "non-willing," a passing-over, but even the rejected corresponds to God's lordship by possessing reality. The reality of the rejected possesses the grade and mode of being God orders for it, of course: it exists as "non-creation," as Nothingness. With this argument, Barth hopes to honor the threat to God's dominion over creation yet still confirm God's mastery and ultimate triumph over the opposition. To use Christological language, the rebellious chaos of creation is enhypostatically assumed and limited by God's will.

Such a formulation, however, threatens to raise more questions than answers. A residual contradiction seems to lie at its base: how can Nothingness exist? How can opposition be defeated yet not eliminated? Such threats of contradiction hardly ruffle a thinker of such dialectical leanings as Barth. The irrational nature of evil actually provides a place to launch his strongest argument.

Nothingness assumes several forms in its encounter with creation: evil, chaos, and sin. In all forms, it exists in what analysts might call "counterdependency." All the time proclaiming its power and independence, Nothingness—like Milton's Satan on the burning lake—lives in craven dependence

---

29. Hegel's discussion of "one-sided infinity" is instructive: "When we say 'infinite spirit,' the word 'infinite' is itself understood in a one-sided way because it has the finite over against it. In order not to be one-sided, Spirit must encompass finitude within itself, and finitude in general means nothing more than a process of self-distinguishing. . . . Finitude is this distinguishing, which in Spirit takes the form of consciousness. Spirit must have consciousness, distinction, otherwise it is not Spirit; accordingly, this is the moment of finitude in it. It must have this character of finitude within itself—that may seem blasphemous. . . . When we view the characteristic of finitude as something contradictory to God, then we take the finite as something fixed, independent—not as something transitional, but rather as something essentially independent, a limitation that remains utterly such—and then we have not properly recognized the nature of the finite and the infinite" (Georg Wilhelm Friedrich Hegel, *Lectures on the Philosophy of Religion,* trans. and ed. Peter Hodgson, R. F. Brown, and J. M. Steward, assisted by H. S. Harris [Berkeley and Los Angeles: University of California Press, 1988], 405, 406).

upon creation and its Creator. Nothingness must live by opposition; its particular kind of reality displays nothing of the spontaneous freedom of a created being. All of evil's reality draws upon creation, though in a distorted and darkened mirror image. This interior "hollowness" reflects the state of being the non-willed of God. But more, it reflects the punishment of opposition to the divine will. Unlike creation, unlike even more the Creator, Nothingness must exist as contradiction. It possesses no rationality, no order, no freedom; it is utterly dark. This, after all, is what existing as the opposite of God must be like. For this reason, Barth insists that theology must be discontinuous, "broken," especially here where it speaks of evil.[30] We cannot expect to erect a system in which evil is rationalized and reconciled into a higher concept. It will always carry the stamp of an alien, irreconcilable element, certainly present, never domesticated, and never welcomed within the plan of creation. Nothingness can never be understood. And though Barth asserts that God is lord even over the rebellious, the creature will never master it alone.

The location of Nothingness at the frontier of creation presents a special danger to the creature. Evil, though delimited by God, threatens to overwhelm created being. The danger springs from both sides. On the side of evil, the danger arises from its inherent opposition to the creature. Evil must oppose; more, it must invade, corrupt, disorder the product of God's will. The irrational existence of Nothingness will always tempt the creature with despair, anxiety, and chaos. The creature, on its side, approaches the conflict as the ambivalent and weaker combatant.

Evil and sin are forces of genuine fascination to the creature. Nothingness repels the creature by drawing it in. Human beings fear yet desire evil. Like the love of filth diagnosed by analysts, the creaturely desire for evil satisfies human pride in its own works, yet covers the creature in shame and disgust. The deeply irrational fascination of the human person, created in obedience, for disobedience and sin make the creature a poor opponent to the forces of evil. In such a battle, human beings will always lose. But they will not, at the same time, be guiltless. Psychoanalytic language, in fact, springs readily to mind when describing Barth's doctrine of sin precisely because it describes human willfulness as at once compelled and free. In his case studies, Freud captured the uncanny experience of those who act as though directed by an unseen hand—those meaningless, necessary acts—yet all the while recognizing and willing their secret purpose in a submerged recess of the self. Like

---

30. Those who look for Dialectical Theology in Barth's mature work will not be disappointed here. Section 50 in vol. 3.3 retains both the language and the thought-form of Barth's early work.

Freud, Barth held human beings accountable, even though "ought may not imply can."[31] Fundamentally, human beings long to be like gods, to flatter their own intelligence with the knowledge of good and evil, to disobey under cover of the elevated idea of mature self-sufficiency.[32] This is the side of creaturely desire for sin and evil.

The other side, too, brings the creature close to the reality of Nothingness. But this is the side of human frailty and passivity, the side Barth calls the "shadow side of creation." Barth cautions that theologians must never confuse the shadow side with evil itself.

> It is difficult to attack a slander on creation which is so old, multiform and tenacious. Yet is it imperative that we should do this at the very outset. No protest can be too sharp or emphatic. It is true that in creation there is not only a Yes but also a No; not only a height but also an abyss; not only clarity but also obscurity; not only progress and continuation but also impediment and limitation; not only growth but also decay; not only opulence but also indigence; not only beauty but also ashes; not only beginning but also end; not only value but also worthlessness. It is true that in creaturely existence, and especially in the existence of man, there are hours, days and years both bright and dark, success and failure, laughter and tears, youth and age, gain and loss, birth and sooner or later its inevitable corollary, death. It is true that individual creatures and men experience these things in most unequal measure, their lots being assigned by a justice which is curious or very much concealed. Yet it is irrefutable that creation and creature are good even in the fact that all that is exists in this contrast and antithesis. In all this, far from being null, it praises its Creator and Lord even on its shadowy side, even in the negative aspect in which it is so near to nothingness.[33]

Trained in the sights are Idealists, early and late, who locate evil within creation and hold that it is only painful for the moment, a defect to be sublated in the end in a higher view, an error forgiven once understood.

31. Kant's own formula, altered in the text, summarized his lofty expectation for the fulfillment of moral duty: "Ought implies can." On the other hand, Kant's late essay, *Religion within the Limits of Reason Alone* mirrors at times this human ability and inability to properly order and enact our moral life.

32. Barth works out this analysis of pride in *Dogmatics,* 4.2, with characteristic sneers at the refined air of bourgeois individualism and moral piety.

33. *Dogmatics,* 3.3:296–97 [*Dogmatik,* 3.3:336].

Barth allows no appeasement with evil, no *apokatastasis* with an irreducible enemy. Instead, Nothingness must be recognized in its true form: an absolutely alien, third force bordering creation. The shadow side, though dark and often senseless, belongs to creation and is good. Nevertheless, Satan stands on the frontier of this shadow side. Nothingness tempts the creature at this boundary. In the experience of loss and suffering, of death in its senselessness and brutality, of injustice in its numbing cycles, in these dark moments of created life, the creature hears the bitter call of Nothingness from across the border and hands itself over.

The creature, after all, is not God. It is mortal, and the fear of death gives human beings their strongest taste of what Barth calls "real death," existence in opposition to God. The risk to the creature cannot be exaggerated. It is genuine life or death—the only absolute danger the human person can face. But the risk is real to God as well. God recognized this risk when he willed to create mortal life. And, unlike the creature, God will vindicate the risk. This act of justifying his creation is what Barth calls election. Through the Son, the Father and Holy Spirit will to be with the creature. In assuming flesh, the Son engages the battle for creation. The victory over Nothingness is secured in Christ, but is fought in history. The story of this war, of the elect who struggle with and succumb to sin, and of the final though unconsummated defeat of the Evil One, is the story of Israel. In Jewish flesh, Christ takes on and confronts the power of Nothingness and sin. In Jewish flesh, the rejected is elected. In the people Israel, the electing life of the Trinity assumes historical reality. In the people Israel, in both its biblical and rabbinic forms, God elects in Christ. But the history of this election, Barth solemnly repeats, is the execution of divine judgment and wrath.

Israel Elected to Be the Rejected Community of Christ

At the head of the section, "The Election of the Community," Barth boldly summarizes his position:

> The election of grace, as the election of Jesus Christ, is simultaneously the eternal election of the one community of God by the existence of which Jesus Christ is to be attested to the whole world and the whole world summoned to faith in Jesus Christ. This one community of God in its form [*Gestalt*] as Israel has to serve the representation [*Darstellung*] of the divine judgement, in its form as the Church the represen-

tation of the divine mercy. In its form as Israel it is determined for hearing, and in its form as the Church for believing the promise sent forth to man. To the one elected community of God is given in the one case its passing, and in the other its coming form.[34]

In his analysis of the "Paradox of Rejection," Friedrich Marquardt aligns this area of Barth's thought with the tradition of Idealist epistemology concerned with "representation" and "reflection":

> *Der Begriff 'spiegeln',* den Barth parallel zu 'darstellen' verwendet, hat in unserem Zusammenhang schon Tradition. "Die Juden bleiben noch immer ein Spiegel, in dem wir Gottes Geheimnisse in der Erlösung des menschlichen Geschlechts als ein Rätsel sehen (J. G. Hamann) u.ä. Wichtiger ist aber "spiegeln" in der Tradition des Erkennens. Im Feuerbachschen Projektionsthema vom Hinauspiegeln der geschichtlichen Wirklichkeit auf die Wolkenwand metaphysischer Phantasie spielt es genauso eine Rolle wie bei Kants Entdeckung von Raum und Zeit als blossen Formen unserer sinnlichen Anschauung und wie in der Leninistichen Abbildtheorie von der Beweisbarkeit der Realität durch die Wiederspiegelung der Basis im Überbau. Barth hat seine Theologie bewußt in die Problemwelt dieser Tradition hineingestellt, als er überging von der Methode der Dialektik zur Methode der Analogie.[35]
>
> [The concept of 'reflection', which Barth uses parallel to 'presentation', has a long tradition in our context. "The Jews still remain a mirror, in which we see the divine mysteries in the redemption of humankind as an enigma" (J. G. Hamann) etc. The concept of 'reflection' is more important, however, in the epistemological tradition. It plays a role in Feuerbach's projection theory, in which historical reality is reflected out onto the cloudy reaches of metaphysical phantasy. It plays an equal role in Kant's discovery of time and space as the mere forms of our sensible perception, and in the Leninist representation theory of the confirmation of reality through the reflection of the base in the superstructure. Barth has consciously placed his theology into the problematic of this tradition when he passed from the dialectical method to that of analogy.]

34. Ibid., 2.2:195 [2.2:215].
35. Marquardt, *Die Entdeckung des Judentums,* 317.

For its part, "presentation" [*Darstellung*] should be placed within the context of higher biblical criticism, and the theological use of the doctrine of analogy. The Bible "mediates" the ideas of theology, giving them substance and historical reality. In fact, this "presentation" of theological truths in historical "objectivity"—the representation of human pride in the history of the Jews— is the "kernel of truth," Marquardt claims "of natural theology within the revelation of grace."[36]

Marquardt displays many of his favorite themes here. The survey of continental philosophy, the sweep of hermeneutics and higher criticism, the compass of the German Protestant tradition; they are all here in characteristic style. And more important, Marquardt points to his later, controversial announcement, that Barth brings natural theology back to life through a sympathetic use of Marx and Lenin.[37] But can we follow Marquardt's direction with equal confidence?

To be sure, this direction points to Marquardt's most serious, sustained critique of Barth. To see Judaism in a mirror, to understand its existence as reflection or projection of another reality, is to trivialize and deny Jewish reality; this is Marquardt's argument. Jews have independent existence, a genuine and voluntary life in God's service, a dignity and responsibility all their own. They cannot be extracted from their own reality in order to serve as a support for Christian superiority—or for Christian self-knowledge and repentence. Of course, the Jews who represent the community that hears, who mirror the flesh that must "pass away," can certainly be granted empirical and historical reality. Marquardt does not claim that Barth contests the intuitive and biblical knowledge of Jewish existence. Of course, the Jewish people exist. But they exist—and this is the heart of Marquardt's critique—as "representation," as "projection," as the mere forms of our perception and the stuff of our alienated consciousness. Their *reality,* that is, lies elsewhere. Marquardt detects German Idealism in Barth's construction of the Jews, and draws out its implication. The Jews are the phenomenal matter of religious reality, making Christian experience possible. They are not "in and for themselves," but confirm, explain, and depend upon Christian reality.

Marquardt has built up a philosophical edifice with an impressive structure.

36. Ibid., 316: "Das Judentum ist die Empirie und insofern: die anschauliche und wirksame Darstellung dieser Situation, anders gesagt: Das Judentum ist für Barth Beweis für den Kern Wahrheit der natürlichen Theologie innerhalb der Gnadenoffenbarung."

37. See Marquardt's later work, *Theologie und Sozialismus: Das Beispiel Karl Barths* (Munich: Christian Kaiser Verlag, 1972), and a lively reminiscence of that controversy by Markus Barth in *Footnotes to a Theology,* 77–94.

But is the foundation sound? He begins with the technical vocabulary of German Idealism, and this point of departure deserves some scrutiny. Barth, after all, does not use these technical terms. Unlike Kant, who uses *Form* for the depiction of time and space, Barth uses *Gestalt* for the shape of the Jewish community. And, although Barth does use *spiegeln* in his description of the role of the Jews in covenant history, he does not adopt the hegelian counterpart, *Vorstellung,* sensible representation, without which Feuerbach's ideas could scarcely be launched out onto the cloudy and empty sky. Barth, of course, does employ the term *Darstellung* to describe the twofold life of Israel, and this *is* a hegelian concept, but it belongs to Hegel's aesthetics, not to his philosophy of religion.

The idea may "present" itself in sensible, plastic form as the beautiful; since art belongs to the realm of reason, it partakes of *Geist,* but not in the manner and to the extent that religion does. Religion—Christianity in particular—requires "representation." Here the Idea presents itself rationally: Christianity takes Spirit as its object, and it holds this object before consciousness in thought. Unlike philosophy, of course, Christianity requires concrete, sensible manifestation; the Spirit must assume flesh. Nevertheless, religion surpasses art. In religion, the Spirit achieves absolute self-consciousness; it endures the "infinite anguish" of complete finitude, death, and takes up even this contradiction into its self-recognition. Only representation at this level could arm Feuerbach with such powerful weapons. The theory of projection would be reduced to a form of wish fulfillment without this alienated labor of self-consciousness.

At the same time, it cannot be denied that Barth knew the "Problemwelt" of Idealist epistemology well; he served, after all, a long apprenticeship in Protestant Liberalism. And he certainly knew enough of radical politics to become involved in socialist circles in his early years. But is this philosophical tradition active in Barth's doctrine of Israel, and does it account for Barth's polemical conclusions? That Barth did not employ the technical language of Kant or Hegel weighs against Marquardt's argument, I think, but it does not refute it. The shape, the direction, and force of Barth's argument must be examined. Is the existence of the Jews, in Barth's thought, an immaterial reflection and an insubstantial representation of human pride and divine retribution?

Barth's treatment of the election of the community can be understood as a sustained commentary on Luther's early and remarkable essay, "Das Jesu Christus ein geborner Jude sei" ["That Jesus Christ was born a Jew"]. The complex and often troubling reversals in Luther's life are well known and have made his doctrines the stuff of rich psychoanalytic interpretation.[38] His attitude and teaching about the Jews illustrates the raw power of Luther's contradictions as well as any. Early in his career, Luther wrote the often tender and well-received essay cited above. The Jews are to be commended for their rejection of idolatrous Christianity, mired and polluted by the papists. Those who love the gospel recognize that Jews are the flesh Christ assumed, a living treasure of the Incarnation. True Christian rulers will treat the Jews with the respect and dignity that the family of Christ commands. Some commentators hold that Luther expected the Jews to convert to Protestant Christianity, as the truth and comfort of a purified gospel would prove irresistible.[39] That Luther was bitterly disappointed by the "perdurance" of the Jews seems unmistakable. But the unvarnished vulgarity of Luther's late essay, "Die Juden und ihr Lügen" ["The Jews and their Lies"] transcends such straightforward explanations. The essay distills the religious and social contempt for Jews widespread throughout late medieval Germany. The murder of Christ, the poisoning of wells, the arrogance and "grasping materialism" of the Jews are all there. Luther gives voice, as only he could, to the fear, respect, and visceral rage Christians felt toward the Jews in their midst.[40]

Barth belongs to this Lutheran tradition. This point should not be exaggerated; Barth is no Luther. He does not advocate violence against the Jews—he abhorred the eerie Nazi reenactment of Luther's clamor for the punishment of Jews. Nor does Barth rely upon the crude mixture of admiration and contempt for acculturated Jews that lay so close at hand. In the decade of the 1930s, when the "lights went out," this time in earnest, "all over Europe," Barth's vigorous and repeated condemnation of anti-Semitism must not be minimized. Still, Barth stands in Luther's shadow, in a complex and inescapable heritage of darkness and light. Much of Luther's medieval world lives on in Barth—the drama of Christian supersession of the Jews, the vigorous claim

38. The best known of these studies is Erik Erikson's *Young Man Luther* (New York: W. W. Norton, 1958).

39. See, for example, the commentary in vol. 47 of *Luther's Works*, ed. Jaroslav Pelikan, trans. W. I. Brandt (St. Louis, Mo.: Concordia Press; Philadelphia: Fortress Press, 1962). This is the English edition of *D. Martin Luthers Werke*, Kritische Gesamtausgabe (Weimar, 1883–   ). See also "That Jesus Christ Was Born a Jew," in *Luther's Works*, 45:99–229 [*Luther's Works*, 11:314–36]; and "The Jews and Their Lies," in *Luther's Works*, 47:137–306 [*Luthers Werke*, 53:417–552].

40. Heiko Obermann, however, in his biography of Luther, *Luther: Between God and the Devil* (New Haven: Yale University Press, 1988), and his historical essay, *The Roots of Anti-Semitism*, does not find such a clear distinction between these two essays, though this means, on the whole, depressing the early essay to the level of the late.

of ownership over the scriptures,[41] the overarching form of prophecy and fulfillment, and, not least, the blindfolded Synagogue of medieval iconography. All but the first of these find their place in Barth's work. But they are rooted in and draw their passion from Luther's early confession, that Jesus was born a Jew.

"It is from Israel," Barth writes, "that this man [Jesus] has come and been snatched [like a brand from the burning]. Not from Greece, not from Rome, not from Germany, but from Israel!"[42] Christians cannot afford to forget or dismiss this "fact" because, as the fourth gospel expresses it, "Salvation comes from the Jews." This understanding of Jesus as the Messiah to and for Israel influences Barth's doctrine of election. Not only has the doctrine been transformed from a drama of the individual soul to a determination within the Trinity, but Barth has placed the community as mediator between Christ and the individual. The concentric circles Barth wraps around the act of Christ, electing and elected, now radiate out toward the community first, and then, finally to the individual. The individual secures election only within the community; the community only within Christ. That Jesus was born a Jew means this, first of all, that the people of God are properly and principally the recipients of Christ's work of election. Israel is the first, the passing, and the rejected object of God's electing will.

Christ's body exists in two forms; under the aspect of the community, these two forms can be discriminated as Israel and the Church, united yet distinct. But Israel is Christ's body, his environment, in a way particular and unique, for "salvation is of the Jews." It is from Israel's "stock" that Jesus comes, and it is on the ground of Israel's election that the Church arises:

> The Church lives by the "fathers" of Israel, by the fellowship of the spirit with Abraham, Isaac and Jacob, Moses, David, and Elijah. They are the great witnesses to the divine calling, preservation and leading of this people. The Church knows that as such, and therefore in the concrete historical form in which they are presented in the tradition, they are witnesses of Jesus for whose sake this people was called, preserved and led by God. These fathers of Israel, and they alone, ought in strict justice to be called the "fathers of the Church." And now, the Church lives by the existence of "Christ according to the

41. Marquardt claims that this is the key debate between Barth and the Jews, indeed between Christians and Jews. See *Die Entdeckung des Judentums,* par. 1, "Hermeneutische Vorerwägung zum theologischen Reden von Israel," and the conclusion in paragraph 5.5, "Die Auferstehung als Schluß strich der Verwerfung," especially 360.
42. *Dogmatics,* 2.2:204 [*Dogmatik,* 2.2:225].

flesh." It lives by Jesus Christ because and so far as He is, as man, the
Son of Abraham and David, and is called Jesus of Nazareth: not in
spite of this; not under the incidental assumption that He is this too
and not only the eternal Son of God; but because and so far as He is
an Israelite out of Israel.[43]

These are strong words, stronger indeed than Luther's, and Barth is of no
mind to moderate them, even in the thick of his condemnation of Israel's
unbelief. Israel is the environment of Christ, and of Christians, too, because
it is the "concrete, historical form" of the one man, electing and elected. Like
the *Umwelt* that composes reality in Heidegger's early thought, Israel surrounds the Church and grounds it in the concrete witness to Jesus of
Nazareth. And, like the "things" [*Zeuge*] in Heidegger's analysis, Israel does
not live an independent existence; it belongs to another: "For although we
can say of the Messiah that He is 'given' to Israel, any suggestion that He
'belonged' to Israel must be completely excluded. He does not 'belong' to
the church either. On the contrary, the whole elected community of God
belongs to Him."[44] Israel, like the Church, lives "close at hand,"[45] as Heidegger might say; it lives for another, and to another's end. Israel serves Christ,
despite the rejection of "its Messiah," much as the stuff of our environment
must answer to our call.

Of course, the assignment of living communities to the category of
"environment" carries a price. Things serve their masters, but they do not
know them. In Israel's service to Christ, it cannot recognize itself, or the
Christ who arose from it:

> It is . . . implicit in the nature of the case that only in the knowledge
> of Jesus Christ and of His election, i.e., in the faith of the Church, is
> the differentiation as well as the unity of the elect community know-
> able and actually known. The bow of the covenant over the two is not
> a neutral area and observation point between them but the history
> which takes place between Israel and the Church. The way of this
> history is, however, the way of the knowledge of Jesus Christ. It leads
> from Israel *to* the Church. Only in this movement, i.e., in practice only
> from the standpoint of the Church, can it be perceived, described and
> understood as the living way of the one elect community of God.[46]

43. Ibid. [Ibid., 224–25].
44. Ibid.
45. An attempt at Heidegger's *Zuhanden,* another of his celebrated and perhaps untranslatable terms.
46. *Dogmatics,* 2.2:200 [*Dogmatik,* 2.2:221].

To be sure, much more governs Barth's understanding of Israel than the use of a term like "environment"; his understanding of history, and, more important, the place of revelation within and beyond it shape Barth's views here decisively. But the use of this term underscores Barth's intention: Christ is the electing subject of his world; he determines its use and value apart from any mundane self-definition. Like the Church, Israel cannot know itself apart from Christ.

And the electing Christ will use his environment: it will "embody" or "mediate" him, the true Mediator.

> The community which has to be described in this way forms so to speak the inner circle of the "other" election which has taken place (and takes place) in and with the election of Jesus Christ. In so far as on the one hand it forms this special environment of the man Jesus, this inner circle, but on the other hand it is itself of the world or chosen from the world and composed of individual men, its election is to be described as mediate and mediating in respect of its mission and function. It is *mediate,* that is, in so far as it is the middle point between the election of Jesus Christ and (included in this) the election of those who have believed, and do and will believe, in Him. It is *mediating* in so far as the relation between the election of Jesus Christ and that of all believers (and vice versa) is mediated and conditioned by it. . . . The honor of its election can never be anything but the honor of Jesus Christ, the selfless honor of witnessing to Him.[47]

The community of God, mediate between Christ and the believer, serves Christ as his mediator in the world. As his environment, the community expresses nothing of itself, but reflects its one Lord, a living mirror of God's glory. Even in its "unwillingness, incapacity and unworthiness," Israel remains a mediating environment, reflecting Christ's own election to the work of suffering and rejection. It mirrors the form of the Person "judged," the form of One who is "passing away."

Barth's provocative language presses the argument forward, but Marquardt's unanswered questions now demand attention. Israel as an environment, as mirror, mediating and reflecting another's will: are these not the terms of Idealism, suitably altered? Does Barth's treatment of Israel, particularly here, not denigrate history, reduce reality itself to the Idea, now chastely called Jesus Christ? Is the particularity of election, of Israel's election, not

47. Ibid., 196 [216].

here eviscerated, to be refilled instead with the Christian themes of disobedience and self-reproach? That historical reality left to the Jews, Marquardt might conclude, is the history of stubborn existence, a refusal that merely confirms them as witnesses to Christian self-understanding. Their reality is to "project" or "mirror"; or, as Barth has written, "There is, then, no independent election of the community. Only Jewish or clerical phantasy and arrogance can try to exalt the community above Jesus Christ into the beginning of all things."[48]

Marquardt touches a delicate spot in Barth's thought. The place of history, of what Barth calls the "concrete historical form," cannot be easily fixed. On one hand, the Jews are a "historical fact": Jesus came out of and for the sake of Israel. And they are another "historical fact" as well: "Sire, the Jews!"[49] Their existence demonstrates God's faithfulness, his sovereign lordship over even an "obdurate people," to make them witnesses by their very refusal:

> Even in this way [Israel's sectarian self-assertion] it really gives to the world the very witness that is required of it. How it is with man, the nature of the burden which God in His great love assumes, the nature of the curse which God has made Himself for the good of man, man himself by whom and for whom Jesus Christ was crucified—these things, and all that they mean, it reveals even in this way, even in and with its unbelief, even in the spectral form of the Synagogue. The existence of the Jews, as is generally recognised, is an adequate proof of the existence of God. It is an adequate demonstration of the depths of human guilt and need and therefore of the inconceivable greatness of God's love in the event in which God was in Christ reconciling the world to Himself. The Jews of the ghetto give this demonstration involuntarily, joylessly and ingloriously, but they do give it. They have nothing to attest to the world but the shadow of the cross of Jesus Christ that falls upon them. But they, too, do actually and necessarily attest Jesus Christ himself.[50]

Those who read Barth's work as the liberation of theology from the constraints of modern culture will find the price of such freedom here. Barth's method cuts deeply and relentlessly at the premises of modern thought, and

48. Ibid.
49. Barth quotes this well-known story in several places, including *Dogmatics,* 3.3:210. Frederick the Great is said to have asked for proofs for the existence of God; the reply: "Sire, the Jews!"
50. Ibid., 209 [230].

he is a tough-minded surgeon indeed. That the Jews do not understand themselves in this way; that the Synagogue is not spectral, the ghetto joyless— or voluntary; that Jews, too, have their own "special theme and task": these arise from the domains outside Christian theology, and their claims have no merit here.

Christian theology, in Barth's work, has found its own voice, a voice medieval in character and tone, canonical, and anti-Judaic.

Nevertheless, Marquardt is right: Barth knows Idealism thoroughly and shows its influence, but Barth's understanding of Judaism belongs to another heritage. Israel and the Jews "mediate" and "reflect"; Marquardt is right to point to these terms, but their "concrete, historical reality" is not mere projection onto an empty, Christian sky. Barth, I think, has real, concrete Jews in mind—not the delicate "ancient Hebrews" of much Protestant imagination—and these Jews have an authentic history. He insists on this point, working the ground over and over, that Jesus was born a Jew. All Jews, *"post* and *ante Christum,"* testify to the particularity of Jesus' birth and mission. The events of post-biblical history—the destruction of the Second Temple, the rise of rabbinic Judaism, the medieval ghetto life, the Jewish life in dispersion—they all gain their significance in Barth's work because they are "facts," they happened in our world. The description of Jews as the "environment" of Jesus pays benefits here. The Jews are historically serious because they are the reality "close at hand"; they people the surrounding world and condition our reception of it. They are "mediators" between Jesus of Nazareth and those who believe in him. They "reflect" Jesus, because they, like him, are Jews; they "reflect" humanity, because they, like all flesh, are sinful. Barth's terms belong to this thought-world, not Idealism, and borrow their problems from it.

Barth's *Israellehre* as Dogmatic Interpretation of History

Barth's portrait of Israel, after all, belongs to the thought-world of Christian history, to what Collingwood has described as the providential conception of history.[51] Like Calvin and Augustine, Barth searches history for its silent motion, flowing out and away from God and returning to Him at the end.

---

51. Collingwood, *The Idea of History,* 50.

God's purpose will out, and history will tell that story. Christian historiography begins with faith, of course; Barth would readily assent. But too much can be made of the premise of faith. History cannot be a "pious fiction," imaginatively placed into the past to serve religious ends. *That* is the history of alienated consciousness, a history of "pure commodity," in which "events" are the objective form of the human mind. Christian history has no room for such "Idealism."[52]

The Christian use of history assumes a common record of the past, visible and ready for confirmation to those within and outside the Church.[53] The events of history are ambivalent and obscure; they are covered by the confusion and corruption of human will and reason. They are *poor* witnesses, Barth might say, but they are *witnesses*. The Christian can discern a pattern, a question mark, perhaps, but one that waits confirmation when God is all in all. Consider Barth's treatment of the destruction of the Second Temple:

> What does not happen, however, is that Israel as such and as a whole puts its faith in Him. What happens, on the contrary, is that it resists its election at the very moment when the promise given with it passes into fulfillment. Israel refuses to join in the confession of the Church, refuses to enter upon its service in the one elected community of God. Israel forms and upholds the Synagogue (even though the conclusion of its history is confirmed by the fall of Jerusalem). It acts as if it had still another special determination and future beside and outwith the Church. It acts as if it could realise its true determination beside and outwith the Church. And in so doing it creates a schism, a gulf, in the midst of the community of God.[54]

"Even though the conclusion of its history is confirmed by the fall of Jerusalem": this is Christian history. The events of the year 70 are part of the public record. The supression of the uprising, the destruction of the Temple, the imposition of Roman rule, all the property of history. But for the

52. Of course it is hardly fair to jump Idealists together in this way, and it is unjust to Hegel, for whom history is a very serious matter indeed. Hegel has his critics precisely at this point—a good number of them—but it is fair to say that Hegel intended to *demonstrate* the life of the Spirit from an analysis of history, not invent events that confirm his thesis.

53. The scientific status of historiography is a controversy all its own. I am not proposing a particular view of historical "objectivity" here, or even less, a Christian "covering law," but simply that, in its traditional use, Christian history has assumed that the records are open for general inspection and interpretation.

54. *Dogmatics,* 2.2:208 [*Dogmatik,* 2.2:229].

Christian, A.D. 70 knits together the biblical and the modern ages and is the origin of much of the material of Christian supersessionism. This year is the "concrete, historical form" of the punishment of the Jews; the fulfillment of the old dispensation; the completion of "late Judaism"; the evocation of the Temple not made by hands, who rises up to complete and fulfill what has passed away. The type of the blindfolded Synagogue, humbled, holding a broken sword takes its place in medieval public life—on cathedral tympanums—because Christians saw their triumph justified in history.

But just what sort of history is this? That is Marquardt's question. It is not a simple matter, particularly in Barth, and the common distinctions between evidence and interpretation, or even, between "husk and kernel"[55] do not take us far. Typology, the complex classical method of biblical interpretation, brings us closer, as it takes up history into enduring patterns, making a narrative of disparate figures and events.[56] Typology grows out of history, G.W.H. Lampe argues, and it is this distinctive admixture of history and figure that distinguishes the type from allegory:

> Typology in this sense of the term would appear to be grounded in a particular view of history which the New Testament writers undoubtedly held themselves and which Christians for whom the Bible is authoritative can scarcely repudiate. On this view a type may be called in the language of the Fathers a "mystery," but it is a "mystery" in the normal New Testament sense of the word. It is a secret in the counsel of God which is being made known in Christ; an element in the hidden purpose of God which has been made manifest in being fulfilled. The prophecies of the Second Isaiah are mysteries in this sense. . . . So, also, we may think, is the story of Jonah who, through

55. Adolf Harnack used this distinction in *Wesen des Christentum* [*What is Christianity?*] to separate the essence of the religion of Jesus from its incidental, historical form. The liberal lives of Jesus are unimaginable without such a distinction; Barth would have none of it.

56. K. J. Woollcombe offers this definition of typology (a notoriously difficult task): "Typology, considered as a method of exegesis, may be defined as the establishment of historical connexions between certain events, persons or things in the Old Testament and similar events, persons or things in the New Testament. Considered as a method of writing, it may be defined as the description of an event, person or thing in the New Testament in terms borrowed from the description of its prototypal counterpart in the Old Testament. Thus, if we were to say that Isaac, who carried the wood for his sacrifice, is a type of Simon of Cyrene, who carried the wood for the Cross, on the grounds of an etymological similarity between the names of their children, we should be using the typological method of exegesis. On the other hand, when St. Matthew and St. Mark described John the Baptist in terms borrowed from the description of Elijah, they were using the typological method of writing (G.W.H. Lampe and K. J. Woollcombe, *Essays on Typology* [London: S.C.M. Press, 1957], 39, 40).

his swallowing up in the belly of Hades and his restoration to life brings the message of repentance to the Gentiles. The author of that story did not consciously foresee Christ as the end towards which his own thought was pointing; but in the light of Christ's saving work it is possible to see that the picture which he painted held elements of a deeper truth than he himself could know, and that it was in fact an adumbration, as St Matthew, if not Jesus himself, pointed out, of what was to come. . . . In such mysteries there is a real correspondence between the type in the past and the fulfillment in the future. Typology of this kind is an expression of the particular view of history held by the Scriptural writers as a whole, and in this expression the type is a genuine foreshadowing; it is indeed a *typos tou mellontos.*[57]

Much has been written on the particular force and significance of typology, and of its contribution to the Christian concern for the unity of the Bible.[58] Hans Frei points to the specific biblical texts used by Barth in his doctrine of election (in volume 2, part 2, of the *Dogmatics*) as examples of "realistic or narrative readings," at once literary and historical, tying together the Word and our words in one story, the type of Christ, elected and electing.[59]

Using typology as a model, Barth's conception of history requires that the Synagogue be seen as a type. It is a historical, material reality that finds its meaning in the biblical story, in the figure of Christ rejected. The typology is historical because it ties together an institution of our experience, the Synagogue, with a figure of history, Jesus of Nazareth; the historiography is typological because the Synagogue receives its meaning from Another, from His isolation, His sorrow, His cry of dereliction. The Synagogue is a type of the one Antitype, who took the "judgment that has overtaken" humanity upon Himself, who sealed up all disobedience in His suffering obedience.

Of course, typology—especially as a "historical" form—is far easier to evoke than explain. It is a teleological system: "It is a secret in the counsel of God which is being made known in Christ; an element in the hidden purpose of God which has been made manifest in being fulfilled." The overarching pattern of promise and fulfillment, the "rainbow," Barth writes, from "there to here" makes typology particularly hospitable to Christian use, and appeals to the strains of biblical realism in Barth's thought. But we would flatten the

57. Ibid., 29, 30.

58. Two classics in this field: Erich Auerbach, *Mimesis: The Representation of Reality in Western Literature,* trans. Willard R. Trask (Princeton: Princeton University Press, 1953); and a book inspired by it, Hans Frei's *The Eclipse of Biblical Narrative.*

59. Frei, *Eclipse of Biblical Narrative,* viii.

remarkable depth of typology if we imagined that past merely pointed to its future, and stood like a pale reminder of its vibrant fulfillment.

The type draws its power—and this, I think, is its attraction for Barth—from its ability to recognize the past in its separate, objective dignity, while enriching, extending, and binding it up with its future. Moses raises up the serpent in the wilderness; Christ stretches out his arms on the cross. Ezekiel hears the rustle of dry bones as they rush into life; the tombs open and the dead become incorruptible. These are types. They work on the imagination because both figures in the pair are real, living images. They evoke one another, despite their differences. The "stubborn" existence of both makes the parallel stronger, more compelling. One figure is bound up—"sublated"—in the other, yet remains true—the contradiction is preserved—to type. Those readers who have felt the power of typology will remember how the figures, type and antitype, grow one into the other, yet live a life of their own. I suggest a hegelian interpretation of the type, one I think that fits the material, but it might be fairer to describe the dialectic itself as typological, rather than the other way around. We might find another example from German letters that would offer more insight into the power, and the mechanics, of typology.

Consider Freud's notion of the "overdetermination" of the conscious mind. Freud's thought is nearly irresistible to many literary theorists, as his representation of the unconscious as commanding, enticing, and enriching the conscious opens a path into the creative act. But the idea of "overdetermination" offers a more specific aid; it reenacts the motion of the type—from there to here—and, more valuable, offers an explanation of its mechanism. I am not suggesting that Freud has *explained* typology, or that typology merely foreshadows Freud. Rather, I offer Freud's theory as a *parallel* to typology, an explanation of unconscious process that may illuminate what kind of history Barth, and other typologists, seem to have in mind.[60]

Freud considered *The Interpretation of Dreams* his greatest work, an idea that "comes to a man but once in his life." Complex and often obscure, it was little read at the time of its original publication, but has remained widely influential, in part from Freud's own estimation of it; in part because of the essay's provocative insights into symbol and story. Freud proposed that dream

---

60. I am certainly not the first to have spotted a connection between psychoanalysis and our conceptions of history. For an interpretation of Freud's work as a historical, rather than a biological, theory, concentrating on the significance of the past for the individual and for a personal sense of freedom, see Michael S. Roth, *Psychoanalysis as History* (Ithaca: Cornell University Press, 1987), especially his generous bibliography on other studies of Freud and historiography on page 22.

images are "overdetermined": they are caused by several agents, from thirst during the night, to daily events (the so-called dream remnants), to the unrecognized and oddly interconnected longings of our unconscious life. Figures in our dreams can stand for several members of our waking friends and family. They may represent past hurts and envies, silently nursed in our unconscious. They may evoke victories dreamed of and unrealized; acts of aggression we would rather not acknowledge. Under analysis, these meanings reveal themselves, but reluctantly. Our "resistance" is the attempt to keep these raw and embarrassing multiple associations buried. Freud considered dreams the royal road to the unconscious; this subtle, retentive power lying outside our awareness, with its elaborations, distortions, and layers of alien meaning—this center of drives fascinated Freud and he saw its force in all areas of waking life.

In his mature understanding of the drives, Freud found new respect for the human "compulsion to repeat," that irresistible desire to work over old ground, to make the same mistakes over and over, to keep discovering an old beloved in someone we claim—this time!—is really new and different. This deep, conservative impulse in human life (what Freud called the "death drive") makes overdetermination a universal element in adult choice and identity. The "repressed material" of our childhood reasserts itself in our adulthood, the unconscious "cunning of history":

A professor's daughter becomes a professor. A child of the modern era, she makes a choice independent of the tradition of family business and apprenticeship; free, perhaps, of the constraints of her father's wishes or of the narrow scope of bourgeois womanhood. This young professor has made a genuine choice, Freud might argue. A relatively healthy personality, of some spontaneity, her decision represents a real weighing of material, historical factors, combined with the influences of taste, opinion, and predisposition we call character. But the father, an authentic and historical figure all his own, lives on in her.

She remembers him, his work, its pleasures and petty tediums, but her unrecognized memories work with greater force. She unwittingly borrows his gestures; she may, in a moment of introspection, recognize her father in her as she speaks with colleagues or students; her research interests may shadow or contradict his own. If, as years pass, she honors her father's influence on her career, she may, like Freud's own daughter Anna, repeat his pattern at depths she may never recognize, and in its subtlety and ironic distortions, never exhaust. Her decision to take up the academic life, in short, is overdetermined. Like a dream image, her adult choice reaches back through conscious agency into the associations of her childhood. Her father, though perhaps still living, retains the mystery he had during her childhood. To her unconscious, a realm outside time, her father still embodies every image once applied to him. Like an archaeological site,[61] the father covers up and reveals the layers of love and rage, distance and tenderness, the dark magnificence that parents become for their infants. This young professor's future has preserved, taken up, and transformed the past. She remains herself, yet embodies another.

She is, in a sense, a type of her father; or, her father is a type preserved in the daughter, the antitype. They have lives of their own—perhaps, some say, they are not so much alike!—yet they are bound up with one another, and their full meaning, for each one, is realized in the life of the other. This complex and inexhaustible association of lives and images points, I think, to the kind of history typology employs.

For the overdetermined professor, let us insert the type of the disbelieving Synagogue. Here, the Synagogue typifies the unbelieving witnesses, those who have seen the truth but refuse it, who testify to their misery in the "joyless and inglorious ghetto." Like the soldiers at the base of the cross, the "disciples who fell away," or the crowd that longed for Barabbas, the Synagogue, in this medieval type, evokes and embodies those who look on the Messiah, but will not receive him.[62] Though they, most of all, should become disciples, they turn against him, condemning themselves to a life of arrogant darkness. They and their type, the Synagogue, are, in Barth's terms, the "elected ones, rejected." Like the professorial father, the Synagogue is a living, historical "fact." It may be examined and understood from a neutral position, and the evidence uncovered in this process matters. But it matters in a particular way. Like the daughter reenacting the father's life, the figure of the disbelieving soldier at the crucifixion takes up the historical form of the Synagogue through the medium of the Christian story. It is not so much that Christian typologists take license with history, any more than that patients fabricate the terrors of their early life—though some of each happens, of course.[63] These events take place, but they take place in the brilliant heat of

61. I borrow an image from a celebrated passage in *Civilization and Its Discontents* (New York: W. W. Norton, 1961), 18–19, in which Freud describes the Unconscious as a city (Freud's beloved Rome) in which buildings are raised one on another, yet magically, never destroyed or lost from sight.

62. Medieval Christian polemicists held that Jews knew full well the doctrines of Christology and the Trinity, but refused to acknowledge them, or Jesus as the Christ.

63. The celebrated "seduction theory" demands a hearing. Jeffrey Masson has charged that Freud abandoned the truth—that his patients had been sexually abused as children—for a pious, politically covenient, and wonderfully plastic fiction—that his patients unconsciously *wished* to be seduced (*The Assault on Truth: Freud's Suppression of the Seduction Theory* [New York:

desire and conviction. These forces need not distort or deny the truth; through their desires, children may experience the terrifying satisfaction of the parents' desire for their children, long controlled and chastely reworked as affection. In the same way, typologists like Barth claim their convictions discover a determination in history that the mere observer cannot find.[64] Where others might see the concrete and neutral reality of the Synagogue, the Christian historian recognizes estrangement. The Synagogue belongs in the Christian story—so Barth argues—and the historical-critical account of its rise in rabbinic Judaism cannot capture the Christian longing for its origin. Like all overdetermined material, this Christian longing preserves, reworks, distorts, and repeats this early object, but it does not forget. The historical imagination used in typology, I suggest, is driven by a kind of love for and aggression directed against its object, and its power to recall and elaborate the past derives from this passion.

Judaism, then, does "mirror" or "represent" Christ, as Marquardt points out, but it is a representation of type, not an estrangement of essence. If the parallel between typology and overdetermination runs true, Judaism cannot be wholly reduced to the terms of Another, nor can it have a purpose limited only to its moral usefulness for Christian doctrine. Judaism "overruns" its image as a type. It has a historical and institutional reality all its own. In fact, it is this "brute facticity" of the Synagogue that forces Barth to assign the unity of the community—Israel within the Church—to a testament of faith.

Of course, such a sturdy defense of Barth's historical "positivism" opens the rear lines to attack. In his effort to take history seriously as a Christian

---

Farrar, Straus & Giroux, 1984]). Peter Gay, in his biography *Freud: A Life for Our Times* (New York: W. W. Norton, 1988), argues that the realities of family life makes such widespread abuse unlikely, and hardly secure as a foundation for psychoanalysis. While I do not share Gay's rather sanguine view of the incest taboo, I think Masson has divided the two positions too sharply. The mutual longing of parents and children for one another is the biological impetus for the creation of families; this power to draw together makes the parent the greatest living force within the child. In Freud's Oedipal triangle, the child *is* seduced by the parents, and the concrete reality of that act is the repetition of the parents, time and again, in the choices, fears, and deepest loves of the child throughout adulthood. This unconscious seduction is a terrible power, and children can be abused by it.

Of course, this seduction is not identical, morally or physically, to the sexual abuse of children. To hold this view would be to repudiate the reality of the material world. Nevertheless, the one reality lies close to the other, and to say that something has taken place in our mind is to acknowledge that something has taken place that is concrete, historical, and very real indeed.

For another account of Freud's "abandonment of the seduction theory," placing the event within the development of psychoanalytic theory, see William McGrath, *Freud's Discovery of Psychoanalysis: The Politics of Hysteria* (Ithaca: Cornell University Press, 1986).

64. So Barth argues in "The Task of a History of Modern Protestant Theology," in *Protestant Theology in the Nineteenth Century,* 2d ed. (London: S.C.M. Press, 1972), chap. 1.

type, does Barth not give tacit support to "natural theology," to the belief that history points to God? This is the second, and I think, more damaging critique Marquardt raises. Again, we circle back on the original question: Just what kind of history is this?

Typology easily lends itself to the demonstrations of natural theology. Those who use natural theology rely upon the doctrine of creation in order to find the impress of God's glory on the works and the creatures of his will. Natural theology comes in many forms, and the argument that leads from order in the universe to an orderly Creator takes another form altogether when the movements of history lead to a governing Lord. That the world is a fit place for its inhabitants is a piece of evidence that in pre-critical days was considered commonplace. All eyes observed that "fact"; its objectivity gave the argument its characteristic attraction well into the Enlightenment, but history has always been another affair. The human past—typology takes no interest in natural history—cannot be relied upon to produce consensus; even the evidence engenders controversy. The broad outlines were considered reasonably secure, but human free will could not be compared to the clarity and order of the heavenly spheres. That a pattern existed *was* common property; typology, pagan and Christian, demanded it. But human corruption, the darkened and disordered will, could never duplicate God's will, but only suggest it, or, worse, defy it. Augustine shared with his Roman contemporaries a somber recognition that a civilization was passing away, but he alone saw God's providential hand. As a form of natural theology, historical typology built an argument on common ground, but in substance it was a "thing not made by hands." An argument from history, though "natural" in form, always required the tenets of faith.

Barthians have called a reliance upon faith, an obedient faith of irreversible relation, the "analogy of faith." Here the relation between the Creator and the creation finds its link—the "analogy"—in faith, the acknowledgement of Jesus Christ, both human and divine, and in the world made through him. He, and neither other human actors nor nonhuman patterns, embodies the place where God's will can be seen in history. In this place, and not another: that is the Barthian response to natural theology. Not any history, not even the history of the Church, but the history of Christ; not any evidence, particularly not the cold neutrality of "scientific" evidence, but the evidence of revelation alone. This is the Barthian's first response to Marquardt's challenge, but it does not capture Barth's argument, nor Barth's own means of escape.

Barth takes up history, post-biblical history, into the Christian drama; his treatment of the Synagogue is typological in just this way and places his thought within the broad tradition of Christian historiography. That tradition, I have tried to show, belongs within the classical and medieval world, in which the creation witnesses to its sovereign Origin. Marquardt's claim to have detected the presence of natural theology rests on its firmest foundation in Barth's use of the historical type. After all, what I have called "concrete" or "positive" history witnesses to God's action in the world; and, with the Christian story firmly in mind, the past *can* lead from below to above, from the plane of human conflict to the realm of God's lordship. But this unmistakable pattern, the motion of natural theology, from "here to there," cannot be applied to any human past. The "natural," typological history Barth applies holds one particular history in view, moves out from one institution and tradition: the history, community, and consummation of Israel. The "kernel" of natural theology in Barth's *Dogmatics* can be found in the history of the people Israel, a history bound up with the doctrine of election and with the Triune God who elects. To speak of Israel, once again, is to speak of election.

But the history of Israel, the "elected ones, rejected" cannot be "natural" as that word was used in its classical sense. Israel's past and future, leading out from Egypt and coming home in the Church—that history can only be the "unnatural" enactment of God's inner life in our worldly time. The story of Israel, from exodus to Synagogue, can be interpreted as a divine witness because Israel, alone of all peoples, is taken up in Christ into the divine life, and alone lives out the divine election of the creature. History indwells in God—it can be stated that boldly—and that history, or divine time, becomes flesh first in Israel and then fully in Christ, Israel's head and promise. "God has time for us," Barth writes, and a living God commands and renews that time, electing in every moment to sustain his body, Israel. It is not so much that God acts in history, Barth might say, as that history begins in God, and unfolds in our time the eternal election of the Son. That, in a suggestive and inexhaustible way, is the kind of history I think that Barth has in mind, and would offer, finally, in response to Marquardt's critique.

Conclusion

The history of the people Israel makes objective the obedient will of the Son in his election of the creature; as such, it is the history of covenant and good pleasure, but of rejection and affliction as well. Christ elects all people in Israel—that is the meaning of the Church—but he elects sin and punishment, too, and that sin, like the election, belongs first to his community, Israel. Although without the doctrine of the Trinity election cannot be made synonymous with redemption, the election of the community takes place in the realm invaded by evil. The entrance of Christ into that realm, to secure and complete that election, engages Evil in the final battle. The rejection and punishment that overtakes Israel in its election is the eschatological judgment, the "wrath that breaks forth" over God's elect. Like the Baptist who stand at the entrance to the end-time, the "ax is already laid to the root":

> They [the Jews] have only the transient life of a severed branch, and the sure and immediate prospect of withering away. This is the existence of all those in Israel who, from Ishmael up to the present-day Synagogue, although they were and are Israelites, have proved unserviceable in relation to what God willed with Israel and finally brought forth from it, so that in their totality they can only form that dark and monstrous side of Israel's history. This is the disobedient, idolatrous Israel of every age: its false prophets and godless kings; the scribes and Pharisees; the high-priest Caiaphas at the time of Jesus; Judas Iscariot among the apostles. This is the whole of Israel on the left hand, sanctified only by God's wrath.[65]

Israel, from "Ishmael to the Synagogue," is history, the history of God's electing will in Christ. But this history, taken up and showing forth the divine inner life, must like God's own self, be event, too.[66] Israel's history, its recurrent and renewed call to election, is the event of "passing away": the Jew, like all others, but more deeply, more truly than all others, is the "passing man," the form of one turning away. The "actualism" of Barth's language is particularly vivid here. The German verbal forms translated as gerunds convey the dynamic, fluid motion that breaks out in Barth's exposition. "Now," Barth insists, "now" is the hour of decision, the moment when the "new Man" comes and the old passes away; now the hour when "Satan is driven out," when the "kingdom of God draws near." In the event of Israel's history, its election, God's will for grace breaks into human disobedience; even now, those who hear will be called to believe, those who are passing away to rise up into new life. The people Israel has a past, of course, and its election in part serves as "preparation" for and "prefiguration" of the one

---

65. *Dogmatics,* 2.2:287 [*Dogmatik,* 2.2:316].

66. Eduard Buess develops just these themes in "Die Erwählung der Gemeinde," in *Zur Prädestinationslehre Karl Barths* (Zurich: Evangelischer Verlag, 1955), 13, 14.

Elect. But it cannot be closed up in the past, for Israel is the community of
the Elect, his body and mediator; as the "passing form" of the one people of
God, Israel witnesses to revelation and represents that revelation to the
world. Like Christ, the true act of revelation, Israel is an event. It hears the
promise of God; it testifies to "how it is with man"; it makes visible the
judgment rendered on human obduracy and self-assertion. In every Jew, not
just the "ancient Israelite" or the "high priest and Pharisee," but in every Jew
present and past Barth envisions the silent drama of turning, passing away,
and the God who turns toward them. This drama, this moment of dying and
rising, at once past and present, our time and God's time: this drama tells the
story of the divine, not human, cost of election. Israel, before and after Christ,
suffers at great cost; Barth does not dispute this biblical and human fact. But
the history of Israel primarily recounts God's will for the creature and the
suffering God assumes in taking the creature's part. Election has taken on
many features in Barth's dogmatic treatment. It has become an element of
the Christological gravity in Barth's work. It has revealed the Object and inner
determination of divine life. It has brought the community of God, Israel and
the Church, into the doctrine of God and the Trinitarian will. But more,
Barth's doctrine of election has served as revelation: election reveals God,
God's plan and mercy, not human decisions or salvation. Of course, human
actors take part in this drama—the "believing and disbelieving Jews"—but
its Subject is God; God alone, his will, his wrath, and long-suffering mercy.

THE
CHURCH DOGMATICS

Barth's Doctrine of
the
Election of Israel

3

Any treatment of Barth must approach his thought with patience and some caution. A reasonable understanding of a work so plain, yet so complex, a theology at once open and layered with disguise, a work in short in Barth's characteristic dogmatic style, requires a good bit of lying in wait, and scouting ahead. Barth's doctrine of the election of Israel waits full exposition; and the poor critic must try to capture it as best she can.

Barth divides his treatment of election in the creaturely sphere into "The Election of the Community" and "The Election of the Individual." Each follows the twofold form Barth pursues throughout the *Dogmatics*. Like Christ, the elected and electing, the community receives a double determination. Elected to this dual form, the community is analyzed under the pairs of "Israel and the Church," "The Judgment and Mercy of God," "The Promise of God Heard and Believed," and "The Passing and Coming Man." Turning to the individual as object of election, Barth outlines the particular dual form of each human life: "Jesus Christ, the Promise and its Recipient," "The Elect and the Rejected," and the somber conclusion, "The Determination of the Elect" and "The Determination of the Rejected."

Discussing the election of the community, Barth refers specifically to Israel and the Synagogue as the type of those who hear and do not understand. Discussing the election of the individual, Barth also focuses on the Israelite and the Jew, exemplified by biblical and post-biblical figures. Taken together, these sections begin the dogmatic treatment of themes considered philosophically and theologically in the *Epistle to the Romans:* the relation of time and eternity; the dialectic of Law and Grace; the definition of sin as human self-assertion; and the reception of revelation as the eschatological moment of judgment. All are reshaped and *inspirited* by his Christological center; all are deepened and determined by Barth's hard-won respect for history and his encounter with "Jesus, born a Jew."[1] Barth's doctrine of God, then, takes history, a particular history, as its stage. God works his will, creating, judging, and showing mercy through the suffering, perdurance, and faithlessness of the Jews. They are the elect whose rejection points not to them, to their "running and willing" but to God, whose own life is to love in freedom.

Barth makes use of several terms in his treatment of the election of the Jews, each with its particular intent and range of meaning. "Israel" is the first, and I think most common and wide-ranging. Here Barth has in mind the biblical people, as tribe *[Stamm]*, nation, and covenant. But that is only its primary focus. Barth can also use this term to represent a figure—those who receive God's promise—or a human position—those who hear but do not believe. Israel can operate as determinate community over against the Church, a community composed of Jew and Gentile; or, it can stand for the elected community as a whole, a "passing and a coming" Israel; a disobedient and obedient people; a true Israel within and beyond the faithless Israel that is sustained by God's mercy. Barth reserves the term "Synagogue" for post-biblical Judaism, though it receives some attention in his discussion of the destruction of the Temple, the most significant type in Barth's doctrine of Israel. To my knowledge, the term "Synagogue" is derogatory throughout *Dogmatics* without exception. The term "Jew," though often associated with the post-biblical designation Synagogue, can serve several functions. "Jew" may be contrasted with "Israelite," though Barth shows little interest in the rather delicate and euphemistic use of that term by other Christian scholars. He recognizes, after all, that Israelites are ancient Jews. "Jew" may also be used to refer to New Testament figures, including Jesus Christ. It may also serve as a link between Israel or the Synagogue and the Church, a community "called," Barth is careful to stress, "from Jew and Gentile." Barth rarely refers to the terms of higher historical or biblical criticism, "rabbinic" or "pharisaic

---

1. Not everyone concurs in this assessment of Barth's "hard-won respect." In "Die Problematik der Prädestinationslehre Karl Barths," in *Zur Prädestinationslehre Karl Barths,* part 3, pp. 42–64, Eduard Buess argues that Barth's overall historical, exegetical position is contaminated by an "unhistorical strain" of systematic thought. It seems to me that to insist, as Buess does, that Barth must leave all questions open to the "darkness and uncertainty" of historical knowledge is to deny him the use of the "analogy of faith" by which theological statements can be wrested from historical events.

Judaism," modern schools of "orthodoxy," the *haskalah,* or "radical Reform." As is evident to readers of Barth, these terms take on the flavor of knowledge apart from revelation, and Barth approaches any such with suspicion. "Ghetto," however, *is* a term Barth accepts and applies to the post-biblical Jew. Though clearly a word with medieval origins, it, like "Synagogue," has entered the dogmatic tradition as these other, more academic terms have not. The "Ghetto," a place Barth inscribed with the character of "joyless and inglorious" witness, shares the work of derogation with "Synagogue" in these chapters. All of Barth's vocabulary related to Jews has specific uses and definitions, but are never fully discrete from one another. As the community of God, Israel unites its disparate parts in a single divine and historical purpose, to "serve the representation of the divine judgment" that Christ alone assumes.

Judas, the Elected Head of Israel, Rejected

Of those judged and rejected, Barth places Judas Iscariot at the head. Like Christ, Judas stands at the head of Israel; he too suffers and dies "for the nation." In a remarkable and complex reading of the Passion, Barth draws the figure of Judas from the deepening shadows surrounding Jesus into the light. Caught in the smoky glare of torches, the light of a nighttime arrest, Judas confronts Christ alone. Face to face, Judas meets the Elected One who is rejected; in the betrayal, Christ meets the rejected apostle, still elected. They are doublets, Barth writes; they belong together. When all the disciples scatter, when the faithful deny their master, when the forces of Jew and Gentile have had their way, when "all has been accomplished," Judas and Jesus are left to their solitary deaths. They alone are the true elect of Israel. They alone embody the elect, each to his own task and his own painful end. And, in their own way, Judas and Jesus are the rejected. By Judas's hand, Jesus is the rejected Messiah of Israel; by Jesus' hand, Judas receives the bread of rejection and goes out into the night. Of course, they are not identical figures; Barth does not claim that. Jesus suffers as the one true innocent. Judas suffers as the demonic, the obdurate, and the traitorous. In Jesus, Israel finds its rejection covered over, assumed, mediated, and redeemed. In Judas, it finds its secret ambitions betrayed, its sins embodied, its history enacted in a crude and unmistakable power. In the story of Judas, the head of those "determined for rejection," Barth encloses the community within the individual, and rehearses, now in sharp detail, the divine intention for the people of Israel.

Judas recapitulates, prefigures, and typifies the history of the Jews, and in his brief span of light and darkness, reveals how it is with those elected for rejection.

Of course, a discussion of Barth's doctrine of Israel need not begin here. Barth's understanding of rejection could arise from any section of the *Dogmatics*. The doctrine of sin, the work of reconciliation, the election of the community, the battle of the Creator for the creature: any of these dogmatic positions could provide the foundation for this discussion. In fact, a substantial argument could be made for beginning where Barth does, in the election of the community. That would preserve the original emphasis of community before individual and would allow the reader to follow Barth's narrowing focus from the panorama of history to the ambiguous and foreshortened view of a single human life. Election is a divine act that belongs first and most completely to Christ alone. It extends to the people chosen in Christ as his body, and then, only then, to the individual members of Israel and the Church. Starting with Judas collapses the history and destiny of the Jews into a single figure, its manifold and complex life concentrated into one bitter story, its form the form of a single "passing away."

But in a dialectic that might have pleased Barth, these disadvantages are also its advantages. He does mean what he says: outside the community the individual is unintelligible for theology. And Jesus has to do with the community; he elects to come to the "house of Israel." It is still risky to place the individual once again at the head and as the subject of the doctrine of election for it might betray Barth's central insight: that Christ alone elects and is elected, judges and is judged in our place. But here, the disadvantage "turns over." To speak of individuals in the Bible, of Jesus and of Judas, of the disciples and of Paul, and the host that followed them—to speak of these individuals is to address the figures and types of revelation. The biblical characters move in a moment Barth calls the "time of revelation." Their light is not ours, and our world and our individual lives can only be taken up in theirs. This moment ends with Paul and his mission to hand over Jesus once again to the Gentiles. It no longer speaks to us directly, but only in figures; revelation now is mediated to the present, to individual believers through the biblical witness. Judas is such a witness, perhaps the most significant of those who followed Jesus. His is an "overdetermined" story in which the intention of God for his people and, in the end, for all people of his creation is typified and made concrete. Judas suffers the judgment that belongs to all things human—the *Epistle to the Romans* comes to life in Judas—and his features are illumined by the fiery explosion of revelation in Christ. A discussion of the election of the community may then begin with the individual, Judas, because his history, too, is given over for the "good of the nation."

Another justification follows from this. Barth has a flair for the concrete. His loving discussions of the history of doctrine, his mastery of source and detail, the scope of his literary and philosophical interests: these remarkable talents are generously displayed in his treatment of Israel and Judaism. But these discussions are quickened by his return to the pictorial and particular. The biblical text with its layers, figures and voices provided Barth a complex and stubborn reality. He encountered these figures; they revealed themselves in the details of meaning and meaninglessness that human lives embody. Barth was at home here—the comfort and vibrancy of his voice is unmistakable—and he sets down, at long last, what he really means. That the Word became flesh, a human person, one royal man, Jesus, is a concrete and solitary fact that Barth never tires of. The individual story, the life of a biblical character can never be exhausted or replaced in Barth's thought. The life of the community, the election of Israel, comes first in Barth's program, but it is with Judas, the individual, that Judaism takes on sturdy reality. To speak of election is to speak of Israel; that still holds true. But Israel, both before and after Christ, encounters revelation in Judas and, as all things must in the brilliance of that One Light, betrays its deepest identity.

Of course, the debate over the individual and the community is hardly the exclusive domain of theology. The *Dogmatics* scarcely acknowledges topical events—there is little evidence of the German descent into Nazism—but Barth was by no means detached from his culture.[2] In a rare direct address

2. Indeed, some interpreters of Barth place political commitment and theory at the center of his work. Barth's allies on the theological left, Gollwitzer and Marquardt among them, belong here, as do North American commentators like George Hunsinger and Joseph Bettis. That Barth was politically active can scarcely be disputed; his letters, not to mention his biography, bristle with political and socialist analysis and initiative. But it seems to me that his insistence on the goodness of the "shadow side of creation," his long view of history, and his lifelong critique of the liberal kingdom of God do not make Barth a reliable political partisan. This may be the "anarchism" Marquardt finds in Barth, although Hunsinger is right, I think, to label Marquardt's analysis "reductionistic." I cannot shake the impression that Gollwitzer's explanation of Barth's "unreliable partisanship" is in fact an act of explaining away and special pleading, although he clearly draws on personal experience closed to me. Nevertheless, Barth's deepest commitments lay elsewhere. I do not see that Barth ever abandoned his assertion that revelation could only enter history in judgment, even after the "analogy of faith"; that there could never be "another word alongside the one Word"; and that allegiance to a "living Lord" came before and made relative any earthly allegiance. In the end, I cannot share Hunsinger's confidence that Barth has begun the "needed reconciliation between the evangelical gift and the socialist task in theology and church," although I need no persuasion that Barth became a socialist in Safenwil and never looked back.

The citations from Marquardt, Gollwitzer, and Hunsinger—and much interesting and valuable material—can be found in *Karl Barth and Radical Politics*.

to current debate, Barth makes plain the theological significance of the individual for political theory. Two distortions of Christian insight dominate the debate. On one hand, modern culture longs for the "secular leader," the "Führer"—Barth could have had only one führer in mind—through whom all other individuals gain their importance and find their true selves. On the other, modern political theory "hungers for wholeness";[3] it longs to find a collective in which individual strivings and sterility are satisfied and compensated for. Both political positions are dangerous because they caricature the truth. They mirror and distort the one true Individual and his community, and their demonic attraction springs from this shadow of truth they each embrace. As usual, Barth adopts a mediating or dialectical position. Christ is the one true individual, the one "man for others," and his community belongs with and to him, rising up to life in him. Both poles, the individual and the collective, are significant, and both are elected and represented in Christ, the only true leader. *Individualismus,* the individualism rooted in the Enlightenment, must be distinguished from the *Einzelne,* the individuals whose dignity and worth cannot be trivialized or erased because they too are the objects of God's decision on behalf of the creature. To begin the discussion of election with a single person, Judas, is to acknowledge that for Barth the "mystery" of the individual is not lost but confirmed in the election of the community of God.

Barth takes up his discussion of Judas in the fourth section of chapter 35, in part 2 of volume 2, "The Determination of the Rejected." In a close reading of the New Testament picture of Judas, Barth explores the details of this life, from the anointing in Bethany to the death by hanging and the reward buried in the Field of Blood. In each moment, the petty and magnificent motives for the pattern of rejection and betrayal are uncovered; in each, the difference from and uncanny resemblance to Jesus are opened up for dogmatic use. Barth concludes the section with an analysis of a final doublet, that of Judas and Paul. Both Jews, both persecutors, both disciples, though untimely born, Judas and Paul complete the handing over of Jesus to the Gentiles. God's will in election is fulfilled through the stubborn misery and inexplicable reversals in these lives. The Church, the true Israel of Jew and Gentile, springs from the moment between these two figures, the "time between the times" when the "passing man" turns toward the "coming" and the election of the Jews is confirmed in its one twofold act of betrayal and commission.

3. An evocative phrase of Peter Gay's, used in his analysis of the last decade of bourgeois liberalism in Germany, *Weimar Culture: The Outsider as Insider* (New York: Harper & Row, 1968), chap. 4.

Barth first draws attention to Judas in the event that opens the Passion narrative in the gospel of John. Jesus has raised Lazarus from the dead—the final, triumphant foreshadowing in the "book of signs"—and it is to this household, of Mary, Martha, and Lazarus of Bethany, that Jesus came to prepare for the Passover feast. During the supper, as Martha served, Mary anointed the feet of Jesus with a burial ointment and wiped them with her hair (a gesture that the gospel of Luke repeats to a different end). In both narratives, an onlooker protests the woman's act of devotion; in both, Jesus rebukes them. In the Johannine account, that onlooker is Judas, "he who was to betray him." Judas raises what Barth might call the complaint of bourgeois piety: "Why was this ointment not sold for three hundred denarii and given to the poor?" The narrator gives even this reading short shrift: "This he said, not that he cared for the poor but because he was a thief." The pericope closes with a teaching that points to the drama beyond: "Jesus said, 'Let her alone, let her keep it for the day of my burial. The poor you always have with you, but you do not always have me' " (John 12:1–11).

Barth draws attention to the character of these two disciples, Mary and Judas:

> This total offering, this gift of the most costly of her possessions, is to Jesus, who goes about on this earth of ours as a man, and to that extent Himself shares its uncleanness, to Jesus in all His condescension, which reaches its final point in His death. It is clear that this deed of Mary's describes the life of the apostles so far as they are wholly clean, so far as the presence and protection and vigilance of Jesus have not been in vain for them. And this is what is to take place in the world through their life—the whole house is to be filled with the odour of the ointment. But it is precisely this, this prodigality, which Judas—as seen by his protest—cannot and will not understand or accept. He is not opposed to the surrender of Mary's costly ointment. But he wants something for it—namely 300 denarii—not for himself, as he explains, but to give to the poor. He is not willing that the complete devotion, which by her deed Mary had in a sense given the apostles as a pattern for their own life, should be an absolute offering to Jesus. For him it is too little a thing that the death of Jesus should be glorified by it. If there is to be an offering, he wants to exploit it. . . . This view, this attitude of Judas is what makes him unclean. It finds relatively innocuous expression. It is not really evil. To correct it would be comparatively easy. But it was because of it that Judas "handed over" Jesus.[4]

4. *Dogmatics,* 2.2:462 [*Dogmatik,* 2.2:512, 513].

Here Barth draws together Judas and Mary of Bethany as the doublet surrounding Jesus. The extravagance and "prodigality" of Mary's discipleship throw into shadow Judas's act of pious frugality. Barth pays scant attention to the narrator's bitter aside that Judas was a hypocrite and a thief—his protest Barth writes was a "relatively innocuous expression." Barth underscores the intention of the act: Judas would hold back; he would see devotion planned and measured.

Turning to the synoptics, Barth finds the pattern once again:

> The Synoptists obviously try to understand the sin of Judas in the same way as John for they tell us that he decided upon this handing-over for a payment of money. According to Mt. 16:15 this was thirty pieces of silver. This obviously means that Jesus was for sale. He had his own freedom in face of Him which he was resolved to maintain. He had indeed turned to Him. But he was not bound to Him. He had not yielded himself to Him. He could surrender Him for something else which appeared better to him. Because he could do this, because he reserved for himself this judgement of his as to what was better, because he did not hand himself over to Jesus, he for his part was able to hand Jesus over.[5]

Judas could not give; he could not give of himself, generously, extravagantly, and completely. Unlike Mary, unlike Paul, and, more, unlike Jesus, Judas "reserved for himself" the right to judge, the right to wait for "something better." These are the marks, Barth insists, of a small man. Judas's "uncleanness" is a petty affair; his view could be "corrected comparatively easily." Barth pictures this model of the rejected as a constricted, restrained, and sadly priggish man.

In Barth's hands, Judas takes on the character psychoanalysts might describe as compulsive and retentive. These are the figures who suffer in an airless and suffocating personality. Rules must be obeyed; they are exacting and limitless. The compulsive conscience demands unrelenting obedience. Their acts of charity must serve established moral ends; their "faith" is a stubbornly bourgeois affair. Every corner of life is contaminated by obligation and the deepening conviction that nothing is ever enough. Indecision and regret invade each moment but the pattern of life is never abandoned. Over and over, the compulsive clings to the past; repeating, controlling, holding back and holding in. In this narrow compass, the sins are petty transgressions;

5. Ibid., 463 [513, 514].

the satisfactions, however pleasing, belong to the modest achievement of tidiness and order.

Judas then is no grand criminal, though Barth insists on the horror and wickedness of his act. His is a "banal" evil: the betrayal of a leader never in hiding, the naming of the Name already known, the denunciation by a kiss, the pious prevention of waste. These are the works Barth assigns to Israel as a whole:

> Within the apostolic group . . . [Judas] obviously represents the Jews, the tribe *[Stamm]* from which both David himself and his promised Son sprang. When he reserves something for himself and therefore in principle everything, in face of Jesus in this characteristic fashion, he merely does that which Israel has always done in relation to Yahweh. He merely does that which has always made Yahweh's rejection of his chosen people inevitable. There never was a time when Israel encountered its God as Mary encountered Jesus, when it was willing to trust Him and therefore to dedicate itself wholeheartedly and unreservedly to Him. Israel always retained the possibility of serving other gods as well as Yahweh. Israel always tried to buy off Yahweh with thirty pieces of silver. It gave Him a modicum of Yahweh-religion which it made as similar as possible to the religion of all other peoples. . . . The paltry and wholly inadequate payment which Israel dared to offer its God for his faithfulness as the Shepherd, the thirty pieces of silver, are themselves returned to Judas and therefore to the people of Israel as a payment for his faithlessness, for his freedom to behave so differently from Mary, for the handing over of Jesus. This is his contribution, his work. This, then, must be his reward.[6]

Israel dares to offer a "paltry" and "wholly inadequate" thanksgiving to Yahweh's faithfulness: this is Barth's recurrent diagnosis of Jewish sin. Even in its royal past under the great kings of the united Kingdom, Israel rebels in a figure of petty and "microscopic sins." It elects Saul as the king to rule over them in order to be like all the nations *[Volk]* of the earth.

Saul, figure of Judas

In an exegesis of 1 Samuel 8–15, the anointing and reign of Saul, Barth insists on the banality of this king's disobedience. Departing from much traditional

6. Ibid., 464 [514].

interpretation of these chapters,[7] Barth underscores that Saul is God's anointed, his *christos*. The rebellion of the people does not lie in its quest for a monarch, its rejection of the judges, or even its wish to be a nation like all others. In Saul, the people find a ruler "head and shoulders above themselves;" he is fit to reign, Barth writes, and Yahweh appoints him to that end. Israel is elected to have a king: that is the divine will in covenant with this people. Here Barth is strengthening his hand. In his Christological interpretation of Israel—that the Jews are the preparation and the environment of Christ's election—Barth stresses that one king shall rule Israel, first in shadow and promise; then in fullness and fulfillment. Saul, in part, serves as a type of Christ, but that does not exhaust his meaning. He enacts Israel's rebellion and rejection, as well, in a drab and "thoroughly respectable" sin.

Commissioned to destroy the Amalekites without remainder, Saul "reserves judgment." He spares the sheep and oxen; they may serve as "sacrifices to the Lord." A pious and very tidy rebellion!—Barth will not let the reader miss the unmistakable parallel. But Saul is caught in his transgressions. With the quiet and masterful irony of these historical books, Samuel questions Saul: "What is this bleating of sheep in my ears? Why do I hear lowing of cattle?" Saul has made a "partial accommodation, a modest *modus vivendi,* with the world of other kings and nations and gods that surrounds him and Israel."[8] Unable to resist, Barth draws Saul into the pious hypocrisy of the modern, modest sinners: Saul allows "small adjustments and accommodations *[adaptation intellectuelle]* to the foreign world which seemed alone to make physical or spiritual life possible."[9] These are the very deeds Israel and the world demand and respect. But Samuel will not relent: "Time was when you thought little of yourself, but now you are head of the tribes of Israel, and the Lord has anointed you king over Israel." But should not Saul "think more of himself"; is it not something to be king of Israel, the Lord's anointed? Barth presses his readers with these questions. Like Judas, Saul commits "microscopic sins," and receives the full blow of divine judgment. "The spirit of the Lord forsakes Saul, and at times an evil spirit from the Lord would seize him suddenly." Rejected and afflicted, Saul falls on his own sword; a "dark prototype of Judas Iscariot," he is a ruler whose transgressions are

---

7. Exegetes have distinguished two separate traditions connected to Saul: the king fit to serve and "set over them" by Yahweh; and the king unfit and sinful, whose very reign is a rebellion against Yahweh. Barth delights in such contrary traditions, finding Christological import in them all. As the first king over Israel, Saul is an irresistible type not only of Judas, but of Jesus, the Royal Man.

8. *Dogmatics,* 2.2:371 [*Dogmatik,* 2.2:410].

9. Ibid.

altogether different from the "crimson sins of David." Yet, Barth repeats, he participates in the twofold character of all biblical witness: he prefigures Christ, the one king and elect of Israel, but he represents the rejected, too, the rejection Christ assumed. Like Judas, Saul is the elect, determined for rejection.

Judas, Rejected Bourgeois

But what is the shape of this "determination," the election to rejection? How can these petty and small-minded rebellions define the rejection of Israel, the judgment that "has overtaken humanity?" Barth develops a complete doctrine of sin in the fourth volume of the *Dogmatics,* where sin is defined and made visible only in the light of Christ's obedience. In the doctrine of election, Barth's object of attention is "rejection," not sin in its strict and independent interpretation. Sin is present in the moment of rejection; Barth does not separate these two human states. But rejection is an act of God, principally, and not a human affair. It is the act of God's "passing over," his proclamation of judgment, his dividing *No* that separates all things human from his self-revelation. In this description of those determined for rejection, Barth sketches in the outline of human sinfulness that tradition has termed "original." This is the corruption that clings to all human beings in their humanity. It is, Barth claims, the most ordinary of failings, a trifling matter in the world's eyes. Original sin possesses no drama, no "crimson" horror. It has no flair for the special—it is a universal condition—and it makes its way through human life and history in silence, an assumed and respectable part of human society. By its definition, original sin implies a quiet acceptance by its sufferers, but Barth had special reason to drive this point home. Human sinfulness is a banal affair. As C. S. Lewis never tired of pointing out, Satan could never possess the energy required for Miltonian magnificence. The representative of evil must be a kind of lifeless bureaucrat, cramped and dull—after all, all joy and power belong to the divine realm.[10] Barth was sympathetic to this position; he too saw evil as a special form of nonbeing. But for Barth this argument takes shape under unique conditions: God's rejection breaks into the history of the Jews; and its dogmatic interpretation reads "justification by grace alone."

Consider Barth's description of the rejected. These are the "people of the

---

10. Lewis outlines these platonic positions throughout his religious works—perhaps, in fact, in everything he wrote—but it is most clearly and delightfully explained in the *Screwtape Letters,* a kind of antidote to those who have overindulged on Milton.

lie"; their lives are false testimony; they bear false witness about "how it is" with them. They live as a kind of "caricature or perversion" and possess no full or independent existence:

> It [the rejection] consists in the fact that the "individual" does not accept as grace, and gratefully correspond to, the distinction and dignity conferred on him by the one and only God. Instead, he desires and attempts to make and vindicate them as his natural possession, as a right which is inherent in his human existence, and therefore as his claim upon God: as if the fact that God regards, intends, wills, loves and chooses him rested upon his own abilities and merits; as if God did not do this for His own will's sake; as if the covenant—the covenant of grace—which God has made with him were one of those groups; as if he could therefore exist on his own account in relation to God, as a partner in God's covenant, in the same way as he is able—by the goodness of God—to do so in relation to the many and even the totality of his fellow-men, with all his obligations and duties towards them. This is the individuality of man which is negated by Jesus Christ, and which is therefore only to be understood and judged negatively. It means his sinful and fatal isolation. It is the essence of man's godlessness.[11]

These are the "godless" of every age, but readers of Barth know that he has particular "godless" in mind, even at this highest level of abstraction. The phrases familiar to Barthians are all here: "as if he could exist on his own account"; "as if his dignity and distinction . . . were a natural possession," "a right and claim upon God"; "as if his [election] rested upon his own abilities and merits." As if, Barth might say, human nature—the natural and accepted way of life—were not godless at heart, a glorification of human self-reliance. These are words familiar and very dear to Barth, embedded in his first essays and never abandoned. They describe an intimate enemy, the Liberals, and an estranged tradition, the Thomists, both of whom Barth struck at directly throughout his early years. But these words also describe the Jews. This depiction of Judaism as the "highest human achievement," the "religion of busy reform," springs from the pages of the *Römerbrief,* and finds a fertile resting place in these segments of the *Dogmatics.*

Saul and Judas after all typify for Barth the godlessness of the rejected. They are the supreme bourgeois: sincere, primly moralistic, duty-bound individuals, preened by their sturdy self-reliance and voice of conscience. They are religious men—who could deny their delicate experience of God! But they are godless

---

11. *Dogmatics,* 2.2:315, 316 [*Dogmatik,* 2.2:347].

and rejected, the determination of those who only worship their own ability. In his exegesis of Romans 9–11, the classic text for the Christian interpretation of Judaism, Barth reiterates his evaluation of the human possibility of the Law first worked out in the *Epistle to the Romans:*

> Israel certainly pursued the law of righteousness. In all its willing and running it was intent on the maintenance and fulfillment of the order of a life under the promise, on the Torah and the temple, on the purity and holiness of the existence of the chosen people, on the preservation, fostering and development of its tradition. . . . "They have a zeal for God" Paul will say in [chapter] 10.2 in express confirmation. If then the possession of the Law does not help after all, if after all it comes short of the Law itself, this is due to the fact that all that it has can be its living possession only in relationship to Him who is the meaning of it all, only in the apprehension of the divine mercy that attests itself in it all. It is due to the fact that the Law itself can be kept and fulfilled only in this relationship and apprehension, i.e., only in faith. But this was precisely what this Israel lacked. . . . What it lacked was that it did not want to rely on the promise, on the mercy of God, but on itself, on its own willing and running in the direction of the promised fulfillment; that it sought by its own willing and running to bring about the fulfillment of what was promised. Therefore, having all, it lacked all.[12]

In every detail, a replication of the *Römerbrief!* Though a legendary critic of all systemizing impulses, Barth displays an astonishing consistency here. But it is no small matter to reproduce these ideas in the mid-thirties, although they origi-nated in the first years after World War I. It may be too strong to say that there are volkist elements in Barth's thought, but George Mosse's contention—that volkist ideology is no aberration in German thought[13]—deserves attention here. The polished surface of bourgeois culture was under attack from all sides, not least from the right and left. But this particular fusion, of the liberal with the Jew, belongs to the core of reactionary German nationalism reaching back into the early nineteenth century.[14] Jews embodied the cancer that fed on the native

12. Ibid., 241 [265].

13. See George L. Mosse's introduction to *The Crisis of German Ideology: Intellectual Origins of the Third Reich* (New York: Grosset and Dunlap, The Universal Library, 1964), 1–10.

14. Of course, anti-Semitism was by no means restricted to the reactionaries; progressives of all kinds shared the belief that Jews were at the bottom of all German ills. And a case could be made I think that Barth's own position owes more to the left than to the right, as his political views certainly do. I am not inclined to this point of view because it seems to me that Barth

German spirit; they weakened it by their participation in and their championing of modern industrial capitalism. They, like all civilized[15] city dwellers, put down no "roots" in the German soil. They undermined the natural order of work and family by their "mobility of land, labor, and capital."[16] The dangerous and heady mix of nostalgia and sentimentality made volkist thinkers long for a medieval past when honest peasants fed a culture of guilds, artisans, mystics, and warriors. This fictional realm honored family and children, but intimated that such primitive communities must be fortified and defended by violence.

Barth, of course, would not tolerate such dangerous pieties about nature, blood, and soil. Indeed, he and the Confessing Church considered his attacks on natural theology to be the strongest possible condemnation of National Socialism and German Christianity. His conduct during the war confirms his position as a tireless member of the Church resistance.

But Barth's evocation of the Synagogue's "empty future"; the "joyless" and miserable Ghetto; the legalistic and arrogant Pharisee; and more, the self-reliant, petty, and self-satisfied Jew cannot be wholly assigned to medieval tropes. Barth's "allergic reaction to Jews" is bound up with the cultural criticism of the interwar years, and the strains in German thought that identify the corruption of modernity with the Jews are not lost on him. We cannot say more than this—to echo Barth's style—but we can say this.

Judas on the Border of Nothingness

At the same time, we cannot lose sight of Barth's theological goal in these passages. He intends to make concrete in the Jews the original and "passing

---

finds fault with Jews as Jews—their Judaism is the cause of complaint—and not with Jews as agents of the transformation of the means of production. Barth exhibits deep conservative strains in his thought: his "high doctrine of authority" described in "Authority under the Word" and his highly differentiated support of the "freedom of the Christian" in "The Freedom of the Word," both in *Dogmatics* 1.2, are only two examples. And I argue here that his criticism of Judaism as "religion" belongs to those strains.

15. "Civilized" was a derogatory term among the volkist right. They contrasted it to *Kultur*, the organic, vital, and genuine social expression of the German people. Freud spoke for many educated liberals when he quietly but "scornfully" denounced such a distinction (*The Future of an Illusion* [1927; translation, 1928; reprint, New York: W. W. Norton, 1961], 6).

16. Marxist anti-Semitism belongs to a separate discussion, but ever since Marx's polemic "On the Jewish Question" (1844; reprinted in the *Marx-Engels Reader*, ed. R. Tucker [New York: W. W. Norton, 1972], 26–52), Marxists at times have allowed themselves the easy equation of Jews with bourgeois capitalism.

form" of universal sinfulness. Human beings arrogate to themselves a divine power: they wish to be their own judges. This theological insight inhabits much of Barth's landscape but rightly belongs to the garden of Eden in the second Genesis narrative. The first couple longed for the knowledge of good and evil; this primal power to judge would make them "like gods." This bit of temptation, promised by the serpent—"the first instance of bad theology"—becomes a bit of dialectical truth in Hegel's exegesis of the Fall. In a remarkable and influential account, Hegel thought he had found the justification for Kant's claim that human beings are both good and evil "by nature."[17] Like Adam and Eve, every person desires the "unnatural," those goods God has forbidden. At the same time, everyone longs to retreat from the tasks of life—to remain at the level of "nature" rather than "thought" and culture. This too is evil, a forsaking of the purpose and ability God assigns to human creatures. For Hegel, and many Idealists after him, the Fall took on the character of tragic greatness: human beings enter history and its burden after Eden; they fail in their calling, but it is failure in pursuit of maturity and noble human morality. Such elegant and nuanced self-congratulations were all too familiar to Barth, an heir of the German preoccupation with history and high culture. To say that they provoked his suspicions, more—his contempt—is actually to say too little: Barth considered this cultivated moral greatness the very portrait of human sinfulness. It is not enough, Barth would write, that human beings desire to judge matters for themselves, to defy God in their knowledge of good and evil. No, human beings want more. They covet the divine role of judge and then flatter themselves that such arrogance should be called "tragic greatness" and the "burden of the Real in history." Barth enjoys himself in these raids on bourgeois piety—the delight is nearly palpable—but his intention is more serious.

Barth traces human godlessness in ever-widening circles, from Judas, to Israel, to the heathen world of philosophers and empires. Without God, human beings rely on their own principles and assumptions. They determine their "positions" or "way in the world," some workable, some corrupted and failed; all human systems nevertheless, all attempts to make the best of this lonely task. Barth's "godless" are the human beings encountered in history, the normal and accepted members of human society. As a universal type, Judas expresses ordinary humanity. He "reserves judgement"; he submits to

17. See Hegel's analysis in "The Story of the Fall" and "Knowledge, Estrangement, and Evil," in his *Lectures on the Philosophy of Religion,* 3.B.1. Kant's powerful, but sometimes puzzling argument is developed in "Concerning the Indwelling of the Evil Principle with the Good, or, On the Radical Evil in Human Nature," in *Religion within the Limits of Reason Alone,* book 1.

his own obedience; he defines his own highest good. He is no monster—
Barth underscores this claim—but rather an accepted and acceptable disciple
who, like the others, "thinks for himself," an act of quiet defiance that ends,
as it must, in betrayal and death.

Judas lives out the path and destiny of the creature who usurps the
authority of the Creator. God alone has the sovereign freedom that makes
judging and, more importantly, being judged possible. God alone can assume
the conflict between good and evil and endure the punishment such cosmic
strife inflicts. In Christ, God assumes this burden; in Christ, human beings
witness its terrible cost.

> [God] knows good and evil. He affirms and helps on the one hand, to
> deny and destroy on the other. But He does not do it as the victor that
> man obviously imagines Him to be when he wants to act like Him.
> That He stands on guard on this frontier means that He gives up
> Himself to be with the creature in this antithesis, allowing Himself to
> be called in question and injured and shaken and assaulted by that
> which is not, taking to heart the weakness of the creature, and more
> than that its transgression and guilt and need, its deflection into
> nothingness, taking to Himself the judgement into which we fell by
> this deflection. He has no pleasure in His being and activity as Judge.
> It is only the most bitter sorrow that He takes to Himself. And the
> world lives by the fact that He does give Himself to bear this sorrow
> for it and with it and in its place—a sorrow compared with which all
> our sorrows both great and small are only shadows, the great and
> fearful sorrow which, because He bears it for us, gives to our shadowy
> sorrowing its place and meaning and hope because in it as the sorrow
> of the Judge, right is really done and the wrong done away. And we
> are such fools—we know not what we do—that we go and try to
> usurp His office as Judge, as though it were something to be desired.[18]

That Christ is the elected means this: he assumes the role of the Judge,
judged in our place. That this is a terrible role—an act of "bitter sorrow"—is
confirmed by the prayers for deliverance wrung out of the "man of obedience" in Gethsemane. Jesus meets the power of Satan undisguised in the
garden; he is tempted as once before to assert his own will, to "reserve
judgement," but this time in earnest. Jesus is not mistaken in his terror. The
betrayal Judas has prepared for him contains a threat far greater than death:

---

18. *Dogmatics,* 4.1:452, 453 [*Dogmatik,* 4.1, 502, 503].

he will become the victim of the only "great powers," God and Satan, in their battle for creation.

> It was not a matter of His suffering and dying in itself and as such, but of the dreadful thing that He saw coming upon Him in and with His suffering and dying. He saw it clearly and correctly. It was the coming of the night "in which no man can work," in which the good will of God will be indistinguishably one with the evil will of men and the world and Satan. It was a matter of the triumph of God being concealed under that of His adversary, of that which is not, of that which supremely is not. It was a matter of God himself obviously making a tryst with death and about to keep it. It was a matter of the divine judgement being taken out of the hands of Jesus and placed in those of His supremely unrighteous judge and executed by them upon Him. It was a matter of the enemy who had been repulsed as the tempter having and exercising by divine permission and appointment the right, the irresistible right of might. It was a matter of the obedience and penitence in which Jesus had persisted coming to fruition in His own rejection and condemnation—not by chance, but according to the plan of God Himself, not superficially, but in serious earnest. That was what came upon Him in His suffering and dying, as God's answer to His appeal.[19]

To be the elected of God, to really know good and evil is to suffer God's wrath against evil, a judgment in which Satan executes God's righteous will. The identity of purpose between God and Evil is the terror of the Passion, a reality Jesus recognizes alone. An agent of this divine justice, Judas prepares the way by his stubborn and godless insistence that he acts on his own. But he is by no means alone.

As a type, Judas takes up the part of sinful humanity and disobedient Jew; as "one of the twelve"—Barth stresses his membership—Judas represents the disciples as a whole.

> The apostle Peter, elect and called, is just as much in need of the death of Jesus, of this perfecting of His love in the slave-service of the Lord's utter and final devotion to His own, as is the apostle Judas, also elect and called. For the nature of Ishmael and Esau, of Pharoah and Saul, whose rebellion breaks out in the person and act of Judas, is no

19. Ibid., 4.1:271 [4.1:298].

less the nature of Peter than it is of Judas. . . . Peter no less than Judas
was inclined to be independent in face of Jesus, as is shown in the
story of his denial, although Peter did not hand Him over but only—
and how emphatically!—denied Him. . . . The basic flaw was revealed
in Judas, but it was that of the apostolate as a whole. At this decisive
point the apostolate was also Israel, and Israel was the world and
therefore of the night. The elect were also rejected and as such
elected. This was why Jesus had to "love them unto the end," to die
for them, and as the One who died for them to be theirs.[20]

Here Barth travels some familiar ground. Judas, though elected as one of the
disciples, gives shape to the determination of the rejected. He is Israel, the
elected ones, rejected. He is also the disciples as a whole, those called to
serve who give but unwilling service. Judas betrays, but the disciples desert
and deny. Judas accepts the bribe, but each disciple wonders, and deserves
to wonder, "Is it I, Lord?" Jesus dies for them all, all disciples, all Israel, all
creatures—all sinners.

Barth does not leave the matter there, however. He enriches his description
with one of his signature marks, the presence of the doublet. Samuel and
Saul; Saul and David; Cain and Abel; Judas and Mary; and now, Judas and
Peter. Doublets are naturally biblical figures and types; they are nearly a
standard in Barthian exegesis. They expand beyond the canon, of course.
The human and natural world "mirror" and "represent" the Creator: our
lights and his Light; our truth and his Truth; our communities and his
Communal Life. These doublets are Christological echoes in the time of
revelation and beyond. To find this imprint of Christ's two natures in the
world made through him is nearly a commonplace in Barthian thought and
scholarship. But this is not a fascination on Barth's part with the number two,
or even with the two-nature doctrine. We come closer to Barth's intention
when we recognize the presence of a living not a static model for these pairs,
but this is still not enough. Doublets are an element of the uncanny in Barth's
thought and they "turn over" into each other. They are types, of course, and
as such contain a diverse and sometimes conflicting history within their own
singular, particular lives. And as the doublets approach Jesus' own life more
closely—there is an order and sequence here, too—they assume more
clearly the force of contradiction and opposition. A hegelian flavor is unmistakable at these points: the doublets deepen and sharpen the antithesis and
at their extremes, at the point of "infinite anguish," they rise up again in

20. Ibid., 2.2:474, 475 [2.2:526, 527].

identity. Judas *is* Peter; both surround Jesus, alike in discipleship and betrayal. Yet they are opposites. In the end, Peter confesses Christ, and leads his disciples; Judas hands him over, and dies, alone, by his own hand. This pattern of opposition and terrible identity finds its center in Barth's last pairing of Judas with another; his pairing of Judas and Jesus himself.

Judas, Doublet of Jesus

Although drawing on several themes within the New Testament record, Barth describes this doublet in an image, an etching of sharp contrast, of brilliant light and darkness that Flemish painters might have appreciated. As darkness settles, the disciples gathered around Jesus grow indistinct, nearly lost in the silence and shadows. Against their muted forms, the last light captures these two faces, Jesus and his opponent, Judas. They stand alone, antagonists and allies, each prepared to go his own way but caught for this moment by the light, facing one another. They are figures turning away; one is to "pass away," one is to come. But they are frozen, stopped for an instant in this act of turning, and we suddenly see them with the clarity and distortion that bright light conveys. They are mortal enemies—we see that now. But they are alike; they belong together; they are somehow the same. The dark, still shadows and the light capture the uncanny identity between the familiar and the strange, the good and evil, the elected with the rejected. Judas and Jesus are a doublet.

Barth describes them this way:

> Is not Judas also, in his own place and after his own fashion, *the* outstanding apostle? Is he not the holy one among them—"holy" in the old meaning of the term, the one who is marked, branded, banned, the one who is burdened with the divine curse and thrust out, the one who is thus brought into remarkably close proximity to Jesus Himself? . . . For all the dissimilarities, is it possible to overlook the likeness in which Judas alone of the apostles stands face to face and side by side with Jesus? Or the more than chronological proximity of his very different death to the death of Jesus? *Mutatis mutandis,* could not the famous utterance of the high-priest in John 11:50: "It is expedient for us, that one man should die for the people, and that the whole nation perish not" be said of Judas too in his relationship to the other apostles? *Mutatis mutandis* for, like the crucified thieves

and even more so, he receives his deserts—death as the wages of sin. He does not really die an atoning death, but the utterly hopeless and fruitless death of one who is not obedient but disobedient even in death, who in death still regarded himself as his own judge. . . . There remains only the similarity that he too, like Jesus, suffered his death in the place of others; that Jesus actually did not go alone to the death which the sin of all the apostles made necessary. Although lacking the power of his death, there went with Him this one apostle, and represented in the person of this one there went all the dead of the old covenant which Israel had continually broken, those whose death could only be a punishment, Ishmael and Esau and Pharaoh, Saul and Ahithophel and all their kind. All that the utter darkness of the death of this one apostle can do is to emphasise the light and life of the death of Jesus. But it can do this. This is the proximity of Judas to Jesus, the resemblance to Him, which he alone knows of all the apostles.[21]

They are both, in innocence and in guilt, elected for rejection.

The drawing together and repulsion of these two figures, Jesus and Judas, provide the form and motion of Barth's entire doctrine of election. The Trinitarian drama of election—the giving over and taking up of divine life—becomes flesh in this doublet. The community of God, the embodiment of Christ, is one and cannot be divided. It is called and formed from Jew and Gentile, a single elected people, but determined for separate tasks. The people of God may be distinguished as Israel and Church or, more tragically for Barth, Synagogue and Church. In the identity and difference of the disciple and Lord, Judas and Jesus, Barth gathers up the distinction and unity of God's elect. They must receive this double impress; Barth's exegesis relentlessly seeks the balance and opposition of pairs. The Church requires a mate and will be satisfied. That the people Israel, or more, the Synagogue does not understand itself as counterpoise to the life and institution of the Church makes little impression on Barth.[22] Revelation has assumed this

---

21. Ibid., 479, 480 [531, 532].

22. Barth is hardly alone in this view. Since the medieval period, the Church has sought an institutional counterpart in Judaism, an ecclesiastical structure to address or condemn. That body traditionally has been the Synagogue. Rabbinic Judaism however does not have a place for such a centralized, sacramental authority; the Synagogue is organized for teaching and prayer but it does not characterize or ground the Jewish life as the Church does the Christian.

The ecumenical and interfaith movements—not to ignore commercial interests!—have renewed interest in the Synagogue as the counterpart to the Church. "Attending the Church or

particular, twofold identity, and the community will radiate that twofold light. Anti-Semitism has no place in the Church, Barth concludes, because a one-sided collection of Gentiles makes a sad caricature of the community God intends. Barth's opposition to the "Ayran codes" in the church of the German-Christians has its theological basis here. And Christians should not delude themselves that this insoluable conflict and connection between Church and Synagogue is a matter for "interfaith dialogue" or "Christian-Jewish relations." No, Jews are not members of another "faith" or "religion," however ancient or honored. They are integral and inseparable members of the Church called, Barth insists, from Jew and Gentile.

That is the significance, Barth thinks, of Jesus being "born a Jew" but that heritage receives its focus and power in this doublet. Judas, Jesus' "second," is a Jew, a disciple, indeed *the* disciple of the Passion. It is through him that Jesus comes to his atoning death; it is through him that Christ is handed over to the Gentiles, to Pilate and then the Roman world. Strictly speaking, Judas is the founder of the Church, and it is for him, and for all Israel, that the community of God exists. Christians do not proclaim a "mission to the Jews,"[23] Barth concludes. The Jews *are* the mission of the Church: the

---

Synagogue of your choice" is a parallelism of good will, though reductionistic in flavor. Making Hanukkah the equivalent of Christmas may smooth some rough spots, but on balance extends the Christian dominance over Jewish categories and institutional self-definition. I am not one to dismiss the importance of good will—the alternative is rarely an improvement—but the desire to subsume the different under a single category is one, I think, to be resisted.

To be sure, this debate has its roots in Judaic culture as well. Nineteenth-century Reform is broadly considered suspect for its interest in "modernizing and westernizing" Synagogue practice. The use of the organ, of choral music, the introduction of the exegetical sermon and clerical dress: all these were viewed as efforts to accede to Protestant demands. They had the effect, critics argued, of finally realizing the Christian program, that the Synagogue is the Jewish Church.

23. Barth discusses the *Judenmission* in volume 4 of the *Dogmatics*. Like all German "questions" about Jews, this topic of a "Jewish mission" takes on its own particular, technical character. Franz Delitzsch (1813–90) organized a systematic approach to the conversion of the Jews based on the argument that only Christians well-educated in the life and thought of Judaism could make Christianity attractive and convincing. Delitzsch's approach gave the New Testament claim, that "salvation is of the Jews," a kind of technical sheen, one that reflected the vigorous debates over that biblical verse in the Confessing Church of the 1930s. Barth had read Delitzsch's biblical commentaries—I can find no reference to his other, missionary works—but Delitzsch's evangelical tone and his insistence that the Church owes a special debt and honor to the Jews may have entered his exegesis of Genesis and through it Barth's work as well. Direct dependence is difficult to prove and, in light of the common texts and culture in which the two men worked, is not as important as it is suggestive. In addition to biblical commentaries and translations, Delitzsch edited the influential journal of the Institute, *Saat auf Hoffnung;* his *Institutum Delitzschianum* continues, publishing works on Judaism and Jewish-Christian relations under the direction of K. H. Rengstorf.

proclamation of grace. They are the rebels God has taken for his own, the self-possessed who testify to human need and who deliver up redemption for the world. They are the mission God has with his creatures, to judge and to save, and it is to this house of Israel that Jesus came.

One community of God in two forms: that is the center of Barth's position. It is two-sided, paired, bound together in similarity and difference, but it is not symmetrical. Barth cautions against an easy temptation, to confuse the two-nature doctrine of Christology with the living Christ or the presence of doublets with an essential dialectical principle in reality. Christ is not a "principle"—Barth never tires of this admonition—and Judas, though a double, is never Jesus' equal. Barth's world is one of rank and order. His distate for the bourgeois lines up with his respect for medieval dogma and type: equality does not stand a chance.[24] Of course, this is a theological critique "from below"; Barth could never justify his dogmatic position by a cultural critique of Enlightenment ideals. He would insist, instead, on the inescapable ranking of figures and events in revelation itself. David is a greater king than Saul; Israel a more favored nation over the heathens; Moses greater than Pharoah; the Church more complete and perfect than Israel: ranking conforms to God's intention for creation. As the biblical witness draws attention to Jesus, this ordered pattern becomes more fixed and distinct. Jesus is greater than John—indeed, his least disciple ranks over John. Judas, of course, is less than his Master; even Christ's own humanity is assumed, taken up "enhypostatically" in his divinity; God's own love is ordered to his freedom. Such fundamental distinctions express themselves in the lives of those gathered around Christ. The relationship of Jew to Gentile, of Church to Israel and the Synagogue, and of the community as a whole to Christ belong to the ordering work of God's will. For this reason, the types and doublets Barth employs "turn over" into the other. It is not so much a hegelian symmetry and opposition, though that is present, too; rather, Christ is the gravity at the center of all things, drawing them in and up to him, exposing their opposition and "turning them over" towards him. The relationship of the Church to Israel and the Church to the Synagogue should be seen in this light.

---

24. It may be a fusion of this type that governs Barth's famous ranking of men and women (see *Dogmatics*, vol. 3.4, par. 54.1). They are ordered to one another like *a* and *b*; both "letters," both members of the "same alphabet," but with *a* before *b*. A more elaborate effort to preserve an idea of equality within the demands of rank could scarcely be imagined.

Judas and Paul,
Doublets of the Church and Synagogue

Though Jews and Gentiles are members of the Church, both full members
through grace, Gentiles, on the other hand, are not silent or "anonymous"
members of Israel. On occasion, Barth will use the language of supersession:
the Church is the new or true Israel. But even in this expression, Barth does
not imply that Gentiles have become the true Israelites; following the pauline
language in Romans, they are "grafted in" and not native to the people Israel.
Jews are the elect, the chosen people of God and they rank before and above
the "nations of the earth."

> One thing is sure, and that is that [the Gentiles] are borne by the root
> of Israel, and are not in any sense its bearers. It is only if they were
> bearers and not borne, restorers of life and not restored, givers and
> not receivers, that they would have occasion to magnify themselves
> and disparage the others. In fact, however, they are such as are borne,
> and therefore this is quite out of the question. Moreover, it is by the
> root of Israel that they are borne, by the holy origin that makes even
> the others holy even though they are separated from it, and holy in a
> way in which they as Gentiles will never be holy. . . . "Unto them (the
> Jews) were (and still are) committed the oracles of God." Even the
> New Testament "oracles of God" are without exception Jewish oracles.
> Whoever has Jesus Christ in faith cannot wish not to have the Jews. He
> must have them along with Jesus Christ as His ancestors and kinsmen.
> Otherwise he cannot have even the Jew Jesus. Otherwise with the Jews
> he rejects Jesus Himself. This is what is at stake, and therefore, in fact,
> the very basis of the Church, when it has to be demanded of Gentile
> Christians that they should not approach any Israelite without the
> greatest attention and sympathy.[25]

The Gentiles are ordered to the Jews; the motion of election flows from
"here to there." Pilate and his Gentile empire must wait on Judas to receive
Jesus. But in the same way, Israel is ordered to the Church. Israel must "rise
up to life in the Church," find its completion and fulfillment there, hear the
words of comfort and mercy for its misery in the Church, even as Judas—

---

25. *Dogmatics,* 2.2:289 [*Dogmatik,* 2.2:318].

Judas, "*the* great sinner of the New Testament"—finds his sins "borne" and "borne away" in Christ.

In his customary way, Barth has let loose a large and lively topic with the wave of a single, evocative phrase: Israel must rise up to life in the Church. Has Barth, after all his protests, given himself over to full-blown supersessionism? Shall we take Barth's turn of phrase literally—to rise up to life—and see the death of one way of life followed by the resurrection of another? Or, if the Church has not superseded Israel—replaced it altogether—how can the Church maintain a place for Israel, "living" within it? What is the role and destiny of the people Israel, distinct yet united with the Church, itself a community of Jew and Gentile? We are faced here with a condition inhospitable to Barth's turn of mind, a question about matters contrary to fact. Israel has not, in fact, "risen up to life in the Church," and Barth shows some impatience with efforts to explain how things might and, in his view, ought to have been. Nevertheless, this phrase reveals more than a thinker impatient with the abstract; in its suggestive, elliptical style, it points with dogmatic precision to the dark testimony of Judas, Israel's head and representative, and to the proclamation of Paul, Judas's double, who "dies to sin, but lives in Christ."

Judas witnesses to this "turning" from Israel to the Church in his act, in death and life, of "handing over" Jesus to the Gentiles. Even in death, Judas finds a doublet: he is the form, the "passing" form, of Paul, the great and final apostle of the time of revelation. The significance of this substitution should not be missed: this is the biblical event that lays the pattern for all relations between the Synagogue and the Church. It is the event in the time of revelation that is interpreted in Romans 9 through 11. In these individual lives, the collective life of the Church, that life formed from Jews and Gentiles, is enacted, signified, and called into being.

Barth sets out his discussion of this final doublet with the appointment of Judas's replacement among the twelve. The story in Acts however names Matthias as the twelfth, not Paul: a "perfectly straightforward account," as Barth himself observes. But in fine dialectical fashion, even this only serves to confirm Barth's position: "This same Acts of the Apostles, which begins with this story of the apostles, becomes the history of the apostle Paul in a way which begins progressively to emerge after the story of the first martyr Stephen and is quite unequivocal after chapter 13, so that we can hardly deny that it is really Paul who took over Judas' place and the work abandoned by him."[26] Paul, as the persecutor Saul, is the "ghost of Judas": he pursues

26. Ibid., 478 [530].

Christians with unrivaled "zeal"; he "hands them over" to the authorities; he draws near to Christ in deepest opposition—"Saul, Saul, why persecutest thou me?" The members of Paul's early communities could not fail to see the parallel: "Those of his readers who knew the gospel stories must have been reminded of the Judaean, Judas!" Barth makes a good return on these parallels, but they are not his major interest. He is not busy with a moral example: see how it goes with the religious! Rather, he looks to the theological pattern caught up in the ambivalent act of "handing over." Judas and Paul are the disciples elected to hand Jesus over, and, in their concrete, historical lives, they determine the forms of the "passing" and "coming" communities:

> Paul—no longer the ghost of Judas, but a regenerate man, freed from his sin and shame, and clothed with another life—is the embodiment of a new Israel, obedient and fulfilling its destiny. For what is Israel's destiny, according to the Old Testament, if not to be a light to the Gentiles, to the world? But according to the Acts of the Apostles and the Epistles of Paul, the special office of the apostles is to bring Israel's Messiah to the Gentiles. This then—in a radical reversal of his own beginning, as of the badly begun work of Judas—is the peculiar and essential continuation of his work. Paul sets out from the very place where the penitent Judas had tried to turn back and reverse what had already happened. He begins by doing what to Judas' horror the high-priests and elders had done as the second links in that chain of evil. He fulfils the handing-over of Jesus to the Gentiles: not this time in unfaithfulness, but in faithfulness to Israel's calling and mission; not now aiming at the slaying of Jesus, but at establishing in the whole world the lordship of this One who was slain but is risen. Judas had been so little able to nullify the appointment and establishment of the apostleship, to destroy or even to disturb it, that when he fell and vanished, not only did the group of twelve re-form at once, but even outside it, in the figure of this supernumerary, there begins the true story of the apostles in the sense of Mt. 28:19, the genuine handing-over of Jesus to the Gentiles.[27]

Both Judas and Paul are Jews; the Church is their community. But it is a community now open "to the nations." Barth sees in the biblical turn from Judas to Paul the movement of Israel from particular to universal people of

27. Ibid., 478 [530, 531].

God.[28] This is not a repudiation of their mission—they were called to be the "light to the nations"—but a fulfillment of it.

Barth holds that Israel belongs to and within the Church; indeed, it finds its fulfillment there. Its refusal to enter the Church gives rise to the Synagogue, Barth's term for the "disobedient remnant" of post-biblical Judaism. This modern parallelism of Church and Synagogue caricatures the true relationship Barth reserves for the Church and Israel:

> The specific service for which Israel is determined within the whole of the elected community is to reflect the judgement *[der Spiegel des Gerichts]* from which God has rescued man and which He wills to endure Himself in the person of Jesus of Nazareth. If in faith in Jesus Christ Israel is obedient to its election, if it is given to it to come to the Church and rise to life again in it, to attain in it the goal of its determination, the special contribution which it will make within the whole of the community to the work of the community will be this. It will express the awareness of the human basis of the divine suffering and therefore the recognition of man's incapacity, unwillingness and unworthiness *[Unfähigkeit, Unwilligkeit und Unwürdigkeit]* with regard to the divine mercy purposed in Jesus Christ; the recognition of the justice of the judgement passed on man in the suffering of Jesus Christ. The Church needs this contribution. It cannot voice its witness to Jesus Christ and its summons to faith in Him without at the same time expressing this testimony which is peculiarly Israel's. . . . But the Church knows of man's misery only in so far as Israel too lives in it— as a reflection of divine judgement.[29]

This is a deceptively simple arrangement. Barth seems to have in mind a double form of a single mission: Israel, as a "mirror of divine judgement," witnesses to human misery; the Church, as the "perfect form *[vollkommene Gestalt]* of the elected community," witnesses to divine mercy. Together, they proclaim the whole gospel, judgment and mercy; wrath and love; misery and reunion. If Israel were obedient, Barth argues, it would "come to life and live

---

28. As is customary, Barth works out the logic of his position from within Christian sources. He disregards and, I think, is unaware of the nineteenth-century debate over the universal mission of Judaism. The claims advanced for example by Abraham Geiger (see *Judaism and Its History,* lectures 1, 2, 8, and 12) and Hermann Cohen (see *Religion of Reason,* chaps. 8, 13, and 14) to a kind of messianic universalism would interest Barth, I think, as a "shadowy doublet" of the "true Messiah" and his "light to the Gentiles."

29. *Dogmatics,* 2.2:206 [*Dogmatik,* 2.2:277].

on even in its form as the Church"; this "negative side" would remain "actual until the end of the world." Both sides count—it is the *Church,* the Gentiles are grafted in, and it is *Israel,* the Jews and their "misery" are taken up and preserved. But we have to ask how this "rising up" and "preserving" should be understood.

Barth insists on the presence of Jews within Israel *and* the Church; they are determined for both election and rejection and cannot be reduced to either term. It is too easy, Barth warns, for Christians to think of Jews as "the Rejected"—those disobedient and stubborn Israelites—and Christians alone as "the Elected." "We cannot" Barth reminds his readers "call the Jews the 'rejected' and the Church the 'elected' community. The object of election is neither Israel for itself nor the Church for itself, but both together in their unity."[30] Within that one community, Israel reminds the world of human need; the Church of divine grace. Jews belong to Israel first, but then the Church. Gentiles belong only to the Church.

But how shall we distinguish these roles and recognize the actors? If Jews are the "hearers" of the Word, how can they also be its "proclaimers"? How can they "rise up to life in the Church" yet remain Israel, without which the Church loses its direction and power? Do not the Jews within the Church believe also in the divine mercy? Have they not also been obedient to God's act on their behalf? How, in short, can Jews live out their election—to witness to their misery—and remain obedient to their fulfillment in the Church? Barth has made a distinction here, an interesting and provocative one, but has he made a distinction without a difference?

One possible solution to the questions raised here might have been assumed by Barth, and by most of his contemporaries. Jews could remain at once members of Israel and believing Christians because they are a separate people, a *Volk.* Barth was not a racist—we must go carefully here—and he knew "racial theories" for what they really were.[31] But it was the common

---

30. Ibid., 199 [219, 220].

31. Consider Barth's discussion of the "true, spiritual" Israel in par. 34.2 The translation, following Barth's treatment of Romans 9:6b–7a runs: "For it is not at all the case that according to the Word and will of God all who belong to the race of Abraham, all bearers of the name Israel were appointed to become members of the Church. They were certainly appointed members of the one elected community of God. This is something that none of this race can decline, not even if his name is Caiaphas or indeed Judas Iscariot, this is what Jews, one and all, are by birth" (214). Now this passage could give the unsuspecting reader some pause, but the German here is *Stamm,* not *Rasse.* While "race" can generally serve as the English for both, *Stamm* is better translated as "tribe" or "stock." By the 1930s, "race" had become a technical term, covered with a "scientific" veneer. Barth indicates his contempt for this term, and all it implies, by avoiding it in its customary sense, a "people by birth." He gives *Stamm* its earlier,

property of Germans, both within the "new Romanticism" and without, to assume that each ethnic group—"nation," to use the language of the day— had a particular historical and spiritual identity that was ineradicable. Jews, too, were a *Volk,* a view shared by some Jews like Martin Buber and Gentiles alike.[32] The expatriated Americans in Paris during the 1920s were often considered "ineradicably" American, and this persistance of national charac-

---

more Romantic connotation, a term of course not innocent by far but thought-worlds apart from the technocratic realm of Race and Blood.

Barth makes this explicit in the next few lines. While acknowledging a special role for "Abraham's seed" [*Abrahams Nachkommen*], he stresses the election of Israel as a whole: "This is God's order in Israel just because Israel is the elected people [*das erwählte Volk*]." But they are elected in Christ: "Not one of them is so by nature; not one in virtue of his Jewish blood; not only as a self-evident consequence of his membership of this people: but each only on the ground of a special election in which the election of Israel as such is repeated and established." [Keiner ist es von Natur, Keiner vermöge seines jüdischen Blutes, Keiner in selbst-verständlicher Konsequenz seiner Zugehörigkeit zu diesem Volke.] The language of people, volk, yes; but not of race: this I think is Barth's inheritance.

A contemporary and more polemical context bears out this point. In his exchange with Gerhard Kittel in 1934, Barth makes explicit his contempt for the German Christian appropria- tion of the Nazi "order of creation" and his theological rejection of the entire "racial theory":

> Vorderhand haben Sie, die D. C. [Deutsche Christen] und die Ihnen Nahestehenden, es reichlich verdient, daß man gegen das Wort *Schöpfung* in Ihrem Munde schlechterdings mißtrauisch ist, wil es in Ihrem Munde nicht das Geheimnis Gottes, sondern eine ganz geheimnislose menschliche Theorie über Rasse, Blut, Boden, Volk, Staat, usw. bedeutet. Mit dieser Identifikation von der Schöpfung haben Sie sich theologisch ins Unrecht gesetzt. Denn diese Identifikation können Sie nur aufrechterhalten, wenn Sie eine besondere zweite Offenbarung darüber empfangen zu haben behaupten. Sie meinten natürlich auch bei Ihrer "Offenen Frage" diese Identifikation. Darum habe ich Ihren Ergänzungsvorschlag abgelehnt. Er besagt faktisch doch nichts anderes als die Forderung, daß die Kirche in Gottes Namen mittun solle, nicht nur im Dritten Reich, sondern im Sinn des Dritten Reiches. Zu dieser Forderung ist Nein zu sagen. . . . Die Kirche hat den Gehorsam gegen jeden Staat, sie hat aber nicht den Glauben an eine bestimmte Staatsform zu fordern. (Karl Barth and Gerhard Kittel, *Ein theologischer Briefwechsel* [Stuttgart: Verlag von W. Kohlhammer, 1934], 20)
>
> [First of all you, the German Christians and your like-minded companions, have richly deserved the absolute mistrust that greets the word "creation" on your lips. Because, on your lips, it does not mean the mystery of God, but an entirely unmysterious human theory about Race, Blood, Soil, People, State, and so on. With this identification between Creation and your own conception of Creation, you have placed yourself in theological error. For this identification can only be maintained if you claim to have received a second, special Revelation about it. You, of course, intend this identification in your "Open Question" as well. Therefore, I have rejected your entire proposal. Factually it means nothing other than the demand that the Church should collaborate not only with the Third Reich but with the spirit and intent of the Third Reich. To this demand, one must say No. . . . The Church must demand obedience to every state, but not belief in any one particular form of the state.]

32. Gentiles holding this view ranged from a position of neutrality or some affection toward

ter within an alien culture may provide a clue to this untranslatable term, *Volk.* It must not be flattened out, however, into a commonplace: Americans, in this example, can always be recognized not simply because they drive on the right, pronounce English in a particular way, or use their forks in a manner odd to Europeans. No, for the expatriates to be considered a *Volk,* they must have a particular *Geist,* a "spiritual" quality that affects both inner disposition and outer behavior, appearance, and ways of life. The often-cited "pragmatic character" of Americans, if understood as a unifying and transcendent quality, might undergird an American *Volk.* This idea has its dangers— the twentieth century is the most somber testament to the danger of ideas— but in its original form it was not an inherently racist ideology. It was, as we might politely term it today, a theory of "identity" or "national character." The union of racial theories, considered at that time scientific, with these mystical longings of the *Volk* produced the ideas of terror we recognize in Nazi claims to Aryan supremacy. But that is not the use of the term *Volk* I am suggesting here. Barth may have assumed a particular, continuing "spirit" of the Jewish people for the reasons that many people of good will reached for the language of the *Volk:* it helped explain the enduring character of regional groups. If this is so—I can find no textual evidence—then Barth may have pictured the continued life of the Jews within the Church as a *Volk,* witnessing according to their character to human misery, but participating according to their belief in divine mercy and reconciliation. The Christian then, and the world beyond the Church, would know who were the Jews among them and why they deserved the Gentiles' "greatest attention and sympathy."

I have suggested this interpretation in part because it is, I think, a more plausible and far more attractive solution than several others available to Germans in the 1930s. It is also, on the positive side, a reasonably coherent explanation for how Israel can "rise up and live" with the Church perpetually. The caricatures of European Jews common to his period, and not so foreign to our own—"Jewish" surnames, facial types, occupations, the long, cruel list of stereotypes—even these would not allow Jews to remain visible within the Church, visible that is as Christians, until the eschaton. That Jews and Judaism exceed the definition of "religion," that they are more than a "belief system" is a claim Barth seems to recognize and honor.[33] But these more cultural explanations of Barth's position should not obscure his theological one.

Judaism to the overtly racist; both George Mosse (*The Crisis of German Ideology*) and Lucy Dawidowicz (*The War Against the Jews, 1933–1945.*) provide ample examples of the full scale of German volkist thought. For Martin Buber's early work, see "Das Judentum und die Juden," in *Reden über das Judentum* (Berlin: Schocken Verlag, 1932).

33. For Europeans, the identity of the Jews took on a different character during the age of Emancipation. Both Christians and Jews sought a definition or essence of Judaism outside the

Like Israel, the Church is an elected community; within Israel, from its beginning, the Church has lived a hidden existence. The Church foreshadows the election of grace within the election of judgment of the people Israel. Though Israel has given rise to Judas, it has also created Paul, the Jew obedient to his Messiah. Judas expresses Israel as a whole; he is the type and determination of the Rejected. But Paul expresses Israel as its future; he "completes in his body" the determination of the Elected, those Jews who "rise up to life in the Church." The figure of Paul, at once a "ghost of Judas" and a paradigm of the apostle, typifies the theological interpretation Barth gives to the place of Israel within the Church. As in *Romans,* he is *the* Jew, turned from disobedient to obedience, from "passing" to "coming" form, from death to eternal life. All Christians learn of Christ from Paul, but the Jews within the Church learn what their election means, at once betrayer and disciple.

Barth of course read Paul through the eyes of the West—through Augustine, Luther, and Calvin. Paul, in his letters certainly, but in his life as well, represents for Barth the source of the Protestant form of the Christian life, the life lived under justification by faith alone. With his synthetic mastery, Barth discerns the radical impulse of the justification doctrine within Paul's own conversion and ministry. A "pharisee of the pharisees"—remember that Barth is speaking "dogmatically"—a zealous persecutor of Christians, a man "untimely born," Paul nevertheless becomes the single authority of the Church, the last apostle, a witness to the Resurrection, and an exemplar of all those sinners reconciled by grace alone, apart from merit and works. In Paul, those members of the hidden and invisible Church within Israel find their head and completion. In his exegesis of Romans 9:6–13—For not all who are descended from Israel belong to Israel—Barth ties together the theme of justification with the hidden elect:

> God is righteous in the fact that when He shows mercy to Israel—for the sake of all men and all Israel as well—He is concerned with his future act of mercy and therefore with this one man [Jesus] and with His Church. God is righteous in the fact that He causes this electing mercy towards His Church in Israel to follow upon His special electing mercy shown to Abraham and all his race [*Geschlecht,* descendents].

medieval ghetto, and this search characterized most of the nineteenth century. Is Judaism a "religion," a "religion of Reason"? Is it "revealed legislation," ethical monotheism, the religion of the prophets? What are the ties that bind Jews together; shall the halakhic life continue in bourgeois society? These questions are a common legacy from the nineteenth century, but are recast and reevaluated of course by the events of World War II.

This sequel, indeed, only renews, establishes and glorifies that beginning. Even in loving Jacob and hating Esau, God is supremely righteous—and supremely righteous in the disregard thereby shown with
respect to all natural and moral presuppositions of the persons
affected. "So then it is not of him that willeth, nor of him that runneth,
but of God that sheweth mercy," if (in addition to the fact that as a
member of Abraham's race *[Abrahamsgeschlecht]* he has a share in the
mercy of God) this special mercy falls on anyone, if he is called to the
Church.[34]

These themes concerning Israel and the Church, so elaborately unfolded
over the last few pages, must now be drawn up again. How do things stand
between the people Israel and the Church called from Jew and Gentile? And
how, in this intricate arrangement of doublets and types, is the Synagogue to
live and be understood? Barth has brought us up to the edge of his final and
most complex interpretation of Israel—the disobedience and rejection of the
Jews—and we must now step back and make sure of our surroundings.

In Christ, the Object and Subject of election, the community is appointed
and determined as the "representation" of Christ in the world. That community is one, as Christ is one; but it is determined in two forms, as Christ is of
two natures and the creation, made through him, reflects his glory in the
dispersion and ordering of doublets. This one elected community in its two
forms conforms to God's intention: in the foundation of election, God willed
to be with the creature, to establish fellowship with humanity through a
community of Jew and Gentile. But it is an ordered community: the Jew
precedes and has precedence over the Gentile. The name and event of that
particular honor is Israel. Israel is the elected one of God; it stands at the
beginning of all God's "ways and works." From that people, the One Elect,
Jesus Christ, is to come. The final reconciliation, the full fellowship of God
with humanity would take place within history, the particular history of
Israel. The recognition of and obedience to this, Israel's Messiah, is the
purpose, honor, justification, and perpetual election of the Jews. Were this
act of divine grace and condescension met with obedience, Israel, like Paul,
would confess Christ. Like Paul, Israel would recognize in its own flesh the
misery and pride that Christ has assumed, and in the Church, it would hear
the mercy that covers it all. The elected people of God, the Jews, would
remain Israel, yet belong to the Church; in their act of turning from wrath to
grace, they would establish the human response that began with God, the

34. *Dogmatics,* 2.2:219 [*Dogmatik,* 2.2:241].

divine act of breaking over, encountering, and reconciling his creatures. One community in two forms; Israel and the Church; Jews and Gentiles: that, Barth stresses, is the divine intention in election.

But that one community of obedience, Barth warns, is precisely what does not happen. The Jews do not believe, they do not confess their own Messiah. They take as their type not Paul but Judas; they deny, betray, and hand over their Messiah but they do not accept his gracious and righteous mercy. They do not "rise up to life" in the Church, but perpetuate their misery in the Synagogue. Like Judas, the Synagogue Jews have no future; they must joylessly repeat their elected witness, that human arrogance will never earn salvation. The Synagogue still finds its partner in the Church, but now only as Judas finds Jesus—in the night. The Church still requires, indeed belongs to Jews. It must continue to honor the people from whom Christ came, and it must remember their proclamation of "how it is with man." But it must recognize that a division has severed the one community of God: not now Israel within the Church, but the Synagogue beside and outside the Church. This disobedience of the Jews, their stubborn clinging to rejection and wrath, the repudiation of their elected purpose—this is the "mystery of the Jews" Barth encounters in Romans, and it is to that classic passage, chapters 9 through 11, that Barth obsessively turns and returns in his final and darkest examination of those "determined for wrath."

Judas, Agent of the "Night"

Thus far, I have been presenting Barth's thought, but Barth's obsession with "obdurate Judaism" is hardly unique. Barth's insistent question: Why do the Jews not believe? may be taken as *the* classic question of Christian interpretation of Judaism. This "mystery of disbelief" courses through the New Testament, in the polemics against "the Jews" in John, in the conflict between the "Church" and "Synagogue" in Acts, in the "stone which the builder rejected," the "stumbling block," and the "Temple not made by hands," and most of all, in Paul's rehearsal of the "hardening of Israel" in the divine plan of election in Romans. The elements of this "mystery" were all too clear. Jesus, the disciples, the first followers and missionaries: all were Jews. By the close of the apostolic age, the institution of the Church governed communal life, and it had passed into the hands of the Gentiles. The second-century apologetic and patristic task of Christian self-definition fell to Gentile believers, and by the late fourth century, John Chrysostom could exhort his congregation to abandon its Jewish practices, rituals now considered foreign and dangerous to Christian identity. The controversial literature with Jews had by now taken on a formal style; they were "dialogues" without partners. Justin Martyr in the second century may have controverted scripture with Trypho, though unlikely, and some medieval debates, like the Barcelona Disputations, were encounters between living partisans, though by this time hardly equals. Nevertheless, Christian polemics against Judaism, particularly on "proofs from scripture," testified to the prolonged and sometimes troubled Christian consciousness of "Jewish disbelief."

What does it mean that Jews did not confess Jesus as their Messiah, or later, that Jews did not convert? These questions, again at the center of Christian anti-Judaism, allow two distinct though related responses. One is represented by the medieval tradition of controversial literature, by debates, and the "teachings of contempt." Though not of course limited to the medieval West, or, more importantly, solely to theological contempt, this tradition of controversy has little in common with the modern concept of pluralism or tolerance. This particular form of anti-Judaism assumes that Jews require a special "mission"; they claim knowledge and possession of the Scriptures but they are wrong. Their own sources prove that Jesus is the Christ—they do not own the Scriptures—and they are unwilling to admit this, or unwitting. Debates with Jews, that is, are significant, if only to demonstrate Christian superiority. Like most apologetic literature, the mission to the Jews assumes a difference—Christians are not Jews or pagans—within a commonality— they, like us, can and must recognize the Truth.

But the second tradition of Christian anti-Judaism relies upon a distinct, more pauline premise about the history and meaning of Israel. Here, the Jews require no special mission, no controversial demonstration from Scripture, no calls to conversion, because they are in God's hands and are God's affair. Christians may debate Jews, may proclaim to them the gospel, offer them baptism, but God will determine when the Jews enter the Church. A divine and sometimes inscrutable plan governs the relationship between Jew and Gentile, and, though Christians glimpse its outlines, its full majesty will be preserved for the end-time. All that Christians may know with certainty is that Jews are "hardened"; they are "closed up in disbelief" and the Gentiles are "grafted in" until the fullness of time when the Jews join the "faithful remnant" in belief and mercy. Jews, in short, are the concern of God's wrath and providence; God will judge and justify them, like all creatures, by sovereign grace alone.

This second tradition of anti-Judaism—the Augustinian reading of Paul— dominates Barth's teaching on the Jews. Its impress, I think, is unmistakable to those who have followed Barth this far, but he subsumes his own thought within these categories with special care in the treatment of Israel, "determined for rejection." Without doubt, Paul's discussion of Israel's election in Romans 9–11 belongs to the core of Barth's position and demands careful treatment. But, with characteristic concreteness, Barth reserves the most relentless and ruthless logic of his position for his exegesis of Judas, "traitor and instrument of Satan."

One of the twelve, one indeed in the closest circle around Jesus, Judas was the apostle elected for the work "of the night." This of course is a biblical phrase—Barth makes eloquent use of it—but it is a repetition too of Barth's most impassioned exposition in the *Epistle to the Romans,* "The Night, its Cause and Operation," an exegesis of Romans 1:18–32. Barth surrounds Judas with darkness, enfolding him in blindness, temptation, and "that which is not."

> This, then, is the sin of Judas. And no matter how we look at it, we cannot say that the universal expressions of horror with which the New Testament surrounds his figure and accompanies his way are inappropriate to their subject. What was done here, as the work of Israel from within the apostolic group, the Church, was really work which belonged to the night. As the representative of Israel within the apostolic group, within the Church, Judas is indeed the "son of perdition," the man into whom the Satan has entered, himself a devil. The New Testament then can only reject his repentance, however sincerely he may undertake it. The New Testament can only record with horror that he came to this miserable end. There can be no doubt that here at the very heart of the New Testament we are confronted by the problem of the rejected, by the question: What is the will of God for him? What has God determined concerning him? And we meet this question at the same central place where the New Testament also raises and answers the question of the elect.[35]

Here are Barth's favorite themes: the Church and Israel; the rejected and elected; the will and purpose of God in election; the sin and betrayal of Judas. But Barth sounds a new note as well. Judas, of course, committed a sin Barth had called "petty" and "small," a betrayal only a bourgeois could execute. Judas was a traitor in the way Saul was a sinner: too prim for God's overflowing, unrestrained generosity. Yet here Barth calls Judas the man "into

35. Ibid., 471 [522].

whom the Satan has entered, himself a devil"; "universal expressions of horror" are not too strong for such a figure. This is the kind of puzzle Barth enjoyed, and enjoyed creating. Its underlying consistency will point to Barth's final word on the "question of the elect," but here we return to Judas's act of betrayal.

Barth's exegesis rests heavily on the Johannine account following the footwashing scene in chapter 13:

> When Jesus had thus spoken, he was troubled in spirit, and testified, "Truly, truly, I say to you, one of you will betray me." The disciples looked at one another, uncertain of whom he spoke. One of his disciples, whom Jesus loved, was lying close to the breast of Jesus; so Simon Peter beckoned to him and said, "Tell us who it is of whom he speaks." So lying thus, close to the breast of Jesus, he said to him, "Lord, who is it?" Jesus answered, "It is he to whom I shall give this morsel when I have dipped it." So when he had dipped the morsel, he gave it to Judas, the son of Simon Iscariot. Then after the morsel, Satan entered into him. Jesus said to him, "What you are going to do, do quickly." Now no one at the table knew why he said this to him. Some thought that, because Judas had the money box, Jesus was telling him, "Buy what we need for the feast"; or, that he should give something to the poor. So, after receiving the morsel, he immediately went out; and it was night.

And it was night: Barth closes up Judas in the shroud of the night, the darkness of Satan's work:

> It was the devil who planned in his heart that Judas Iscariot, the son of Simon, should hand over Jesus. It was Satan who led him as he actually went about the deed. Therefore Judas himself, the "son of perdition" of John 17:12, can be called a "devil" in John 6:70. "He then having received the sop went immediately out: and it was *night.* Even in Paul it is surely not just a chronological observation: "The Lord Jesus the same *night* in which he was betrayed. . . ." What the Johannine Prologue announced is now manifestly realised and fulfilled: "The Light shineth in the darkness." . . . We are told of course that this work of darkness does not mean an overpowering (a *kata-lambanein*) of the light. But the work of darkness is certainly that of His own—of His own in the strictest meaning of the term, of His own in the figure of the apostle Judas.[36]

36. Ibid., 461 [511].

The drama of light and shadow, enacted in so many scenes before, in minor turns of misfortune, in acts of bitter treachery—in all these scenes, this one drama, "Judas went out and it was night," was prefigured and in this one sharp exchange of light and dark all other shadows are comprehended and put in their place. *This* is the event of revelation for Barth: "[N]*ow* is the hour when Satan is cast out." The sequence of the Passion—the betrayal, the arrest and trial, the crucifixion and burial—all these particular events are taken up in one cosmic moment: Satan enters in, and the work of the night begins. This cosmic battle between God and Satan, the one real judgment of good and evil, is the terror Israel calls down on itself when, in Judas, it wills to be the Judge:

> [Judas] wills to take even the judgement of God into his own hands, and himself executes it upon himself. It is in this light of a usurped self-judgement crowning all previous offences that Matthew evidently sees the corresponding downfall of Jersusalem and the whole national and relgious life of the Jews. With the killing of its Messiah, Israel has entered a road on which not only is God's judgement on its whole existence inevitable, but in sheer self-consistency it must end by committing suicide. That is what Israel finally did in the revolt against the Romans and particularly in the defence of Jerusalem against Titus in A.D. 70. Unable to live any longer, it gave itself up willingly and wittingly—we have only to think of the account of the end of the last high-priests—to the death which in itself could not be an expiation for its sins, but only their consummation.[37]

In the one, destructive moment of satanic betrayal, Judas enacts the long, cruel history that Barth assigns to the Jews. The "joyless ghetto," the "monstrous side of Israel's history," the "ghostly Synagogue of every age": all these Barthian rebukes find their source in this individual Jew in whom God and Satan, for a single sovereign and terrible task, execute judgment as one. Barth has a stake in this, the most familiar medieval teaching of contempt: the Jews as killers of Christ. He actually uses this phrase—the passage cited above is one example—and we mistake him if we do not recognize that Barth utters it in full seriousness. That "Jesus was born a Jew" means this, too: that the rejection, betrayal, and handing over to death of Jesus was a Jewish act as well. Historical responsibility for acts of human cruelty is a controverted topic, one that cannot be settled here, but it cannot be easily solved by a

37. Ibid., 470 [521].

simple identification of the perpetrators. Barth would acknowledge this point, I think—he is, after all, concerned with a divine, not a human drama—and would repeat his earlier, equally serious remarks, that Judas stands for all the apostles and, indeed, for all human beings, all sinners. But Barth insists on the Jewishness of the New Testament figures—of Jesus, the disciples, the apostles, the "oracles" and "promises," the true "fathers of the Church"—all of them, Barth stresses, Jews. Advocates of the Christian-Jewish dialogue find comfort at times in such remarks, but Barth is a most unreliable comforter. He forces this "scandal of particularity" to its ruthless conclusion: Jesus a Jew; Judas a Jew. In Paul, Christians may see what obedient Israel is like, and to him, all Christians, Jew and Gentile, owe their life in the Church. But in Judas, Christians see what disobedient Judaism is like, and Barth does not allow the reader to forget the stark end of this traitor's life. The judgment on the Jews is the wrath Christ "bears and bears away"; Barth will never let judgment have the last word. But history is a powerful tool, the concrete historicity of the gospels particularly so, and Barth wields it like the "two-edged sword." The Jews typified in Judas are determined, in Barth's somber words, for the "work of the night."

This work, though on the historical plane the task of the Jew, Judas, is supremely the affair of Satan. The Night is the time of cosmic battle. The Creator will defend the honor of his creation; he will enter the battle for the creature with Satan. In Christ's passion, the punishment for sin—death, real death—and the defeat of Satan will be executed in one act. In the resurrection, Christ is victor; Satan has been overthrown, the creature ransomed. The threat to the creature, the Chaos that awaits humanity at the border of creation, has been met and defeated in Christ's work of obedience. The remainder of human history, the "time that God has for us," is actually only the "time between the times." Since the resurrection, creation has waited for the final consummation when God's victory over Satan is completed and made manifest. Until that final revelation, human beings live their course, in the shadow and the light, more in shadow no doubt than light, looking back to this one cosmic moment in which Satan fell "like lightning," and Christ began his reign. No suffering, no sorrow or tribulation, can stand alone or apart from this cosmic victory. Creaturely ills are evil, "nothingness," but they cannot be victorious; in Christ, God is victorious, and every future evil in creation is but a vestige, a shadow of the Night that is overcome by the Light.

Once again, Barth has elegantly worked the results of higher criticism into his figural and dramatic exposition of the text. The stirring proclamation of Bad Bolle, Christ is Victor!, rings out in Barth's early work. It is present here, in the second volume of the *Dogmatics,* and is explicit in the work of Barth's last years, volume 4, the "Doctrine of Reconciliation." The Blumhardts, father and son, were far from academic practioners of higher criticism. The church of Liberal respectability, the theological faculties, the adepts of scholarly criticism, they were all accorded a kind of thin contempt by the Blumhardts. But their emphasis upon the cosmic victory of Christ over evil belongs to that great divide in nineteenth-century academic criticism—the recovery of eschatology.

For German academics like Barth, the work of Johannes Weiss and in a different form, that of Franz Overbeck, brought the question of eschatology to its sharpest expression. The influence of Weiss's *Jesus' Proclamation of the Kingdom of God* is evident throughout Barth's treatment of the Passion. A son-in-law of Albrecht Ritschl, that monument of Imperial German Liberalism, Weiss found his own conclusions about eschatology painful but inescapable. The confidence with which academics like Ritschl approached historical sources, particularly those of the gospel, would never be recovered. The brooding, ecstatic, and truly alien figure of Weiss's eschatological Jesus had changed all that. Jesus preached the kingdom of God, a future reign of God that would crush the power of Satan and bring this world to a close. The little band of disciples gathered around Jesus would prepare the Jews for this final battle; Israel must repent, put its hand to the plow, and not look back. God would usher in his reign, and put his Messiah at his right hand. The judgment, punishment, and reward of the living and the dead was the Messiah's majestic task, and when he returned on the clouds of glory, all people would witness what Jesus had privately known, that he had been appointed to this final work.[38]

A particular feature of Weiss's exposition is the elaboration of the "two-story universe": a realm of divine or cosmic powers anticipating and controlling the second, earthly realm in which human beings are the actors and patients of history. A two-story universe operates something like a theater in which the audience—ordinary mortals—observes the fascinating drama of

---

38. This is a highly abbreviated treatment of that controverted question, the "messianic consciousness of Jesus." Weiss, though speaking in very tentative and cautious terms—at least in the first edition of the *Preaching*—held that Jesus knew he would *become* the messiah in the eschaton. All biblical scholars of this period, indeed down through Bultmann, developed a position on this question, many of them recorded in Albert Schweitzer's classic work, *The Quest of the Historical Jesus* (New York: Macmillan, 1968). This is another theological topic, it seems to me, in which certainty is demanded, a quality that history, and certainly historical criticism, is ill-equipped to provide. Barth opens up new ground here in his reliance on the revelation of the Resurrection, a kind of theological certainty apart from and beyond history. But this is a solution that engenders fresh problems, as I have tried to show.

the heavenly forces as they battle for control of creation. Although this is far from a platonic universe, some elements appear in common. Historical human beings belong to a world far more shadowy, more ambiguous, and in a sense far less real than the world above. In the heavenly realm, the real struggles are fought in bitter earnest; in our world, we receive and rehearse that verdict. The heavenly realm, however, is no platonic world of forms. This is a world of actors, of events, of conflict and defeat. Like other human creatures, Jesus lived in the earthly realm, that place in the cosmos subject to Satan's dominion. But he was an ecstatic: in visions, he was granted a glimpse of the other world; what took place there would eventually take place here. In his preaching, Jesus would proclaim what he had already witnessed: that Satan was cast out, "falling like lightning from heaven" and God in triumph would soon bring his victory to earth. Jesus' ministry was the beginning on earth of that heavenly battle; in casting out demons, in healing sinners, in proclaiming the kingdom, Jesus performs signs of the approaching cataclysm. The eschaton, the kingdom of the end-time, draws near.

In the moment of betrayal, when Satan enters Judas, Barth infuses this "eschatological theory" with life. The struggle between Jesus and Judas reflects the battle between God and Satan; it is a cosmic battle, *the* cosmic battle between good and evil that marks the beginning of the end-time. The captivity of Judas to the Night reflects the reign of Satan over the creaturely realm, the reign Jesus alone will overthrow. Through Christ's obedience, God will restore the order of his rule; his kingdom will cast out the chaos, disorder, and disobedience of Satan and his followers. The judgment on evil will be rendered, and justice restored.

In matters of eschatology, however, Barth is no purist. As in many theological debates, Barth mediates between scholarly positions. He is not, like Weiss or Schweitzer, a "thoroughgoing eschatologist."[39] He does not consider the kingdom of God an event confined to the end of history. Nor is he a "realized eschatologist." He does not hold that the kingdom entered time in the ministry of Jesus. And, while Barth clearly sympathizes with Bultmann's view—"already" we have signs of the kingdom; they are "not yet" fulfilled— he is not merely looking for "proleptic in-breakings" of the kingdom. Barth holds that revelation *is* eschatology: that is the significance of the resurrection. The time of revelation may at first be broadly understood as "biblical

39. I have used this term as it is commonly defined in exegetical work. More properly, however, Schweitzer considered himself the "thoroughgoing" eschatologist; *all* Jesus' life, his words *and* deeds, showed forth the end-time. Weiss, Schweitzer argued, had not pushed his thesis to its radical conclusion.

history"; then, more specifically, as the witness and mission of the early Church; and, in its sharpest form, revelation is the moment of Christ's passion and resurrection. This moment is eschatological because it is the explosion of God's wrath and God's judgment and righteous vindication into the human world of dishonor and disobedience. History cannot comprehend such divine rejection; it cannot receive such divine reconciliation. This revelation—not miracles, not oracles, not mystics or prophets or final trumpets—but this revelation of the Passion and of God's wrath and mercy is the end of history. God alone can suffer this moment; God alone can make it susceptible of human reception. For this reason, in the handing over of Jesus to suffering and death, Judas inaugurates the eschatological conflict. Christ's victory, in obedient death and resurrection, is a permanent and real, indeed the only real, triumph over evil. This revelation of God's justification of his creation is the end of history: it is the purpose, will, goal, and realization of God's love in freedom. Human time, of course, has not ended. Barth does not imagine that human history has undergone a silent transformation or change of name; it is not now "the kingdom." Our time continues, and it is really our time, but it exists because God wills it: He has "time for us." But our time is not eternity. It will someday end.[40] Barth reserved this dogmatic material, the fulfillment of the eschatological events, for his final volume, the "Doctrine of Redemption." It remains unwritten. By the title, Barth may have intended to work out in his own consistent and novel manner the conclusion of the "redemption achieved in Jesus of Nazareth." But in general, Barth takes up the story of Judas, and in him the election of Israel, as the content of eschatology. In this history, this particular figure and people, the Father's election of the Son and the creature is made real and made righteous. This fellowship, too, between Creator and creature is the end, the goal of history; in Judas's act of betrayal and rejection God's will for creation is made manifest. For these reasons—and many others—the election of Judas, the election of the rejected, is the beginning of the eschatological moment.

Judas, the Determination of Rejection

But what does it mean to be the rejected of God? That is the question Barth brings to the biblical text on Judas. In pursuing the answer to that question,

40. For a complex synthesis of Barth's dogmatic work under the aspect of time and eternity, see R. H. Roberts, "Barth's Doctrine of Time: Its Nature and Implications," in *Karl Barth,* ed. S. W. Sykes, (Oxford: Clarendon Press, 1979), 88–146.

we encounter the issue at the heart of Barth's doctrine of Israel: what does it mean for Israel, the elected people of God, to be the rejected? Now, "rejection" is an odd term in Christian dogmatics. It has a long history of course, a history that reaches back through the medieval period to Augustine and, perhaps, to Paul. But its long history has not eradicated or resolved the ambiguity in the term, "the rejected of God," and this ambiguity recurs in Barth, now explicitly and with full force. To be rejected by God has meant to be "passed over"—a term with its own ambiguities!—to be judged or punished; to be damned, in Calvin's thought; to be declared sinful, evil, that "which is not"; to exist, in Barth's works, on the "left hand of God." But many thoughtful readers of Christian dogmatics have been struck by the difficulties in such expressions. They are metaphorical, to be sure, and that is a weakness as well as a strength. They are also oddly contradictory: these rejected states and persons *exist;* they are contrary to God's will yet they exist and, in fact, flourish. Critics have not failed to spot this weakness and have raised a variety of objections. The classic problems of Christian systematics—the presence of evil; the freedom of the will; the extent of Christ's saving action; the origin of and responsibility for sin—all have their place in this debate. Under the aspect of rejection, however, the debate runs along these lines. What is the meaning of human disobedience? And, do these human sinners merit their rejection? For Barth, these questions take shape under biblical types. What is the meaning of the election of a disobedient people? And, does Judas—and in him, all Israel—deserve their rejection? Using classical Reformation language, Barth presses his point: Why has God hardened Israel's heart?

Consider the figure of Judas. Here is the figure Barth has named "*the* sinner of the New Testament." He is the petit bourgeois, the small-minded, self-willed autocrat; he is the type of the rejected, the one who judges for himself and whom God judges in wrath. But Barth would hardly consider Judas unique—the sinner without equal. Judas is significant, as a figure and as a type, because he refuses to serve as a unique or supreme example of any wickedness. Judas represents and enacts the type of the rejected—"*the* sinner"—because he represents humanity; Judas is the sinners' Everyman. Barth, as he often does, expresses both contradictory impulses in a single form: Judas stands alone in his commission of the supreme sin, the handing over of Jesus to death, precisely because he stands for the whole; he represents Israel and, more, he represents all humanity, all those who do the "work of the Night." And Barth does not rest there. We should not allow the role Barth assigns to an individual actor and his psychology to distract from what is, at heart, a cosmic event. Barth narrows his attention to one man, or more correctly to one doublet, but in that twofold figure, Barth records a divine decision. Satan enters Judas and possesses him; Judas goes out quickly into the night to do the work of the "ruler of this age." It was an Evil deed Judas performed: Barth means that quite literally. He considers it a hollow comfort if Christians isolate Judas as the traitor; they have passed by the disciples who ask, "Is it I, Lord?" But more is at risk than Christian ignorance or self-satisfaction. Judas demonstrates the range and strength of the Protestant Gospel at its frontier. He may be *the* sinner of the New Testament, but more, he is the living declaration of justification by grace alone. Or, in Barth's language, Judas is the rejected one, elected.

Judas must not be seen as one possessing special, evil powers, or a unique weakness to temptation, or the flattery of Nothingness. No, in this case too, Judas stands for Everyman; he like all creatures stands at the frontier between Creation and Chaos; he hears the call across the border, as every person does. But Satan enters him. Judas does not merit this wickedness; indeed, his life is a rather stuffy and self-serving affair that is only cruder—or more refined!—than many others. Satan enters him and uses him for his ends: the Gospels are unified on that point. But Barth does not let the matter rest. Judas serves the forces of the Night, but they serve God. It is God's good-pleasure that Judas betrays Jesus; it is God's will that Judas serve evil ends; it is God's sovereign election that Judas is hardened, obdurate, and lost. Judas, in his very alliance with evil, demonstrates the meaning of grace: *that* too, his life teaches, is God's freedom over the creature, the divine grace that acts beyond, apart from, and against the merit of the creature. Barth began his theological career insisting that grace implied judgment. He never relented. Grace is a "hard saying": it does not rely upon human achievement—a comfort for most achievers—but more, it rejects achievement and condemns it, using its true name, rebellion against God. God is a sovereign judge and brooks no competitors. Human beings rebel against their Sovereign not simply in wicked and stupid acts, though Barth is far from ignoring them; more, human beings rebel in their best works, because the high culture of human achievement reflects creaturely confidence in its own opinion, will, and mastery. The order of human society masks its disorder and conceals its arrogance and conceit. All human rebellion lies under layers of deception, from the serpent, a master of concealment, to Judas, who would give more to the poor. God's truth unmasks and judges, and this act of grace is a brutal comfort indeed.

Judas, after all, is led by Satan, owned and commanded by him; yet Judas is the one rejected and condemned. Barth considers him at once powerless and responsible for his acts of betrayal and rebellion. This is a classic conflict in the concept of rejection, and Barth delights in the opposition. Satan and

Judas are both responsible; Satan the overlord, Judas the slave; Satan the embodiment of evil, Judas the type of the creature. Both rebel, but the power rests with Satan. This ambiguity in the concept of moral agency surfaced in Barth's doctrine of Nothingness and he views the story of Judas as the enactment of that doctrine and the New Testament reenactment of its roots in the Fall. Like the first parents, Judas belongs to creation; he is a creature, ordered and made to the image of God. More, Judas is elected; he is chosen as one of the first. But, like the first parents, Judas stands at the frontier of creation. The powers of Chaos that threaten creation, striving to disorder and corrupt it, now have invaded it. Satan, once concealed under the form of a creature, a clever serpent, now rules openly over the world. Judas, a human creature like all others, hears the temptation to flattery, to self-assertion and satisfaction; he listens to the voice; he judges for himself. Judas, in short, hands himself over to "that which is not." Nothingness takes hold, empties him, and leads him to hand Jesus over. Judas is responsible for his actions because he declares himself responsible. The judgment that falls on Judas conforms to the ruthless logic of his own decision: he will be Judge. That, after all, is what the dominion by Satan means: the creature is ruled by Nothing. Chaos captures Judas and draws him into the Night; he does quickly what any creature must who is left in his own hands: he hands Jesus over. Judas's heart is hardened; he does Satan's will. But this evil is like all others. It is concealed, rationalized, and distorted: it appears to the creature like its own will; his slavery is the experience of freedom. This too, Barth warns, is the "cunning of history."

And Barth *has* history in mind in this discussion of Judas, the betrayer. Not only Judas, but Israel is hardened. The history of the elected people is the story of its obduracy, disobedience, and misery. All Israel is elected for rejection; it is chosen from all the peoples of the earth to exhibit its hardness of heart. Like Judas, Israel's own misery and achievement is used by God for his own ends: he wills that Israel be hardened. Barth of course is drawing out, in his own ruthless mastery, the Augustinian voice in Romans 9 through 11:

> As God confirms His election of Israel by the apostolic proclamation of the good tidings sustained by the Word of Christ Himself, so Israel confirms its election, its identity with the people of former times of and to whom Isaiah spoke, by the disobedient act of its unbelief. The converse can and must also be said, that, seen in the light of the prophetic word addressed to the chosen people of former times, Israel confirms the fact that its unbelief, its failure to confess Jesus,

has the character of disobedience. It confesses therefore that it is still and supremely the people from which the prophet could only turn away in order to turn with his heart full of questioning to God, to cry out for His mercy. But precisely because this is not put into words, but remains latent, we can say that the decisive result of this part of the Pauline proof from scripture is to be found in the other point, that even the undeniable guilt of Israel as it is mobilised against the Church in the Synagogue belongs in its own way to the fulfilment of prophecy, and in all its dreadfulness is also a confirmation of its election. This very people, disobedient to the Gospel and therefore unfaithful to its own election, was and is, as the natural root of the Church called and awakened to faith by His mercy, God's chosen people.[41]

Its disobedience is a fulfillment of prophecy and a dreadful confirmation of its election: this fusion of contradictory elements—of disobedience and fulfillment, of rejection and election—is Barth's reworking of the pauline theme of the hardening of Israel:

"Therefore hath he mercy on whom he will have mercy, and whom he will he hardeneth." The saying obviously looks back on the one hand to Isaac, Jacob and Moses, and on the other to Ishmael, Esau and Pharaoh. . . . On both sides, although in different forms, God wills one and the same thing. . . . As will be stated in Rom. 11:32 with complete unambiguity, this purpose is the purpose of His mercy. It is just this purpose which according to vv. 15–17, both Moses and also Pharaoh must carry out. They do so in different ways and to this extent the single will of God has a differentiated form. He chooses Moses as a witness of His mercy and Pharoah as a witness of the judgement that in and with this mercy becomes necessary and is executed. Thus He determines Moses as the voluntary, Pharoah as the involuntary servant of His power and His name. He renews His mercy with regard to Moses. He refuses this renewal to Pharaoh. If it is self-evident that for the men concerned it means personally something very different to be dealt with and used by God in these different ways, there is no mention of that here. . . . But the point at issue here is precisely how the diversity of the personal situation and destiny of Israelite man, which, conditioned by the divine predetermination, is

41. *Dogmatics*, 2.2:255 [*Dogmatik*, 2.2:280, 281].

so characteristic of the history and life of the chosen people Israel, does not contradict but corresponds to the election of Israel and the righteousness of the mercy of its God. . . . *Sklarunein* means to stiffen, harden, make obdurate, petrify and describes the isolation of the original and the withholding of the special new act of mercy as a result of which the same purpose of God with Israel takes effect in its negative aspect, in the constitution of Israel for itself and as such, the prefiguration of the judgement which God, on the same day of His future—in the course of showing mercy—will send forth upon man, to which He will on this day submit Himself of man's behalf. Verse 18 is therefore to be paraphrased as follows: . . . Whomsoever God's merciful purpose in the election of the community determines for the prefiguration and reflection of His judgement, for the unveiling of the impotence, unworthiness and hopelessness of all man's will and achievement as opposed to God's, for the unveiling of the severity of His sovereign dealing, of the freedom of His grace, to him He refuses fellowship and denies himself, so that like Pharoah he must serve Him as God's enemy, involuntarily, with an unthankful heart and therefore through the medium of his sin and guilt and under the curse and punishment of God.[42]

That Israel on the whole finds its representation in Pharoah, not Moses, is relentlessly pursued in Barth's treatment of Paul's example of the potter and the clay:

If the "vessels of dishonor" are appointed to demonstrate the impotence and unworthiness of man, of the "lump" out which they and the "vessels of honor" are taken, "the vessels of honor," shaped by the same hand, stand in relation to them as a demonstration of what God's will and purpose are with this man. . . . What option has the man who is determined as a "vessel of dishonor" except by his witness to the impotence and unworthiness of man—which he must give involuntarily in any case—voluntarily to corroborate the witness of the one who is determined as a "vessel of honor" as he sees God Himself, not cancelling his Yes by his No, but corroborating it? To provide this corroboration is Israel's appointed task in the elected community of God. Israel in itself and as such is the "vessel of dishonor." It is the witness to the divine judgement. It embodies

42. Ibid., 221, 222 [243, 244].

human impotence and unworthiness. For by Israel its own Messiah is delivered up to be crucified.[43]

All the pieces were suggested before this, but Barth has finally spoken directly: God wills to harden his people Israel, and his will has been executed in Israel's disobedience, in its rejection and dishonor. Barth will not allow an escape from this somber conclusion: Israel is elected for rejection. He casts a cold eye over the long and complex history of Israel and sees a procession of rebels, of Cain and Esau, of Pharoah and Saul, of David and David's descendent, Judas. They proceed from Israel, and they represent it. God's people should not be regarded in its faithful remnant, in Moses, in the prophets, in those Barth calls the "Church hidden within Israel." No, Israel as a whole must be gathered together on God's left hand; it is a "vessel of wrath," and its long line of doublets finds its dark completion in Judas Iscariot. Barth's doctrine of evil, after all, requires it. The nature of God's action *ad extra* expresses the motion of God's inner life: it acts to determine, to distinguish, and to divide. In creating, God separates. The heavens part from the earth; the waters from the dry land; the creation itself from the "formless and void." In electing, God chooses. The Father determines the Son; in the Son, the form of the elect is determined from the rejected, the "coming" from the "passing man," the "right hand of mercy" from the "left hand of wrath." We do not understand God's freedom, Barth warns, if we imagine that divine actions do not divide and that divine grace does not judge. To posit is to negate, and Barth repeatedly stressed the great, triumphant *Yes* in the divine plan. In Israel, we encounter the *No*. This is a stark picture, a portrait of contrasts and of a light made brilliant by the surrounding darkness. Barth acknowledges the harsh judgment he has exercized in his doctrine of Israel; he points to it in the pauline objection of Romans 9: "What then shall we say? Is there unrighteousness with God?"

Paul responds to this question with his full rhetorical vigor—God forbid!—and this is Barth's answer as well. But the question itself deserves more attention than this ready answer. What does it mean in Barth's doctrine that Israel is elected for rejection? What can it mean to elect, if "dishonor" and "wrath" are its signs? Once again, Barth has taken up a classic question in Christian dogmatics—the election of the Jews—and transformed the very terms of the debate, sharpening the conflict, infusing the forms with passion and with power.

43. Ibid., 224 [247].

Judas, the Determination of the Elected

Election, of course, has served many theological offices in the past. Israel was elected to be a "nation unto God," to be set apart, to teach and obey the One God. In Christianity and Judaism, the idea of election has denoted the special task of witnessing to monotheism, or, in the terms of the nineteenth-century debate, to ethical monotheism. To be elected meant to be called to this one service and way of life, the prophetic or messianic defense of the One God. Under the form of Christian supersessionism, this task was understood to have passed from Israel to the Church, the body that fulfills, replaces, and continues the mission of Israel. Such an abrogation of Israel's election was, certainly, vigorously rejected by the Judaic thinkers of the nineteenth century, and the contested claims to the major prophets reflects in part this pointed dispute over election. But the concept of election has carried another, more individual burden as well in Christian thought. To be elect in Reformed thought meant to be saved, to be numbered among those souls spared from the damnation they surely deserved. Election and reprobation stood at the entrance to Protestant theology, the great symmetry framing the Reformed doctrine of salvation. Though a collective was implied by these two terms, the Christian faced the Judge alone; salvation or damnation was the comfort or terror of the individual soul.

Always the historian, Barth masters these traditional themes but sets them to work on his own tasks. Barth's doctrine of election expresses both collective and individual reality, and it makes contact with the doctrines of sin and evil. But election is not collapsed into soteriology: election is not the work of salvation, either of Israel or the individual. For Barth, election actually has neither a human predicate or subject; properly, election is a divine work, and expresses the divine life. To speak of election is to speak of Israel; Barth never relinquishes that insight. But to grasp these terms, Israel and election, we must consider both as the object of divine will and self-revelation. Only by looking away from these human representations to their divine Subject—following Barth's direction, pointing from here to there—can the image of election, and more, the expression of Israel's election as rejection, become plain.

Barth's doctrine of God implies, first of all, that he does not hold that Israel's rejection is a divine damnation, or that God has hardened the Jews in order that they may suffer in disbelief and the Church triumph in faith. The medieval teachings of contempt and supersession are not altogether alien to Barth—he made room for several forms of anti-Judaism, old and new—but they are not the foundation or center of his doctrine. Barth claims to describe the life and internal order of Christ, elected and electing; only in Christ can Israel's election to wrath take on form and substance. The Christological coherence of Barth's thought demands that Israel, too, its election and rejection, be taken up in the divine determination and revelation of the Triune God.

To be sure, the doctrine of the Trinity is primarily a doctrine about *God,* but it is the God of Jesus Christ. The Trinity, then, is also a doctrine about humanity: God wills to be with the creature. After a long career at the *Dogmatics,* Barth never tired of that refrain. The divine determination in the giving and receiving of the Father and the Son is complete but not exhausted in the Trinitarian life. The Son wills the obedience of the incarnation; in Christ, God becomes the One who does not cease to be God while becoming man. Readers familiar with Barth have heard this all before, but a new light at times makes fresh what we had seen so many times before. Consider the Trinitarian impress on the doctrine of Israel.

Barth does not hold that the Incarnation is dependent upon soteriology: God willed to be in covenant with the creature in the Son, before the Fall and apart from human sinfulness. But we know creation only as it is confronted, threatened, and, in part, subdued by Chaos. Nothingness has tempted the creature, and it has succumbed; that is what Barth finds in Genesis and claims as the basic fact of human existence. Human beings are in rebellion against God, and God alone will judge and vindicate the rebels. But we do not understand this sovereign work of reconciliation if we imagine it as a universal, "spiritual" event. Time and again, Barth underscores this point: the Bible witnesses to a particular God, who governs his creation in concrete acts with specific actors. For Barth, the doctrine of the Trinity means this, too: God is the Lord of Abraham, Isaac, and Jacob and not another. *This* is the God who triumphs over Chaos, and breaks Satan's power; this victory is achieved through Israel and no other. To be elect is to be a particular, determined people: God chooses, elects Israel for this work.

All this sounds familiar enough. Barth rehearses some classic, biblical themes here about Israel's special place among the nations. But Barth cannot touch a theme without leaving his mark; Israel's election has been transformed in purpose and in character. Israel's calling is now instrumental. It is elected to form the theater where God will secure victory over evil. No longer called to a special nature or relationship—to be God's beloved; to enjoy his special favors—Israel now is set apart to establish the flesh Christ will assume and judge. Of course Israel's election will become a universal role; it will serve as a "light to the nations." But it is a reflected light, mirrored from its source in Christ, one of its descendents. On its own, Israel represents the work that it was sent to do: to raise up sinful flesh that God will condemn.

That is what Barth intends when he echoes the pauline phrase, "God has hardened the Jews," and he does not draw back from its cold exterior. Calvinists are not likely to find this severity uncongenial, and Barth shows his tough-minded lineage here. God has determined to put down human rebellion in the life and work of this one Jew, Jesus of Nazareth, and this divine decree required a preparation in time. The Jews are elected to be that preparation. They are elected to bring into history the cosmic forces of evil that Christ will engage and conquer. They are called to be disobedient, to be stiff-necked and hardened, to hand themselves over to that which is not; the people of Israel are elected to be rejected.

"Is there then unrighteousness with God?" Barth forces this question with particular sharpness. God's wrath and judgment fall on Israel; yet God has appointed them to this task and closed them up in disobedience. How are we to reconcile this concept of election to be permanent "vessels of dishonor" with any coherent concept of human responsibility and divine justice? That is the question Barth forces into open view.

The figure of Judas provided Barth an arena to demonstrate his justification of individual responsibility in human sinfulness. On the historical, not individual level, Barth turns to Israel to answer the charge of divine injustice. His justification, I think, can only be understood if election is removed from the plane of salvation and established on the plane of history. The divine decree enacted in Israel is not reprobation—the damnation of Israel and Israelites to eternal punishment; rather, the divine election of Israel is the meaning of history—God will create "time for us"; he will have mercy on his enemies. The nations of the earth, their peoples and stories; the great rise and decline of empires; the shadow and light that fall across all human lives: all these events and figures of history find their meaning and true existence in God's will to have mercy, to justify his creatures by grace. This, not individual reprobation or salvation, is the "secret decree" of God; this election of grace is the divine act Barth calls the "great Yes," and it is the meaning of Israel's bitter sufferings. The "hidden Church" within Israel is not a secret selection of the saved within the damned. They are, instead, a glimpse, a foreshadowing of this great act of mercy—the "condescension inconceivably tender"—that God will undertake in the midst of his enemies. Barth offers this as his first justification of the divine hardening: that Israel is elected to receive mercy for its disobedience.

But this is a one-sided and inadequate response if we understand Barth to argue only that the elect may suffer God's wrath if it also receives God's mercy. These are the problems embedded in a system of symmetry that Barth sought to avoid. The classical Reformed understanding of the divine predestinating will balanced God's wrath with his mercy, and covered over human objections to this balance with an inscrutable majesty. Such election apart from Christ, Barth claimed, only deepened suspicions of divine injustice and erupted in the open rebellion of the Enlightenment. No, election was properly the work of Christ and must therefore be ordered to him: wrath must give way to mercy; rebellion to obedience; sin and death to resurrected victory. Israel's election to rejection must be understood under the aspect of this divine asymmetry, the great motion from *No* to *Yes*. That, too, is the meaning of history represented and fulfilled in the elected people.

Of course, Barth has not handed dogmatics over to the philosophy of history; he is the last theologian, I think, who could be discovered in the secret act of building a universal history of *Geist*. The election in history of the people Israel, an election to rejection, becomes the meaning of creation and covenant because it is the community of the man Jesus. The Christological center of the doctrine of election demands that all other elections, of Israel, the Church, and the individual, serve that one divine decree, that the Son would obey the Father through the power of the Spirit and assume sinful flesh. In Barth's thought, the doctrine of election is infused with the content of the Incarnation—the birth, lineage, and heritage of the man Jesus, taken up in his life, his person, and his reconciling work. God's predestinating act in Christ means this finally: that God has determined to become the rejected "vessel of dishonor," to suffer himself the verdict rendered on sinful flesh, to be the Judge, judged in Israel's and humanity's place. The justice of the divine hardening of the Jews is vindicated in this act of substitution, in which Christ suffers the punishment Israel and all flesh deserved. What Barth calls the "disobedience" of the Synagogue Jews—their refusal to put their faith in Jesus—prolongs their misery and sharpens their rejection because they renounce the mercy offered them in Christ. Their punishment is paid, and yet, he adds, they perversely reject their pardon. Barth considered that Jews laid particular claim on Christians for several reasons; chief among them is their tragic insistence on exhibiting their election to wrath, while passing by their reprieve in stubborn silence. The Jews are used by God—they are made to represent God's judgment—but they are instruments for Christ's use alone and for his lonely work of self-sacrifice, the task Barth movingly described as the "journey of the Son of Man into the far country."

What then does Barth intend to say about God in this work of election? To place the doctrine of election within the doctrine of God implies that the being of God is revealed in this predestinating act. The election of Israel is an act of divine self-revelation as well. We must be careful, of course, not to read history, even Israel's history, as a "natural" description of God; Barth would not tolerate the witness usurping the dignity of the Object witnessed. But he means to point to some qualities of the "God of the Bible" through the doctrine of election, and the significance of history to the divine life is, I think, a place to start.

The election of the Jews is irrevocable. Barth asserts this permanent election on the exegetical warrant of Romans 9–11. We can also discern a consonance of this theme with a favorite dynamic element in his doctrine of God: the Trinitarian God is God of the living, not the dead; this God is the Lord of history. The Bible gives witness to a God who on a divine plane creates and inhabits temporality; God sustains "eternal time" as well as "time for us." The divine decisions to elect humanity in Christ, and, more, to elect suffering in humanity's place are decrees this God enacts in time. They will be represented in human history; they will evolve and take on human character; they will name individual actors: they will all rise up and fall under God's stern providence. Barth speaks with his most Augustinian voice here. The sweep of history, its majesty and bitterness, its mediocre and silent victims, its commanding figures—in all of history, God will work his purpose out. Israel and its people, the Jews, are that purpose. They are the realization of eternal time—the time of Christ's election—in human time, the history of the suffering, disobedience, and rejection of the Jews. For this very reason, their election is irrevocable. It is not of course that divine decisions are immutable; Barth zealously attacked the static timelessness of the "God of the philosophers." Such a changeless God reflected the "superstitions about the number one"—Barth loved this theme—and had no place in Christian dogmatics. God could change the decree; the Jews could loose their election. But the God attested in Scripture is "faithful": God will each day affirm and sustain the decisions of the last. In being true to the divine nature, God will remain constant and sure. The divine decision to elect the creature for mercy and for fellowship is such a decision: it will be sustained and perpetuated by God's faithfulness. The election of the Jews, though an election to punishment, is bound up in the giving of grace, a divine self-giving that will not end or fail.

The permanent election of the Jews serves as a sign of God's providence; Barth has made use of this theme in several places. The Augustinian majesty of this providence, however, reserves its full voice for the assertion of divine power: that God alone is able to work good out of evil. The sovereign lordship over history means that the threat to creation of Nothingness, the corruption and disorder of human sinfulness, the weak and petty resolve to rebel: all these will remain under God's authority and will serve his ends. That these forces of sin and disorder remain in history is a tribute to God's mercy, not to their power; God alone can allow time for repentance. This sovereign providence extends to all created life, but it belongs to the Jews. Barth recounts their history as a story of rebellion. They stone their prophets, disobey their kings, reject their judges, and dishonor their temple. Time and again, the "Lord stretches out his hands to a stiff-necked and disobedient people." This melancholy story is certainly part of the divine plan, but Barth does not consider the Israelites to be puppets of a divine master. They turn away from God, and it is a genuine turning; they judge for themselves; they hand themselves over, and it is a genuine betrayal and possession by another. But God will bring his purposes to fulfillment, even with unwilling and unable servants.

In the election of Christ, God decided to take on himself the punishment for sin, to bear it and to bear it away. That eternal decree demanded that evil will serve good: all human disobedience will witness to Christ's work of reconciliation. More, the rebellion that consumed Israel will break out, finally, in Judas Iscariot, and in him, the deepest and most bitter sin will be covered in Christ's reconciling death. Christ will suffer for the sins of Israel: that is the "triumph of grace" that concludes all disobedience. Under God's providence, the disobedience of the Jews will deepen and harden; they will turn from God more quickly, listen more readily to their own voices; they will take more comfort in their own achievements and insights: they will, in short, become a finer and closer approximation to the man Judas, the type of all human sinners. The election of the Jews serves to make them more fully and truly themselves, the representative of God's judgment and the embodiment of sin.

Were the doctrine of election concerned with individual or even collective salvation, Barth's selection of Israel for divine service would be a cruel caricature of covenant theology. Barth's doctrine of Israel remains a relentless piece of work—no reader of Barth can mistake his eager pursuit of the most unwelcome conclusion—but Israel takes its place in the doctrine of God and the divine rule over history. Jews are elected to prepare the flesh that Christ will assume; their rebellion is designed to bring salvation to Jews and Gentiles. God will act, in one solemn moment, in concert with evil. In the crucifixion, God will give the rebels their head. In the figure of Judas, the Jews will make their sins manifest, and the powers of Chaos will find their agent. In the betrayal, the Jews will execute their election: they will hand over their Messiah, as they handed over their prophets and kings many times before. All the forces of decay, disorder, and destruction will meet in that

Night, and God will give them rein. Israel's Messiah will suffer and die; that is the meaning of Christ's election. But the Messiah will also rise up in victory; that, too, is the meaning of election.

The doctrine of election is a doctrine of grace. Christ, elected and electing, has determined to walk this path into the far country, to suffer and suffer punishment in order that mercy and redemption from sin might triumph. *That* singular and sacrificial decision, not the determination of the individual soul, is the sovereign and inscrutable mystery of election. That good should triumph through evil; that Satan should be overthrown through defeat; that punishment should be borne by the innocent; that history should reveal divine mercy and grace: these are the permanent mysteries of election. In Barth's doctrine of Israel, they are also the permanent mysteries that belong to the election of the Jews. Barth's doctrine of Israel, though often medieval in tone and trope, is no supersessionist decree. Jews carry the permanent, irrevocable election of God; to them are given the prophets, the Law, the judges and kings, and more, the apostles, doctors, and fathers of the Church; and to them, first, and from them alone, Jesus Christ came, and took their part. The Church that will not recognize these gifts of Israel, and see in Israel and Synagogue the family of Christ, rejects its Lord. And the Christian who does not understand that, in Judas, *all* flesh passes under judgment will not recognize the grace that surpasses all rejection. Barth's doctrine is a judgment bounded, assumed, and closed up in mercy, a twofold doctrine of rejection turning over into election. Barth consigns Israel to the form of one who is "passing away," to the flesh condemned and rejected, to the community that finds its head in Judas Iscariot. But all reality created in Christ rises up to life in doublets. The election of the Jews is an election to mercy, as well. Christ has assumed their rejection, and reconciled their rebellion. This people, called to prepare the way, can recognize their redemption already achieved, and find their head in Jesus, its Messiah; they can obey their election and enter the Church, gathered from Jew and Gentile; they can "pass away" from Judas and "come" to life in Paul. In the *Church Dogmatics,* Barth patiently, masterfully, relentlessly follows the one Form and Object of theology, and in a lutheran discipleship all his own, devotes his doctrine of election to that simple and revealing declaration, that "Jesus Christ was born a Jew."

"JEWISH-CHRISTIAN SOLIDARITY TODAY!"

4

Karl Barth never stood still. A thinker of deep conservative strains, of sober realism about all human possibility, Barth nevertheless went his own way in theology. At times, it was a journey of remarkable innovation and remarkable freedom from the constraints of a system, political or philosophical; he served a "living God." To those who acknowledge Christ, "he speaks the same word: 'Follow thou me!' "[1] and Barth followed this living form of Christ along some unpredictable and unfamiliar paths. One of these paths followed the direction that led out from the *Dogmatics* to the land and state of Israel, the Israel founded and defended in 1948 and toward which Barth found himself in surprising, stubborn, and controversial solidarity.

Late in life, Barth wrote a brief, but revealing note intended to accompany an essay collection entitled "Jewish-Christian Solidarity in the Third Reich." It never appeared there, but Friedrich Marquardt included it among the footnotes to his essay "Christentum und Zionismus." As one of his "final testimonies,"[2] this note reflects the introspection characteristic of Barth's later years, with its tone of somber regret, its complex historical judgment, and its undiminished theological passion. Barth declares the irrevocable

1. So Schweitzer concluded his classic work, *The Quest of the Historical Jesus,* 403, a lyric evocation of the Jesus who comes to us as "One Unknown," who calls for disciples who hear his historic voice and follow.

2. I borrow from the English title of a collection of Barth's last writings, *Final Testimonies,* ed. E. Busch, trans. G. W. Bromiley (Grand Rapids, Mich.: William Eerdmans, 1977).

"solidarity" of Christians and Jews, a theological alliance that demands a political commitment to the state of Israel. Written directly after the 1967 war between Israel and five Arab nations—the "Six Day War"—Barth makes public his support for Israel, a position not widely shared by his allies on the Left, and scarcely to be expected by those who have read the second volume of the *Church Dogmatics*. That Barth did not work from philosophical principles, that his theology was left open to a new Word or to "better instruction," that his theology, in short, was dogmatic as Barth would have us understand that term: these characteristics could not find clearer illustration than in Barth's declaration for the state of Israel. I include a translation of this remarkable note.

> I was unfortunately not able, and I also consider myself not competent, to supply an essay of my own for the book proposed here, *Jewish-Christian Solidarity in the Third Reich*. I would only be able, of course, to confess that because I occupied myself more with other aspects of the Church Struggle taking place in those days than with these, I had neglected—I think of it today with shame—to powerfully point out this aspect directly. In this regard, I am implicated in the guilt for much of what was neglected then on the "Christian" side concerning the Jews. All the better that in this book such voices speak who were active then and, with particular earnestness, were attentive precisely to this issue and are in the position today to testify in a credible way that in those days, in matters of Jewish-Christian solidarity, some of what was possible was earnestly undertaken and accomplished, even if it fell far short of what was required. There were in fact not a few courageous and helpful things said and, above all, done by good Christians. To that end, may the pages of this book render witness after that fact. Were the Swiss to be included (in their way also implicated in the guilt), the names of Frau Dr. Kurz in Berne and the untiringly effective pastor P. Vogt should also be mentioned here. — In this sense, I welcome the appearance of this book with its uplifting and, in the best sense, edifying report from the Hitler era.
>
> I want however not to do that without adding the following, which is immediately and utterly inseparable from the above: If this report is to be meaningful and not only an artifact, the "Jewish-Christian Solidarity" of that period must be understood by those here to call unconditionally for "Jewish-Christian Solidarity" today! That must be expressly stated because recently a group of otherwise respectable Christians—I mean the Working Committee of the "Prague Christian

Peace Conference" held on July 3, 1967 in Sagorsk (I do not know—by which evil spirits were they led astray?) has sent out into the world a Pronouncement of the East-West Crisis of which I can only say that I acutely missed any deep theological meaning as well as any practical-political reason in its negative position on the struggle for the existence *(Daseinskampf)* of the state of Israel. If one follows the intent of the Jewish-Christian solidarity described in this book, one would not and could not speak in that way; even not in view of the partially nasty neighborhood in which one may find oneself in a resolute support for that state, especially in West Germany. Such tactical considerations have never been good advisors! Fortunately, a clear and well-grounded opposition statement signed by K. Immer, H. Gollwitzer, E. Wolf, M. Rohkrämer among others appeared on the scene immediately. But how sad that it is over the matter of "solidarity," the solidarity once tested of which this book speaks, that among us "Christians" it has come once again to serious division! The good direction taken in those days must today be held to theologically and politically; it must not be broken off again today under any pretext. Without this reference to present events, I would not nor could I recommend this book lying here before me. Hic Rhodus; hic salta!

Basel, August 1967   Karl Barth[3]

3. The original to this note is as follows:

Es war mir leider nicht möglich und ich fühlte mich auch nicht kompetent dazu, zu dem hier vorgelegten Buch, "Jüdisch-christliche Solidarität im Dritten Reich" einen eigenen Beitrag zu liefern. Ich hätte ja auch nur gestehen können, daß ich, mit anderen Aspekten des damals geführten Kirchenkampfes mehr als gerade mit diesem beschäftigt, es—ich denke heute mit Beschämung daran—unterlassen habe, kräftiger gerade auf ihn hinzu-weisen. Ich bin insofern mitschuldig an Vielem, was damals von "christlicher" Seite den Juden gegenüber vernachlässigt worden ist. Umso besser, daß in diesem Buch Stimmen solcher zu Worte kommen, die damals mit besonderem Ernst gerade nach dieser Seite aufmerksam und tätig waren and darum heute in der Lage sind, glaubwürdig zu bezeugen, daß damals in Sachen der "Jüdisch-Christlichen Solidarität" wenn auch lange nicht alles Erforderte, so doch einiges Mögliche ernstlich gewollt und mit Erfolg getan worden ist. Es ist tatsächlich damals von guten Christen nicht wenig Mutiges und Hilfreiches gesagt und vor allem getan worden. Davon mögen die Blätter dieses Buches nachträglich Zeugnis ablegen. Wären die (in ihrer Weise auch sehr mitschuldigen) Schweizer einbezogen worden, so wären die Namen von Frau Dr. Kurz in Bern und der des unermüdlich wirkenden Pfarrers P. Vogt hier auch zu nennen gewesen.—In diesem Sinn begrüße ich das Erscheinen dieses Buches mit seinen erfreulichen und im besten Sinn erbaulichen Berichten aus der Hitlerzeit.

Ich möchte das aber nicht tun, ohne sofort and schlechthin untrennbar vom Vorangehen-

Well! Can this supporter of Israel be the same thinker who described the Synagogue as a "gruesome relic," who saw rabbinic Judaism hurrying to an "empty future," who understood the history of Israel as one long chapter of "disobedience" and "refusal of its election"; who declared—in affirmation of the teaching that "salvation is of the Jews"—that the Church "contests the vaunting lie, the nationalist-legalistic Messiah-dream of the Synagogue, which has aroused the hatred and envy of every kind of Gentile arrogance, yet also been the subject of its own dilettante dreaming"? Can this "Jewish-Christian solidarity" built up on the "struggle for existence" of the state of Israel actually put down roots in Barth's deep anti-Judaism? How, in short, can Barth's defense of Israel be reconciled with and derived from his dogmatic theology?

Several obstacles stand in the way of answers. The published sources, including correspondence, for Barth's position on Israel are brief and few, and often contain little more than passing remarks.[4] The few commentaries

---

den hinzufügen: Die "Jüdisch-Christliche Solidaritat" von damals, von der hier berichtet wird, ruft, wenn dieser Bericht sinnvoll sein und nicht nur museal wirken soll, unbedingt nach: "Jüdisch-Christliche Solidarität" heute! Das muß ausdrucklich mitgesagt werden, weil neulich eine Gruppe von sonst respektablen Mitchristen—ich meine den Arbeitsaus-schuss der "Prager Christlichen Friedenskonferenz"—am 3. Juli 1967 in Sagorsk—ich weiß nicht: von welchen bösen Geistern irregeführt?—ein Pronuntiamento zur Nah-Ost-Krise in die Welt gesetzt hat, von dem ich nur sagen kann, daß ich in seiner negativen Stellungnahme zum Daseinskampf des Staates Israel jede tiefere theologische Besinnung, aber auch praktisch-politische Vernunft schmerzlich vermisse. Auf der Linie der in diesem Buch geschilderten "Jüdisch-Christlichen Solidarität" konnte und durfte nicht so geredet werden: auch nicht im Blick auf die teilweise üble Nachbarschaft, in die man sich bei einer entschlossenen Stellungnahme für jenen Staat besonders in Westdeutschland befinden mag. Solche taktischen Erwägungen sind noch nie gute Ratgeber gewesen! Eine klare und wohlbegründete u. a. von K. Immer, H. Gollwitzer, E. Wolf, M. Rohkrämer unterzeichnete Gegenerklärung ist zum Glück sofort auf den Plan getreten. Aber wie traurig, daß es unter uns "Christen" gerade in Sachen der Solidarität, von deren einstiger Bewährung dieses Buch redet, nun noch einmal zu so ernstlicher Entzweiung kommen mußte! Die gute damals eingeschlagene Richtung muß heute theologisch wie politisch durchgehalten, sie darf unter keinem Vorwand heute wieder abgebrochen werden. Ohne diesen aktuellen Hinweis würde ich das hier vorliegende Buch nicht loben und empfeh-len können. Hic Rhodus; hic salta! Basel, im August 1967. Karl Barth. (Friedrich Wilhelm Marquardt, "Christentum und Zionismus," *Evangelische Theologie* 28 [1968]: 654).

4. The note I included is one of the more substantial sources. Others include: "The Jewish Question and Its Christian Answer," in *Against the Stream* ["Die Judenfrage und ihre christliche Antwort," in *Der Götze Wackelt*]; letters to Marquardt, Merrill Miller, Eberhard Bethge, and Henry Poms in *Briefe;* brief sections in *Dogmatics,* 3.3, 4.1, 4.2, and 4.3; a comment on *Nostra Aetate* in *Ad Limina Apostolorum;* the discussion between Petuchowski and Barth at the University of Chicago (in *Criterion*); and the comments on the World Council of Churches conference in Amsterdam with Jean Daniélou and Reinhold Niebuhr, *Amsterdamer Fragen und Antworten,* a special issue of *Theologische Existenz—NF 15* (Munich: Christian Kaiser Verlag,

on this subject often assume knowledge of Barth's position gained from
seminars and the more intimate circle of German Academic Theology.
Students of Barth knew very well that he supported the state of Israel—a fact
the English-speaking audience of another generation may not know so well—
but they puzzled over its theological basis. Do Barth's political convictions
correspond to his theological convictions, or are they, in fact, independent
and fully contingent acts arising from the free obedience of a Christian? Can
we say, as Eberhard Jüngel—a member of the "right-wing Barthians"—
proclaimed: "In the freedom of the children of God . . . , I declare, *Ich bin
ein Bürger*"? Or, as the "left-wingers" maintain, must we find an indivisible
link between dogmatics and politics, by which Barth's theology entails a
commitment to democratic socialism? If we accept the correlation of dogmatics and radical politics, how shall we weigh each contribution to theology?
Are these the "two sources" or "two natures" of Barth's theology, as Marquardt maintained? Is Barth's commitment to Israel, or to any socialist
position a form of "natural theology" to which dogmatics turns for another
source of revelation? Can we, in the end, really look from the world to God,
from human history to divine action, from the human—the altogether
"natural" human—to Christ? Does Barth, in his partisanship for Israel, accept,
at long last, another word beside and apart from the one Word of Jesus
Christ?

These are living questions for Barth scholars and hardly minor points for
interpretation. The scarcity of sources, and the brevity of their theological
argument—a rarity in Barth studies!—makes the controversial topics more
important and more stubbornly insoluble. A good bit of proof texting has
been practiced on both sides of the "two sources" debate, and the meager
evidence hinders a quiet and peaceable truce. Barth hardly welcomed such
truces. He had the polemicist's taste for controversy and sharp prosecution
of one's point; his letters are filled with memorials to old battles and
platforms for fresh attacks. In fact, from this distance, some of Barth's
attraction for his contemporaries appears to rest in his irrepressible love for
his unvarnished truth. Barth seems to have delighted in the controversial
forays: he writes almost impishly of warning Anglican bishops about "too
much love for the Pope" or debating about the Ten Commandments with
several "great figures" in the Soviet sector of Berlin after the war.[5] In the

---

1949). Secondary works that address Barth's postwar position on Israel include Busch's *Karl
Barth;* Marquardt's *Die Entdeckung des Judentums* and *Theologie und Sozialismus;* Helmut
Gollwitzer's *Vietnam, Israel, und die Christenheit* (Munich: Christian Kaiser Verlag, 1967), which
includes the Sagorsk Peace Conference statement and counterstatement; and Klappert's *Israel
und die Kirche.*

5. Busch, *Karl Barth,* 330–40.

matter of politics, and of the Christian commitment to social action, Barth held and expressed a good many sharp and at times contradictory positions, all at varying levels of theological precision. In short, Barth's support for the state of Israel, a position at once theological and political, deserves cautious attention.

We begin with the theme of solidarity, "Jewish-Christian solidarity, today!" This is hardly a fresh departure in Barth's thought, at least for theological analysis. Throughout the starkest anti-Judaic polemics in volume 2.2 of the *Dogmatics,* Barth insisted on the indivisible bond between the Church and Israel. Christians and Jews, even the Jews of the "blindfolded Synagogue," are bound together in one community, the living "environment" of Jesus Christ. Together, they witness to this one Jew, Jesus, who as Israel's Messiah, reconciles both Jew and Gentile to the God of Abraham. Salvation is "of the Jews," Barth argued in the 1930s—God remains faithful to his promises— and Christians can never arrogate to themselves God's ways and works with the people Israel. Rather, the Gentiles must accept their place as guests, "grafted in" to the history and deliverance of the covenanted people. This "organic" solidarity between Jew and Gentile grounds the life of the Church, a body "called from Jew and Gentile." But more, it extends even to the "distortion" of the community of God, to the Church and the Synagogue. Though Barth held that Israel was to "rise to life" in the Church, the Synagogue, the form of the elected people disobedient to their election, remains essential to the Church. In the Jews of the Synagogue, Christians are to hear the testimony of the flesh Christ assumed, the living reminder of human inability and disobedience that Christ elected for himself. The Jews may take the form of those "passing away," but they are not alone; all flesh "passes away" before God, to die and rise again in Christ. Christians, then, live in solidarity with Jews, both in and without the Church, because Jews mirror the sin all creatures share, and they reflect the One Light, shed over all, that came first to the house of Israel. To paraphrase Barth's position in volume 2 of the *Dogmatics:* the Church must never leave off reflecting on this one, central fact, that "Jesus Christ was born a Jew."

In the postwar writings, Barth develops this earlier theme of solidarity in two areas subordinate, but not alien to his support for the state of Israel: his analysis of anti-Semitism, and his critique of the *Judenmission,* the special Christian evangelical mission to the Jews. Barth treats these two themes as opposite sides of a single theological object, a decision that already marks off his position from his contemporaries. On the one hand, German policies of anti-Semitism were based on racial, not theological, categories; that was their devastating and all-encompassing power. On the other, the Christian mission to the Jews, particularly in German-speaking countries, appears to be a uniquely religious, not political affair, dedicated to bringing all souls to Christ. That they both represent a unified political and theological reaction to Jews and Judaism is Barth's contribution to the debate.

Barth turns to these themes in the later volumes of the *Dogmatics,* and in his shorter addresses, all written after the war. The *Judenmission,* Barth declares in volume 4.3 of the *Dogmatics,* is "unfortunate" and "insulting": [I]n relation to the Synagogue there can be no real question of 'mission' or of bringing the Gospel."[6] In its place stands the *"Judenfrage"*—Barth did not shy away from the terms of the Wilhelmine and Nazi debates—the question of the Jews which is the "recurrent question of Christ and the Church which has not been and cannot be answered by any of its ministries. It stands as an unresolved problem, and therefore as the shadow behind and above all its activity in foreign missions."[7] The link between the "Jewish question" and the "Jewish mission" is made visible from the beginning.

There can be no Christian mission to the Jews, Barth writes, because the Synagogue is not—"as some fools say in their hearts"—another "religion or confession" to which the true God must be revealed. Reaching behind the Enlightenment, a gesture so dear to him, Barth rejects the eighteenth-century compromise that allowed Judaism to take its place among the religions of reason or revelation in Europe. As with many of the achievements of Liberalism, this compromise, too, was vulnerable and unstable; Judaism became a religion, perhaps a tolerated religion, but not an equal. After all, its inferiority in the eyes of the Christian West, among liberals and the orthodox, defined the modern Jewish mission and encouraged missionaries to consider the Jews a people misunderstood and shamefully treated, who wait only for a sympathetic guide to the full truth of their religion. Barth sweeps aside such modern developments, and in an act familiar to his readers, clears away his path by moving both forward and back. Judaism is not a religion or confession; it has no independent status outside the Church. Judaism is the Synagogue—though it should not be—and it finds its place next to the Church in the one body of Christ. But, the Jews cannot be the object of the Church's evangelism; in Christ Jews already possess the true worship, promises, and election of God. "What have we to teach [the Jew]," Barth asks, "that he does not already know, that we have not rather to learn from him?" A mission to the Synagogue assumes that Jews worship an idol, not the "King of Israel," and that they have not received the Word, when *"kata sarka*

---

6. *Dogmatics,* 4.3:877 [*Dogmatik,* 4.3:1005].

7. Ibid., 878 [1007].

[according to the flesh] he is first their Christ." The *Judenmission,* then, is insulting and unfortunate, not because Judaism is a religion Christians tolerate, but because the Jews have already received the promises and heard the truth: they are the elected people, disobedient to their election.

Though this is a familiar theme by now, Barth's use of the Christian description of Jewish disobedience takes on new form in the world defined by the second World War. Barth will take up this theme of disobedience, free it from its place in Christian supersessionism, and move it to the dogmatic analysis of anti-Semitism. But Barth's remarkable transformation of Christian anti-Judaism into a critique of political and racial anti-Semitism draws on an equally remarkable presupposition.

The solidarity between Christian and Jew that Barth so vigorously advocates is based upon the quiet assumption that Judaism does not exist. Jews exist, the people Israel exist, even the Synagogue exists in error, but Judaism—an independent religious system and institution—does not. It is easy, too easy perhaps, to emphasize the honor Barth gives to Jews in his theology; it is an honor, however, that is built upon denial. Christians accord Jews "special sympathy [!] and attention," they honor them as the flesh Christ assumed, they unite with them in covenant and election, but Christians protect only what is theirs. Barth rarely uses the term, Judaism, and he never speaks of it as a reality with separate status within Christian dogmatics. Israel is the true form of the Jewish people, and it belongs with and indeed within the Church. The Synagogue, however, is a "gruesome relic," in part because it parodies Israel; it claims to stand alone, but it cannot. The "essence" of the Synagogue remains with the people Israel, those Jews and Gentiles called into Christ's service. Because they are one people, Jews and Christians belong together: they live in solidarity. They worship one Lord, the King of Israel; they honor one covenant; they await one Messiah, that One who has already come. "Salvation is of the Jews," Barth often repeats, but Judaism is the tragic and perverse denial of that truth. Barth may have "discovered Judaism for Christian theology"—as Marquardt claims—but the discovery exacts its cost. Though Christians may owe honor to the Jews, Judaism remains an "impossible possibility"; it exists as disobedience.

Barth resorts to Paul's eschatological language to bring this "impossibility," the contradiction of Judaism, to resolution.

> If the Jew is to go back on the rejection of his Messiah and become a disciple, is there not needed a radical change in which he comes to know the salvation of the whole world which is offered to him first as a Jew and in which he thus comes to read quite differently his own

Holy Book? Is there not needed the direct intervention of God Himself as in the case of the most obstinate of all Jews, Paul himself? Can there ever be a true conversion of the true Jews, therefore, except as a highly extraordinary event? Can we ever expect a gathering of all Israel around the Lord who died and rose again for this whole people of Israel except, as Paul clearly thought in Rom. 11:15, 25f., in and with the end of all things and as the eschatological solution of this greatest of all puzzles?[8]

"The greatest of all puzzles": Judaism takes on life only as a riddle in Barth's thought and, indeed in all theology of Christian anti-Judaism. God alone can bring the Jews out of the contradiction of disobedience into obedience to its Messiah; God alone can complete his work of election, reconciling to himself even those who are hardened. Echoing Paul's drama of completion in Romans 11, Barth calls on the Christian community to take up the one task left to it, to make the Jews "jealous." Christians are to witness to the "fulfilled Word of God," confront the Synagogue with the "monument of the free election, calling and grace of God," make "dear and desirable and illuminating to it Him whom it has rejected." But the Christian community cannot convert the Jews: they are God's people and must be left to his will. Christians, above all, must not despise the Jews, the "root from which [the Church] has itself sprung."

In his treatment of this "division in the body of Christ"—the disbelief of the Jews—Barth expresses in theological passion the obsession that troubles the Christian consciousness of Judaism. The Synagogue is "at once so promising and yet so alien"; it is "so near and yet so distant." Like all parents, the Jews are subject to the ambivalent piety of its offspring. The Jews, Christians claim, are disobedient and faithless; their rejection of their Messiah is a "shattering fact"; their absence is a "penetrating pain," a "suffering more serious than the absence of Rome" from the ecumenical movement. The failure of the Church to make these Jews jealous is "concealed perhaps by all kinds of justifiable or unjustifiable countercharges against the Jews"; it is one of the "darkest chapters in the whole history of Christianity and one of the most serious of all wounds in the body of Christ." The Jews in short are expressed in the language of desire: they fascinate and attract; they fill their beloved with longing yet they inflict pain and rejection. In its darkest side, this fascinated repulsion of the Christians toward the Jews—toward their origin, their salvation, and their election—this ambivalent reaction to one of their own is what Barth calls anti-Semitism.

8. Ibid. [1006].

He turns to the issue of anti-Semitism at some length in two postwar writings, "The Jewish Problem [*die Judenfrage*] and the Christian Answer,"[9] a radio address, and in section 49.3 of the *Doctrine of Creation*, the "Divine Ruling," an expanded and more technical version of the shorter address. Barth speaks over the radio directly about anti-Semitism, dogmatically and homiletically, and the effect on his audience must have been electric. This talk is remarkable in several respects, a taste of vintage Barth. His dogged pursuit of his topic; his delight in its sharpest contradictions; his rhetorical mastery and colloquial frankness: they are all distilled in this address, and it is hard not to quote it in full. Barth intends to shock, I think, and even in 1949, he must have had his way. After discussing the perennial "Jewish question," Barth turns to his central theme:

> What are the origins of anti-semitism? I need not say that in all its forms it is the senseless and evil work of man's utter blindness. But where exactly do its roots lie? How is it to be explained that it has broken out again and again like a plague and was able, even in the middle of this enlightened century of ours, to break out again worse than ever? What is our quarrel with the Jews? Every nation [*alle Völker*] has some unpleasant characteristics, yet these do not arouse the antagonism of others in the same way as the Jews bring forth the animosity of other people just because they are Jews. But why do we object to their being Jews? Why are we so hard-hearted, why so unforgiving? Do they not possess good characteristics, too, like other races [*Völker*]? Why then are these not taken into account? Why are the moral arguments against anti-semitism of no avail at all? Anti-semitism seems to be just as inexplicable as the very existence and character of the Jews, and there are grounds for the supposition that there is some connexion between the two.[10]

The "mystery of the Jews," language as old as Paul, has been brought to bear on the "mystery of anti-Semitism." Barth suspects some connection between the mysteries, and present-day readers may suspect that Barth is preparing

---

9. In *Against the Stream: Shorter Post-War Writings, 1946–1952*, trans. R. G. Smith (New York: Philosophical Library, 1954), 195–201. The original can be found in *Der Götze Wackelt*, 144–49.

10. "The Jewish Problem and the Christian Answer," 198 ["Die Judenfrage und ihre christliche Beantwortung," 147].

the "blame for the victims."[11] But Barth is rarely drawn to such straightforward explanations.

To his mind, anti-Semitism is a product of some complexity, arising both from the faults of Jews and the projections and denials of Christians. In fact, Barth makes use of the psychological defense of projection with some agility. The Jews have flaws and failures, but "no worse than any other people." But they are a "mirror" for all others in which "we see how bad we all are." That is the meaning of election: the Jews are chosen by God to realize the sinful humanity Christ must redeem. Human beings are "rebels" and "transgressors"; they do not deserve the grace and mercy extended them in Christ. And the Jews typify that sinful rebellion. Christians hate Jews, they "suspect and dislike . . . the stranger in [their] midst" because they hate the truth the Jews reveal about themselves, about all humanity. For this reason, violence against the Jews is both "folly" and unwitting truth: "What is the good of turning the mirror to the wall, or even smashing it? That will not alter the fact that we are still what we saw ourselves to be in the mirror. However, the folly of turning the mirror to the wall and smashing it is the only bit of sense in all the nonsense of anti-semitism."[12] A bit of sense [*der eine Sinn*][13] in anti-Semitism: Barth could hardly show greater respect for the "labor of the negative."

This Christian work of projection, however, extends beyond the denial of human sinfulness: Christians hate Jews because they are "rootless." Fearlessly, Barth reproduces the organic metaphors of modern anti-Semitism in his portrait of Jews as the world's mirror.

> [W]e find it uncanny that the Jews live among us and move like shadows through world history with that unheard-of historical permanence, yet without roots, without security; without roots because they are sustained by the free grace of God—so persistent because that grace holds them so firmly. Why do we find that uncanny? Because in this connexion also they are the mirror of our own life and that of

11. The phrase, widely used, belongs to William Ryan, who first applied it to white racist theories that assigned blame to the black victims of racial hatred. In brief, the victims of injustice are understood as the cause of their own suffering (William Ryan, *Blaming the Victim* [New York: Vintage Books, 1971]).

12. "The Jewish Problem and the Christian Answer," 199 ["Die Judenfrage und ihre christliche Beantwortung," 147].

13. The final sentence read: *"Aber eben dieses törichte Umkehren und Zerschmettern ist jedenfalls der eine Sinn im grossen Unsinn des Antisemitismus."* Smith's translation works to soften Barth's position, as it has in other places as well. Barth's sense is stronger: "Even this foolish reversal and destruction, however, is in any case the one sense in the great nonsense of anti-Semitism.

all mankind. This people without roots, the Jews, tell us—and we too suspect—that we, who believe ourselves to be secure on the bank, are in fact not so, and that our own roots, our own security, are in a rather bad state. . . . No wonder this idea is repugnant to us![14]

Friedrich Marquardt had complained that, at times, Barth is tempted to reduce the Jews to a cipher, to a mirror that reflects life but lives none of its own. In fact, Barth has entertained a temptation far stronger. The Jews live their own lives—a life to be sure that mirrors the Christian—but the reality of the Jews is an uncanny mirroring of what anti-Semites taught. Here are the stock images, given full reign: the rootless cosmopolitan, the rebel, the disbeliever, the "defiant people" whose existence is a "permanent and terrible riddle," the stranger who moves a shadowy form across world history. Though Barth offers no comfort to racial hatred, he allows a form of volkist and dogmatic anti-Judaism full expression. Christians, that is, have understood their subject well, but Barth cautions, they have missed its significance. The "contempt, scorn, and hatred" directed toward the Jews belongs to them, yes, but to the Christians, too. Like the Jews, the Christians too are rootless—they must live on grace alone. Like the Jews, they are defiant disbelievers—only Christ can heal such wounds. But the Jews exemplify this life of "lostness and persistence" as no other people can because they are the elect of God. Christians take up this form of the stranger, the unrooted, because they are "guests" in the house of Israel, and assume and mirror the life of their hosts.

These hosts, the Jews, cannot be understood without the Church. Apart from Christian doctrine, he repeats, anti-Semitism cannot be contained or resolved. Barth's long-standing distrust of bourgeois ethics resurfaces: anti-Semitism will not yield to moral suasion, however "fine" the words; it is a theological question and demands a theological response. Jews and Christians are united—and divided—by a single Jew, Jesus of Nazareth. For this one Jew, the people Israel was chosen from all the nations of the earth—they are the "rock of divine choice"—and non-Jews can participate in God's election only if, "for good or ill, they be heart and soul on the side of the Jews." Those who despise the Jews despise their own redemption and redeemer; anti-Semitism strikes at the root of Christian salvation. But this solidarity, forged in theological unity, demands a sharp rebuke: the Jews do not believe. In a stinging reply, Barth draws together his condemnation of Judaism and of anti-Semitism:

14. "The Jewish Problem and the Christian Answer," 199 ["Die Judenfrage und ihre christliche Beantwortung," 148].

The Jews, who ought to be the first to do so, do not acknowledge this one Jew. Therefore, they are not so ready to accept the fact that they can live only by God's grace. That is why the Jews are to this day so defiant a people, and why their defiance is so closely allied to anti-semitism. [*in ihrem Trotz den Antisemiten nur zu verwandtes Volk.*] That is the essence of this permanent and terrible riddle of Jewish existence. We Christians from among the Gentiles cannot, however acknowledge that one Jew, the Lord Jesus Christ, without knowing that we are one with the Jews. In their defiance we recognise the same emotion as works in us. But we also know Him, who has already overcome all human defiance and thereby healed all divisions among us, and first and foremost the division between the Jews and other nations [*Völkern*]. He alone can make self-evident what the other nations without doubt owe to the Jews, and just for that reason we Christians greet the Jews this Advent-tide—in the name of Him, over whose Cross the Gentile Pontius Pilate had the inscription set up, "Jesus of Nazareth, King of the Jews." When the Jews protested against this, Pilate replied, "What I have written, I have written."[15]

Turning to the New Testament, Barth has circumscribed the worldly event of anti-Semitism with the inscription of Pilate. Like the anti-Semites, the Jews refuse the sign of God's election; an unwitting instrument of God, Pilate has written the truth both defiant peoples reject.

Such biblical rhetoric comes easily enough to many Christian thinkers; the Scriptures themselves are a ready store of somber sayings about contemporary, worldly events. But Barth does not come by his biblical world view cheaply. The relationship between the biblical witness to revelation and the natural, historical basis of that revelation occupies a good bit of the *Dogmatics,* and a great deal of the "Doctrine of Creation." That the Bible is particular—the story of the covenant between Israel and God—yet universal—the story of the reconciliation of the world to God—is a problematic Barth never exhausts. In his understanding of the Jews, he searches tirelessly for the points where the long history of the Jews makes contact with the "doctrine of Israel." The connection made between the biblical story of election and the worldly history of Jews and Gentiles is never direct or reversible: we cannot read the word of God in either the book of nature or history. Yet, the connection remains. These Jews of Synagogue or Church, these "pantheists, atheists or skeptics,"[16] these citizens of the modern secular

15. Ibid., 201 [149].
16. Ibid., 197 [146].

state, these people like all others, these Jews in short, are the living Israel of God, the elect. For a theologian like Barth, for whom apologetics of all sorts is suspect, and for whom natural theology, even in its guise as the Spirit of history, is disobedience to the One Word of God—for such a theologian, the "persistence of the Jews" is *the* problem in the dilemma of faith and history. This dilemma, evoked in the rhetorical conclusion to Barth's radio address, is taken up and treated with theological precision in volume 3 of the *Dogmatics.*

In chapter 9 of the *Doctrine of Creation,* "The Creator and his Creature," Barth turns his full attention to this complex relation of the claims of faith to the facts of history. Indeed, as some have seen in the *Epistle to the Romans* a massive effort to reconcile time and eternity, so in volume 3 of the *Dogmatics,* we can see a thoroughgoing attempt to reconcile the world with the King of Israel. It might seem ironic that a theologian of Barth's convictions would spend so much of his later life on the Christian analysis of creation, and the realm of "worldly occurrence." How much better, they might say, if Barth had completed, the *Doctrine of Reconciliation* or begun his *Doctrine of Last Things!* Though the critic might object to this wish on other grounds—yet another volume!—I think it is a wish based on a common misunderstanding about Barth. That he is "unhistorical," that he has no patience for the secular world, that he rejects the achievements of humanism: these are familiar and I think misguided complaints.

Barth could express his loyalty to the great programmatic of the nineteenth century in no clearer way than in his volume on creation. Here, though he begins with "faith"—the doctrines of providence and covenant—he keeps his eye on "history," the history of Jew and Gentile under the lordship of God. That there is a natural world at all, or a secular history in any form apart from or hostile to sacred history, that God, Barth writes, has "space and time for us": these are facts Barth cannot tire of, and they express a living tension he cannot let go. These two realms are related, yet not united; they are joined, yet not reduced to each other; they speak of one God, yet not in one voice. The arena of worldly occurrence—our world—is the great theater of God's hidden glory, of his indirect communication, of his unspoken providence. Human history, in its partial, tragic, and altogether common failures, is a world of "many lights, reflecting the One Light." In this history of many lights, the "stubborn persistence" of the Jews, their sufferings and present-day vindication in the state of Israel, represents for Barth the "most astonishing and provocative indication of the world-governance of God."[17] In treating

17. *Dogmatics,* 3.3:210 [*Dogmatik,* 3.3:238].

this dimension of the "divine rule," Barth uncovers the dogmatic foundation for Christian solidarity with Jews, and with Israel itself.

With deceptive simplicity, Barth sets out the dogmatic significance of world-occurrence [*Weltgeschehen*]. He is careful about his terminology here; he does not address the "religious significance of world-historical events." Such hegelianism has tempted Barth before, and he has given way, but not here. In fact, Barth's central convictions about history and the created order defend him against Idealism at every point. On the subjects of the individual, the meaning and intelligibility of history, and the contribution of human spirit to its *telos* Barth is unyielding. Like Kierkegaard, like Rosenzweig, Barth will break open the System for revelation, and shelter the individual from the pitiless advance of Spirit to the Absolute.[18] World history will not become transparent, even to the philosopher; the grand events of human civilization remain dark and silent witnesses, pointing only to their own partial and broken nature. God rules history and everything within it; all things receive life from the divine rule, and return to it in the end. Barth forbids the hegelian realization of Spirit: God is the eternal and absolute sovereign. To be sure, world occurrence has meaning and goal. It is neither chance nor blind fate. But, striking at Hegel's dynamism directly, Barth will not lift up its one meaning into the progressive motion of Self-consciousness, however complete. World history is governed by the King of Israel. Solitary and sovereign, this world Ruler enacts the meaning of creaturely reality in one place—Israel—and reveals the particular and boundless mercy of this free Lord in one, unsurpassable event, the saving King of the Jews, Jesus of Nazareth. History has no other center, no other goal. Cut off absolutely is the Idealist sublation of this final revelation into a further age, a further community or philosophical world view. Alone in history, Jesus Christ, the elect and electing, calls his community from Jew and Gentile and places them as witness to the world of this one history, one covenant, one unsurpassed redemption. Apart from this single time of revelation, world occurrence lies still, made relative "vertically" and "horizontally," a world of light and shadow whose reality speaks not of the rational but of the one Lord of Israel.

And yet: is the border really closed? I speak so firmly of Barth's repudiation of Hegel, his rejection of the Idealist system, his consistent defense along the front. But Hegel's wonderfully synthetic thought insinuates itself in any room

18. One place, among many, to find this emphasis in Kierkegaard is *Philosophical Fragments,* trans. and ed. H. Hong and E. Hong (Princeton: Princeton University Press, 1985). See also Rosenzweig's "On the Possibility of the Cognition of All," the introduction to part 1 of *The Star of Redemption.*

it enters. Barth's pronounced taste for the concrete; his insistence that the general rests on the particular; his implicit trust that the negative, too, finds meaning in God; and finally, his love of history itself, its lively movement from here to there, its great figures and peoples, its unity amid the random, its meaning taken up in the God who creates and embodies history—all these elements of Barth's historiography pay quiet tribute to Hegel. Idealism has left its mark on Barth and his doctrine of world-occurrence, and I suppose it would be more accurate to say that Barth rejects a system he cannot fully leave behind.

This dialectic between expression and repudiation of the world-historical event provides the frame for Barth's doctrine of the divine rule. Its subject, however, derives from a favorite source, the "older dogmaticians" of Protestant orthodoxy. Barth looks to them for the terms of this debate, the role of providence in the divine governance of creation. In what way, the dogmaticians might ask, shall Christian theology understand the rule of God? Does God's determining hand rest on every created thing and event? Or is there creaturely freedom to "will and to work"? What is the goal of human history, and in what way does this history enact the divine plan and government? In these questions, and their technical distinctions, Barth expresses the dogmatic form of this distinct Christian occupation with history.

Against this framework and background, Barth portrays the human experience of history and the "absolute miracle" of revelation. These are spheres and worlds apart; one indwells the other, but they do not touch. The human experience of history—our historicity—cannot demonstrate or provide God's revelation. We cannot, from experience, rise up or turn within to the reality of divine rule: it must come from without, from the event of God's "self-demonstration." Those who seek the voice of the young Barth in the old will listen to the sharp division in this section and hear echoes of a generation ago: "We ought to speak of God. We are human, however, and so cannot speak of God. We ought therefore to recognize both our obligation and our inability and by that very recognition give God the glory."[19] We humans stand in history, enclosed in darkness; our world, Barth tirelessly repeats, is a realm of complete relativity. It is easy, I think, to overlook Barth's radical insistence on this point. Not content with the corrosive historicism moderns like Troeltsch so painfully confronted and accepted, Barth plunges deeper. The events of human history are leveled, finally and really leveled, by the sovereign holy otherness of God. Our historicity is made relative

19. These famous lines come from "The Word of God and the Task of the Ministry," in *Word of God and the Word of Man*, 186.

"vertically"—God as transcendent ruler "subordinates all creatures to Himself" and "in relation to God . . . all creaturely occurrence and all creatures are relegated to a position of lowliness and dependence and relativity. This means that in themselves they are nothing, and that of themselves they can neither mean anything nor do anything. God is the 'yonderside' of all creaturely being and activity from which alone the light and life and power of creaturely occurrence can derive."[20] But we have not exhausted the relativity of human history if we point only to "God in heaven, and human beings on the earth." Historicity is made relative "horizontally" as well. "Each activity and effect of individual creaturely subjects," Barth writes, "is allotted [by God] its own place and time and function in relation to all the rest. And this means that we can speak of the significance of any one thing only in the light of its connexion with all other things."[21] Such relativity, however radical, does not reduce the creature or its history to meaninglessness: "It is the glory of the creature to be lowly in relation to God." Indeed, the thoroughgoing relativity Barth applies to human experience underscores its one meaning and "glory." God alone is the source, guidance, and goal of all things. From this solitary Ruler, all history and nature graciously proceed, and to this End, and this End alone, all are subordinate and ordered and returned to its only Lord.

Such high-minded dogmatic formulation might give us pause. Does Barth mean to embrace the consequences of his position? He is a fearless and tough-minded thinker—we could hardly fail to notice that—but does he actually mean to pursue such relativity to its end? To fully follow this path: "This means that in themselves they are nothing, and that of themselves they can neither mean anything nor do anything." I believe he does, and that his early polemic against the two sources of theology has never weakened or moderated, despite the cost. Those who look to Barth's political commitments and activity in the world for a "second word" in theology will find scant comfort here. Nevertheless, Barth, a man of earnest morality and outrage, must have known the risk of relativism to political action. Can it "mean nothing" to assassinate Hitler or not; to bomb Dresden or London; to march on Czechoslovakia, or Poland, or the Soviet Union; to make war on Jews; or to have peace? Are all these relative, genuinely relative in the long view, the view of eternity, the view from above? That Barth, a man by no means passive in his resistance to the war, should argue for such a historical relativism points to the theological urgency of his position and the sophistication of its argument.

20. *Dogmatics*, 3.3:170 [*Dogmatik*, 3.3:193].
21. Ibid.

Barth's argument here turns on two simultaneous and apparently opposite poles: that "there is no such thing as secular history, [*Profangeschichte*] . . . history apart from, or opposed to [the divine] economy"; and that "the Father, the Almighty, the Creator of heaven and earth, about whose lordship over all things we have been speaking, is the King of Israel."[22] The whole of volume 3, the *Doctrine of Creation*, may be understood as a dialectical antithesis and resolution of these two poles, the sites Barth variously calls "the general and the particular," "world-occurrence and revelation," "the *gubernatio* and the messianic kingship," or, as Lessing called it, "the truths of reason and history." The balance and distinction Barth maintains between these sites must be made clear if any resolution is to be gained on the problems of natural theology, and the relationship of political commitment to dogmatic affirmation.

On the one hand, "there is no such thing as secular history." Everything is under God's rule and directed toward that End. Returning to the Romantic imagery so close to the heart of the German academic *Wanderer*, Barth describes the creation as an "organic" whole, a tree perhaps or a river, running to the sea. We misunderstand God's creative providence altogether if we comprehend the world under lifeless metaphors, images of similarity and indifference. The created world could not be a sphere, for example, each point equidistant from the center, each equally prominent to the eye. The world ruled by God has direction, roots, and limits; it conforms to one plan; it exhibits one organic order: it is living and lives to God. It cannot, then, be apart and opposed to God's ordering plan. The creation does not tolerate any true, secular history.

The mission of the Church in this world under God's providence cannot be devoted to bringing those outside the faith into the shelter of divine grace and protection. God orders and rules history: all nations are already under the grace and judgment of their creator. Indeed, the Church in its worldly place as witness to this providence, must follow the path laid out for it in the covenant itself. It must take the "journey into the far country," from here to there, offering its life and witness for the sake of the world. No event or place in history is outside the Church's concern; no commitment to human beings "in general" takes the Christian beyond the loving freedom of God.

But the "particular" gives the Church's witness its focus and foundation. In a hegelian motion, Barth overturns the classical model, that the particular is understood by the terms of the general. A piece of Aristotelian logic, this rule has survived its original setting to quietly influence modern scientific

22. Ibid., 198, 176 [224, 200].

and theological thought. A bit of mineral is compared to all others like it; it is understood and delimited by its place within the general, the "universal." Particulars may yield the universal, but it is the universal that provides the definition, the category under which the individual is subsumed and judged. These are elementary examples, of course, the coarsest bits of the modern model of scientific method. But it may not be so widely recognized in its theological guise. It is, after all, the basic form of all theological apologetics, and it is in this role that Barth raises his hand against it. In theology, Barth warns, the particular must not illustrate the general, nor the concrete receive definition and meaning from the universal. All is lost in dogmatics if the individual is swallowed up in the ruthless sea of the ideal, the universal, the world-historical spirit. If the Church is to witness to the providence of God over all creation, it must turn to the King of Israel: the general must listen to and receive its form from the particular.

Why this is so human beings cannot really say—the particular cannot be derived from the general!—but if Barth's dogmatic program can actually admit to a governing principle, this might be the one. God acts in the facts of history, governs through the concrete, reveals the grace and judgment of election in the Individual, elected and electing; dogmatics witnesses to *this* God and no other. For this reason, Christian apologetics however earnest and adept cannot draw its audience to the intended goal: the general will never yield the particular of God's act in Christ. Again and again, Barth circles and redescribes the actualism of revelation. In the rejection and death of Israel's Messiah and in the resurrection of the Son of Man, God is self-demonstrated and justified. All history is relative, subordinate, and confirmed through this single and unsurpassed event of God's being, love, and freedom. To this Center, this one Light, all created lights and centers are drawn, and from this single Source, they receive their dignity and reflected light.

The field of history, then, cannot be level; it cannot stretch out flat and uninterrupted between creation and consummation. Though in itself it is relative and dark, from its center, human history can be seen to form a circle, along whose circumference "signs and witnesses" have been raised up. These signs are "no second revelation of the divine world-governance, no second Bible."[23] They are creatures of history, hidden and broken like all others. But they "stand nearer" to the center of history, the time of revelation, than do any others, and, while they too can be overlooked and misunderstood, these "elements" and "mysteries" along the border can point to its Ruler.

23. Ibid., 198 [225].

Though committed to an organic metaphor for creation, Barth cannot resist the appeal of human civilization. From the days of the *Römerbrief,* he found the language of border and territory, frontier and occupation, congenial to the description of God's victorious ways with creation. In this mature account of the relationship of history to revelation, Barth envisions a drama within a city, a holy city, encircled—but not walled in!—by a border of obscure outposts; from this center, the frontier is defined, and from the frontier, the beyond of world-occurrence. The center spreads its light from the border to all the world; indeed, this drama takes place for the sake of this beyond. But the witnesses to this fact take up their post on the frontier. They are themselves nothing but distant outposts, but they border the place where God was pleased to dwell. Though Barth could not grant theological validity to a Holy Land—revelation cannot be a human possession—his fine ear for biblical idiom and thought form has perhaps guided his hand here. That God has acted in one place, with one people, and that place is not "Greece or Rome or Germany but Israel" is a declaration Barth repeats and reflects in his doctrine and metaphor.

As the conclusion to this section on the Divine Ruling, Barth lays out four of these "enduring elements" that give witness to all history of the one King of Israel: "the history of Holy Scripture; the history of the Church; the limitation of human life; and the history of the Jews." In all four, Barth affirms their singular but hidden character. They all may be understood in their historical, material, or psychological dimensions; they may be reduced to these. They are genuine creatures of history and as such they are "no dearer to God than other creatures." But they take on their particular character as sign and witness because, in their location on the border, they stand as "permanent riddles" [*konstante Rätsel*] in the course of world-occurrence, and can be explained fully only from the center point where God's rule once was made manifest. Such public witnesses, comprised of individuals and events that belong entirely to the natural and historical realm, bring Barth to the threshold of a natural and apologetic theology. Indeed, at times Friedrich Marquardt and Barth himself have felt compelled, for different reasons I think, to describe the Jews as the "only natural proof for the existence of God."[24] But when Barth is speaking carefully, with dogmatic precision, as he does here, these signs and witnesses are restrained along that threshold.

---

24. Barth's is a less formal, less theologically precise remark, used for example in the "critical questions" raised about *Nostra Aetate* in *Ad Limina Apostolorum,* 36; Marquardt's is a more sustained, critical interpretation of Barth, raised in *Die Entdeckung des Judentums,* 316–20, and in another form in his political redescription of the early Barth.

They are "mysteries" and "riddles," irresolvable outside the claims of faith, and that description serves Barth well.

We should understand these four elements, I think, as bits of undigestible evidence in our rationalized world-explanations. They refuse to be fully comprehended under a single system, and stand guard against any completely secularized account of human experience. Brought face to face with these mysteries, we admit the limitations of human reason and acknowledge the shimmering and impenetrable presence of a witness to the One beyond the frontier. Secular explanations of course apply to these elements and may give credible accounts of their enduring presence. But they do not exhaust their meaning or testimony; indeed, their inexhaustibility defines their character as sign.[25] Barth can tolerate such "natural" signs within dogmatics because, in part, they remain permanent mysteries. Like the crater left from the exploding shell, these riddles are silent witnesses; they point to a place, they bear marks of an encounter but they are neither a possession nor a guide. Those who confront them cannot find answers there, or a foundation on which faith can be built or made respectable. Early on in the *Dogmatics,* Barth toyed with the "vestigal signs of the Trinity"—the near universal and abiding presence of the number *3* in human thought and experience—and comes to a fuller and more sophisticated understanding of such "natural wonders" here.[26] They do not prove but "confirm" what faith acknowledges, that God rules, and rules from one place, the covenant history of Israel.

This dogmatic proclamation—that the King of Israel rules creation—is what Barth calls, a "fact" [*ein Faktum*]. We are meant to hear Lessing here, I think, and separate such concrete events from the truths of (human) reason. Indeed, the contingent facts of history are the sole foundation of theology; they alone are not self-evident and cannot be derived from reason. They are, then, the world elements dependent upon a living God, who takes up creaturely reality into the act of revelation. The signs and witness, however, are not divine acts of revelation, but in their mysterious and irresolvable character, they point to and reflect these underived "facts." One of these signs, the "permanent riddle" of the history of the Jews—a history of "very special cogency"—provides, at long last, a location within Barth's dogmatic

25. Barth does not offer such an explicit phenomenology of the sign, but the similarity is suggestive.

26. Barth's occasional use of the term "traces"—the "traces of God's rule within these enduring elements"—may reflect this earlier discussion as, strictly speaking, these elements are fully historical and share with other human experiences the relativity and subordination to God's hidden rule. They do not bear "traces" of God's rule, but only the riddle, insoluble by human systems.

project for his solidarity with modern Jews and his support for modern Israel.

Much of this territory is familiar ground. Barth speaks here of a people [*Volk*] that "was not meant to have any perceptible existence."[27] After the destruction of the Temple, and more, after the defeat of Jerusalem in A.D. 70, which "corresponded in so sinister a way to the death of Jesus,"[28] the remnant of Israel was to take up life within the Church. But it would not. It became a people disobedient to its election, stubbornly clinging to its Synagogue existence, entering world history as a "minority submerged amongst other peoples and nations, great and small."[29] The history of Israel now becomes the history of the Jews; from this form of "persistence" and "disobedience" it will not, cannot vary. "From now on the Jews will be that which they became in the year 70. And what is that? What have they been during these last 1900 years? What are they still today? This is the problem [*das Problem*] with which we are now faced."[30]

The permanent riddle of the Jews, the "problem" of their existence and persistence, receives a biblical title: they are those who once were "not My people" and became "not a people." The mystery, Barth writes, lies in this, that this "remnant of Israel," this shadow in world history, exists without any worldly signs of existence. The Jews exist as citizens of other countries; they have no "connected history as a single community" and even the events in "Palestine [are] provisionally only the work of a comparatively small proportion of Jewry as a whole."[31] The Jews have no single "religion," a fact Barth considers "obvious." Even the founders of the state of Israel did not consider the "Mosaic religion"—Barth will travel some distance to avoid the idea of Judaism as a religion—to be "constitutive for its inauguration." They are adherents of the major philosophical schools of the "Goyim;" they are Liberals, skeptics, and atheists; they take part in the Synagogue and the Church. Yet, "they do not cease to be Jews."[32] The particular amalgam of volkist thought Barth adopted in the 1930s remains largely untouched through the 1940s. Even in denying that Jews constitute a "race" [*Rasse*]—"an idea of a specifically Jewish blood is pure imagination [*ein reines Phantasieprodukt*]"[33]—Barth retains an odd bit of volkist reasoning. Jews cannot be a

---

27. *Dogmatics*, 3.3:212 [*Dogmatik*, 3.3:240].
28. Ibid.
29. Ibid., 217 [246].
30. Ibid., 211 [239].
31. Ibid., 214 [243].
32. Ibid., 214 [242].
33. Ibid., 213 [241].

semitic race, he appears to argue, because they lack what others have called "fellow feeling," or more darkly, "race consciousness": "the Semites [are the "race"] to which their former enemies also belonged, and to which the most bitter of their modern enemies belong."[34] Even in this sense, they are a riddle; a people without a race.

Again, the Jews have no single "culture or language." They have contributed to the nations in which they have lived, their professions, artistic life, and intellectual achievement.[35] But they have not developed a Jewish culture "as such," and "it has yet to be seen whether or not something of this kind will happen in Palestine."[36] Hebrew retains only a "cultic" significance; Jews speak the language of their "hosts." At most, a "degenerate form of Hebrew"—Yiddish?—has been "preserved in certain well-defined areas of Jewish life." Even in the state of Israel, Hebrew is little more than an "Esperanto"[37] and only serves to confirm the fact that Jews have "no mother-tongue."

The Jews, in short, live out a Christian *typos:*

> As the history of this people was determined in the year 70, it seems to consist in the fact that the people then took up its existence again, and yet ceased to be a people in the usual sense of the term, and has never been one since. It necessarily continues to exist in this unique way, as a people which in the usual sense of the word is not a people [*Nicht-Volk*]. It necessarily has history which strictly speaking is non-historical; the history of a guest and alien [*Fremdling*] and stranger [*Unbekannt*] and exception amongst the nations, with the eternal Jew, perhaps, as its legendary pattern [*Urphänomen*].[38]

34. Ibid. It is interesting that the translation leaves out Barth's pointed reference to the modern "enemies," *die Araber,* the Arabs.

35. Barth adds an ominous, though obscure, parenthesis: the Jews have contributed to "the development and purification—and often to what for other reasons, and not through any fault of theirs, turned out to be the dissolution—of the cultures of other peoples" [*Zersetzung der Kultur anderer Völker*] (Ibid., 214 [242]).

36. Ibid.

37. For a decidedly different view of the use of Hebrew in the newly founded state, see Gerhard (Gershom) Scholem's greeting to Franz Rosenzweig on his fortieth birthday, "Bekenntnis über unsere Sprache" ["A Confession on Our Language"], in which the language is described as an "abyss" [ein Abgrund], sharpened to an "apocalyptic edge" [der apokalyptische Stachel], and "filled with meaning to the point of bursting" [die zum Bersten erfüllten Worte]. This letter is in the birthday album for Rosenzweig, *Franz Rosenzweig zum 25 Dezember 1926: Glückwünsche zum 40. Geburtstag* (reprint, New York: Leo Baeck Institute, 1987). I thank Robert Schine, a colleague at Middlebury College, for this reference.

38. *Dogmatics,* 3.3:215 [*Dogmatik,* 3.3:243]. This is not to deny that Judaic thinkers, particularly

To the Christian, to the dogmatician especially, the Jews are an inexplicable fact, an impossible possibility. They cannot disbelieve, yet they do; they cannot persist against empires and states, pogroms and inquisitions, yet they do; they must dissolve into the cultures of the Christian West, yet they do not. Even the "weaknesses" in Jewish thought and culture—observations about life in the diaspora and Israel that amount to little more than crude clichés—these are understood as implicit strengths. The grudging admiration accorded Jews by European Christians finds its place in Barth, as well.

> We have to think how small [the Jews] were. We have to remember how unfavourable the conditions were for their continued existence. We have to remember what had become of the powerful nations which had once been their enemies, the one-time Assyrians, Babylonians, Persians and Syrians, not to speak of the lesser peoples [Stämme] which had once been their neighbours and oppressors. They had all long since lost their identity. We no longer know any of them as they once were. But in spite of the destruction and persecution and above all the assimilation and interconnexion and intermingling with other nations the Jews are still there, and permanently there. And how active [wirksam] and prominent [sichtbar] they are!—an isolated element in history; a leaven which maintains itself and in its own way succeeds amongst other elements; not often loved or even assisted or protected from outside by the others, but quite the reverse; usually despised for some obscure reason, and kept apart and even persecuted and oppressed by every possible spiritual and physical weapon, and frequently exterminated in part; yet always and everywhere surviving; again and again demonstrating its continued existence by the fact of it; again and again winning for itself an involuntary respect.[39]

Even the state of Israel wins reluctant admiration: How quickly it established itself! Against all odds! How effortlessly it achieved the fruits of long-lived civilizations—a "self-sacrificing youth," a courageous military, heroic leaders! For Barth, this ambivalent praise, this expression of distorted and mirrored realities, this projection of riddles and reasons has theological significance.

---

the liberals, made use of the concept of a "people without a nation." Barth, however, rehearses these elements within an exegetical and theological tradition that functions and endures as a type.

39. Ibid., 211–12 [239–40].

The "permanent mystery" of the Jews can be understood and acknowledged only from the foundation of revelation: the Jews exist, and exist in this way, because they are the elected people of God.

Only the elect can live without nation, language, or culture; only the elect may bear the signs of their Messiah's afflictions and persist; only the flesh Christ judged and assumed may disobey yet thrive. The Jews, after all, are the community and body of Christ, the people called for rejection, and they carry the marks of their simultaneous office, to suffer and to save. In every culture and age, in other nations and their own, the Jews will survive, the people that is not-a-people, because God wills it. The stiff-necked flesh of disobedience that God took for himself cannot perish; it must endure as the sign of God's free and justifying grace.

For this reason, the state of Israel, too, offers silent witness to the sovereign reign of God. In response to a question by Jakob Petuchowski, a respectful and frank questioner, Barth repeats this dogmatic interpretation:

> Rabbi Petuchowski: [O]ne realizes how, from the traditional Christian point of view, which sees the destruction of Jerusalem in 70 A.D. as a punishment for Israel's rejection of the Christ, there must be certain difficulties in coming to terms with the existence of the modern State of Israel. Just as, *mutatis mutandis,* Reform Judaism is at present involved in the difficult task of reconciling the nineteenth-century ideology with twentieth-century reality. It would be of great interest to hear how you, sir, view the establishment of the State of Israel, particularly in light of your seeing in Jesus the fulfillment of Old Testament prophecy, and of your description of the Synagogue as existing on a "powerless continuation of Israelite history."

Petuchowski's summary could hardly be more pointed or more deferential! Barth replies:

> Answering the question of Petuchowski, I shall consider the creation of the modern State of Israel in the context of the fulfillment of the Old Testament. A possible explanation is that it is another and new sign of the electing and providentially ruling grace and faithfulness of God to that seed of Abraham, a very visible sign, visible for every reader of the papers, the whole world—a sign which is not to be overlooked. After the horrors of Hitler's time the reappearance of Israel, now as a nation in the political realm, even as a state, may well be called a miracle for all that have eyes to see this evidence, and a

> scandal for all those who have not eyes to see. Remember the answer, mentioned yesterday, given to Frederick the Great, "The proof for God's existence, your majesty, are the Jews." And we could now add today, "your majesty, the State of Israel." The Jews have always owed their existence to the power of God alone and not to their own force or to the might of their history. And here we have another case of this kind of existence of Israel. God alone can help it to exist and it seems that he will do so.[40]

Such language—the informal and unfamiliar speech of a Swiss national at an American colloquium—invites thoughts of natural theology and the nagging suspicion of "two sources of revelation." But considered against its formal, dogmatic presentation, we must resist such ideas, I think, and consider them so many friendly asides. History is the site of revelation, to be sure, and in Christ, world-occurrence is taken up into the electing work of God; but only in Christ, and from that place of reconciliation, and no other. In the creaturely world of partial freedom and necessity, of light and shadow, of responsibility and discipleship, we are confronted by mysteries, of the Church, the Bible, of death, and of the Jews, and no historicism, however relativizing, can fully corrode these mysteries into their component and intelligible parts. We stand before them, at the limit of human explanation, and fall silent; Christians with the eyes of faith see God's sovereign rule under the hidden sign of mystery. In the people of the Jews, and in the modern state of Israel, Barth raises up before his readers, the "most astonishing and provocative" sign of God's election, that Jesus Christ, the Judge judged in our place, was born a Jew.

---

40. "Introduction to Theology: Questions to and Discussion with Dr. Karl Barth," *Criterion*, no. 1 (Winter 1963): 21–22.

CONCLUSIONS AND EVALUATIONS

Barth's Doctrine of Israel as the Divine Act of Justification by Grace

Karl Barth has brought us this far, with his theological mastery, his brooding judgments and shafts of light, his exegetical realm of doublets and types, his history sparked by signs and mysteries—all in service of his dogmatic interpretation of Judaism. Barth traveled some distance in his thought, from the days of the *Römerbrief* to the years of the *Church Dogmatics,* and the changes he announced in theological method and object influenced his "doctrine of Israel." I have not emphasized these changes—indeed it is his consistency that has repeatedly drawn my attention—but Barth was not one to minimize how "his mind had changed," nor the length of the road from Safenwil to Basel. As he mused on his life and world in his last years, on his old age, on the future of his disciples and his theology, on the opening of the Second Vatican Council—an event he could have scarcely imagined in his younger years—Barth reflected on his own transformations with the wistful irony he reserved for his own life. How sure I was then! How things have changed! Like discovering the bust of Schleiermacher in the rubble of postwar Bonn, unexpected things happened to Barth, and he rarely hesitated to draw bittersweet self-deprecations from these "lessons of history." Like most people, I suppose, but more than most, Barth revealed a life of vigorous activity tempered by a bemused acceptance of the irresistible force of change. His conservation of the past and openness to the future made Barth a theologian of real complexity, with an attitude toward innovation at once revolutionary and reactionary. Such ambivalent and sometimes obscure convictions find their place in his attitude, interpretation, and evaluation of Judaism, within and beyond the Bible. Barth altered these views over time, of course; but he also preserved, at times lovingly preserved, his earliest and strongest convictions about Jews and Judaism. These convictions, centered around the Christian appropriation of Law, election, judgment, and grace, have appeared in separate strands in the *Epistle to the Romans,* the *Church Dogmatics,* and later essays and addresses; we now have the task to bind them together, to see what was lost and what will remain.

Despite my arguments for continuity in Barth's thought, I recognize that a strong case can be built for the position that Barth altered and developed his understanding of Judaism over the major phases of his theological career. Not constancy, but change, the argument runs, characterizes Barth's doctrine of Israel.

This is an interpretation of Barth that begins with the claim that in *Romans* Barth uses "Jews" and "Judaism" to stand for the heresy of bourgeois Liberalism. To be sure, the Jews addressed in Paul's letter are real figures in history. Their actions in obedience or opposition to the Gospel determine the pattern all later belief and disobedience will assume. But they are the Jews of Christian polemics: the "Judaizers," the "legalists" imposing on converts fidelity to a Law now superseded or fulfilled. This Judaism is a Christian symbol; it stands for all those who put their trust in works. In his book, *Karl Barth,* T.H.L. Parker presents this reading of *Romans,* blending in a nearly indiscernible way his own derogation and expansion of Judaism with Barth's:

> Barth stands, then, in that line of men to whom the message of Romans has been a word creative of liberty. In the first century Paul had cut the Gospel of Jesus Christ free from the bondage of Judaism by binding Judaism inescapably to Jesus Christ. In the fifth century Augustine, himself first liberated by Romans 13:11–16, applied the Pauline doctrine to the neo-Judaism of Pelagius. Eleven hundred years later the Reformation turned the same doctrine against the neo-Judaism of the late medieval Church. At that time many commentaries on Romans were published. One, however, lay unprinted and in comparative obscurity. From Easter 1515 until September 1516 Luther lectured on Romans in Wittenberg. His lectures were virtually lost until they were at last published in 1908. It would not be over-romantic to see in the fate of these lectures a symbol of the substance of the Epistle itself, shining in such brilliant light in the Reformation, but dimmed and obscured thereafter for three centuries.

Barth's *Epistle to the Romans* takes up again the task of Augustine and the Reformers. But now the doctrine is directed against the neo-Judaism of religion itself, specifically of Protestantism under the sway of Schleiermacher and Ritschl, but this as representing religion itself, any endeavour whatsoever of man to make his knowledge or experience of God the basis of the knowledge or experience of God.[1]

It would be too strong, I think, to argue that in this interpretation, Jews and Judaism function as mere allegory, lacking all particularity. Indeed, actual Jews appear to be very much in mind here, embodying and carrying forward the heresy of works-righteousness that all "neo-Judaizers" imitate. But the reality of Judaism honored by Parker is an instrumental one: it is put to work on Christian tasks to Christian ends. Granted no independent existence, no self-definition, Judaism "represents" the religious disguise of human pride; it is self-assertion in its most elegant form. This is the understanding of Judaism that Friedrich Marquardt condemns, an Idealist conception that strips Judaism of all content but the projection of human misery and need.

Such Idealist trappings fall away when Barth turns to the *Dogmatics*—if we follow this line of interpretation. In his mature work, the history of Israel and the people of the Jews put on the weight of reality in their role as chosen people. Barth's interest in particular Jews—in David, Saul, Judas, and Paul—increases; he gives full dignity to Israel's election; he stresses that the Messiah came first to the Jews because he was one of their own. Though the Gentiles are ingrafted, the root and branch belong to Israel in an irrevocable covenant. The philosophical apparatus, put on display in *Romans,* is now stored away in footnotes or discarded. The *Dogmatics* speaks in full biblical idiom, in narrative, type and figure, giving voice to the history that belongs first and properly to the Jews. "The Prophets are the true Doctors of the Church," Barth wrote, and the prophecies, Law, and theater of redemption are all Jewish gifts. That the Jews were disobedient, that they refused their election, that they rejected their Messiah, that they pursued the "joyless phantasm" of the Synagogue: all these harsh facts about the elected people must not blind Christians to the honor all Jews deserve. This interpretation places emphasis on the positive, on the *Yes* over the *No.* The solid anti-Judaism of the *Dogmatics*—the round condemnation of Israel as "vessels of wrath" and rabbinic Judaism as unwitting sign of human misery—this theological rejection of Judaism must not lead, Barth warned, to anti-Semitism, the hatred of Jews based on pseudo-scientific mythologies about blood, race, and soil. A

1. Parker, *Karl Barth,* 32.

Church that expels its Jews, and supports the secular expulsion of its country's Jews, cannot be Christian. The Church is called from Jew and Gentile, because Christ elected to come to them, to the Jew first and then the Gentile. Like the apostle Paul, the Church rejoices at the presence of Jews within its midst, and waits for the day that God will consummate his election and allow all Jews to rise up to life in the Church. On that day, the one community of Jesus Christ will be complete, binding together Israel that hears the Word promised, with the Church that receives that Word in gratitude. The proud flesh of Israel, the "form of one passing away," will join the "form of one coming," the Jews and Gentiles forgiven their pride by grace. The one body, judged and redeemed, will represent its One Lord, the redeemer and the judged; in its unity, Israel and the Church will at last live out its election in faith, to be a "light to the nations."

This interpretation of change draws its final evidence from Barth's remarkable and unwavering support for the state of Israel in his postwar years. Despite the "nasty neighborhood" he visited in such political declarations, Barth considered Christian "solidarity" with Jews—though not with Judaism!—an essential discipline of those who acknowledge the Elected One of Israel. The people raised up, called, and confirmed for the covenant will receive the irrevocable signs of its election. While empires and reichs, cultures, and peoples perish, the Jews will endure: they are the permanent and inexplicable "mystery" on the border of revelation. Again and again, God will raise them up; they will "persist" as the visible and historical witness of God's gracious condescension in Christ. That the Jews survived every attempt to "exterminate" them, that the "riddle of their existence" resists all secular explanation, that they "rise up to life" not in the Church but in the modern state of Israel—that all these "facts" confront us from the plane of history is silent testimony to the King of Israel and the providential rule of the world from its center, the people of the Elect.

This is an attractive interpretation of Barth, drawing attention to his characteristic generosity and Christian self-criticism. It demonstrates a flexibility and creativity in Barth's thought, growing from a youthful flair for the abstract to a mature tempering by the language of faith. It puts Barth's thought in motion, from the *No* to the *Yes,* a motion that repeats the divine life of grace. His deepening respect for Jews and Judaism as living realities gives powerful testimony to the significance of the concrete as a Christian and biblical mode of thought. Not least of course, this reading of Barth allows his moral commitments a complete hearing; his anti-Judaism, however forceful, does not take the upper hand. In his later years, Barth stood some risk in his repudiation of the Christian Left and its predictable and rather cheap criticism of Israel; they were, after all, his more natural allies. But it is in his war years, particularly in the terrible decade of the Weimar collapse and the rise of the Reich, that Barth's moral example stands out clearly. Barth's denunciation of anti-Semitism, his bitter contempt for the German-Christians, his theological leadership of the Confessing Church: all these signs of Christian courage during a period of Church vacillation and cunning are honored and given their full weight. I am one of Barth's admirers—it must be obvious by now!—and I am far from denigrating moral examples or theological convictions. To risk security for the sake of principle is a rare event, and Barth, though his principles are more obscure than they appear,[2] left the security and privilege of German university life at a time when many academics found new roles as collaborators.

My sympathies, that is, lie with this interpretation of Barth and I acknowledge the weight of its evidence and moral suasion. But I do not agree with it, nor do I think it captures the texture of reality—the complexity, ambivalence, and depth of Barth's hard-won "doctrine of Israel." No theological position is straightforward in Barth; simplicity was not his hallmark. But consistency

2. Barth's correspondence at the time of the university loyalty oath and the so-called Dehn affair reveal the ambiguity and complexity of most human decisions made under fire. Helmut Gollwitzer recounts his memories of Barth's reluctant compromise with it in his essay, "The Kingdom of God and Socialism," in Hunsinger, ed., *Karl Barth and Radical Politics*. As Gollwitzer remarks, Barth's political positions were often difficult to determine and open to several interpretations. Barth's letter to von Soden and Bultmann tell of conflicting reactions to the loyalty oath, that he might have signed it under certain conditions, and that it might have ambivalent content (*Karl Barth–Rudolf Bultmann Letters, 1922–1966*, ed. Bernd Jaspert, trans. G. W. Bromiley [Grand Rapids, Mich.: William Eerdmans, 1981], 78–80, 133–39). Barth refused to sign—that is the point; and had he signed, he would have been forced to resign by the late 1930s—that much is clear. But the details of history are rarely kind to sentimentality and to the romance of great deeds of great clarity—that is the point too. Aside from Barth's correspondence, much material on these controversies can be had in Arthur Cochrane, *The Church's Confession under Hitler* (Philadelphia: Westminster, 1962), Martin Niemöller, *Wort und Tat im Kirchenkampf* (Marburg, 1967), and Eberhard Busch, *Karl Barth*.

As these books illustrate, opposition to the Reich and to German-Christianity arose from several motivations, as the documents from Barmen testify. It is easy to attribute an opposition to anti-Semitism to all opponents of the Reich, but this I think serves modern apologetic ends rather than historical accuracy. In the "Fundamentals" of *Church Opposition 1933*, in his *The German Church Conflict*, trans. P.T.A. Parker (Richmond, Va.: John Knox Press), pp. 16, 17, Karl Barth explicitly rejects opposition based upon the "heresy" of the "Aryan paragraph," the "rejection of the Old Testament," and the "Aryanism of German Christian Christology"; rather, Barth directs the attention of the Pastor's Emergency League to the "single source of all German-Christian errors," its "second source of revelation *beside* the Holy Scripture." This may be the foundation of any theological protest against a totalitarian regime, but it is not a protest based upon the enormity of race hatred, and the two very different motivations, though clearly tied together, should not be confused or collapsed, one into the other.

of a certain kind is. The one Object of theology, the living Christ, dominates Barth's vision from beginning to end, deepening, enriching and broadening the center of Christian dogmatics. A living Center cannot be static—Barth made much of this point—and I do not mean to impose a scholastic unity upon Barth's work. Instead, I argue that Barth in his early reaction to Liberalism brought together the doctrine of revelation with the Protestant principle of justification by faith, the "faithfulness of God," and this powerful fusion of Christological revelation with the sovereignty of grace never diminished in strength or lost its twofold identity. That God's revelation in Christ speaks a free and gracious word is a doctrine that shapes Barth's understanding of election and of sin and reconciliation, and governs his interpretation of the biblical text. In his doctrine of Israel, Barth draws together the history of the Jews, and their preparation for the life and work of Jesus in such a way that divine wrath and free grace are the two movements of God toward his creatures, at once suffered and enacted in Christ. The second volume of the *Church Dogmatics,* in the massive reformulation of the doctrine of election, devotes itself to this union of Christ and gracious judgment. But the *Epistle to the Romans,* though less explicit and concise, presents both Jews and Judaism as historical types and fulfillments of the divine wrath that leads to mercy. This interpretation of Barth, the "argument from consistency," is the conclusion, less sentimental and less attractive, that I hope to advance here.

That Barth was tough-minded about Jews can scarcely be debated; as with most topics, Barth spoke his mind about the "Jewish question," and it is a Christian polemic of unflinching character. Prodded by Rosemary Ruether, Gregory Baum asks whether Christianity is inherently anti-Judaic;[3] if Barth represents the Christianity in view, the answer must be a ringing yes. This answer, the unmistakeable conclusion from Barth's positions, confirms Ruether's second hypothesis as well, that Christian anti-Judaism—and, though less likely, anti-Semitism—rests on the premise of "realized eschatology." Ruether argues that the early Christian confession of Jesus of Nazareth as the Messiah, the fulfillment of the eschatological age, split the Jesus movement from its Jewish origin and set them on separate and rival paths. Had the Church preserved the "thoroughgoing eschatology" of the earliest New Testament tradition, Ruether argues, recognizing in Jesus the one who will be named Messiah in the final days, Judaism may have found in this Jesus-sect a companionable or at least tolerable minority. In more doctrinal terms, we might say that the orthodox affirmation of the Trinity gave birth to Christianity, an independent and often vigorously anti-Judaic institution and system of

3. Ruether, *Faith and Fratricide,* 8.

thought. That this must be so—that Christianity entails the repudiation of Judaism—is not my argument here, and many Christians are now at work demonstrating that such an argument cannot stand.[4] But if Barth is the theologian in view, and if his dogmatic interpretation of the task of theology is accepted, Judaism will find its criticism, its honor, and its fulfillment in the Christian proclamation of Jesus as the Christ of Israel. This is hardly the gospel of tolerance or of world religions and it scarcely needs repeating that Barth liked things that way. Our task, rather, is to follow the internal logic of Barth's dogmatic position, to discover how the affirmation of Christ as the beginning of all God's ways and works upholds, rebukes, and transforms the existence and the election of the people Israel.

My argument in brief is this: that Barth's position has demanded a sustained critique of Judaism; and that from his break with Liberalism to his mature period, Barth's anti-Judaism has reflected his unwavering commitment to the doctrine of justification by grace through faith alone.

Of course, such an argument, so briefly stated, will raise protests from those who know Barth well—and rightly so. Did not Berkouwer point out the precise place where Barth finds the justification doctrine "a problem"?[5] And does not Barth himself complain about the doctrine's one-sidedness, its monopoly on Protestant dogmatics, its divisive part in the history of the Church? And, with these critics, should we not lodge protests of our own? Does not the doctrine of reconciliation move into the center of Barth's mature thought—as Hans Frei has noted[6]—driving out the remnants of justification from his early work? In fact, and more pointedly: has not Barth's career, from beginning to end, shown a pronounced distaste for the center-pieces of culture-Protestantism, from the rise of "faith" to the liberty of the "justified"? His insistence upon the "vacuum of faith"—a phrase from the early days, emphatically repeated in the *Dogmatics*, 4.1; his contempt for the bourgeois confidence of the justified; his sharp polemic against a domesti-cated doctrine of sin: all these attacks upon the high ground of "relational theology" make Barth a poor advocate for the primacy of the justification

4. No footnote could do justice to the breadth and vigor of this debate within Christian theology and exegesis. Paul van Buren has testified to the vitality of this task in his *A Theology of the Jewish-Christian Reality* (San Francisco: Harper & Row, 1980–88). This question, he writes, brought him back to theology and, in a barthian note, to its "special theme."

5. G. C. Berkouwer, *The Triumph of Grace in the Theology of Karl Barth* (Grand Rapids, Mich.: William Eerdmans, 1956), chap. 5.

6. Frei argues that in Barth's mature thought reconciliation has replaced revelation as the central doctrine ("Barth and Schleiermacher: Divergence and Convergence," in Duke and Streetman, eds., *Barth and Schleiermacher*, 65–88).

doctrine. Indeed, his interpretation of Calvin and Luther[7] suggests that he considered sanctification of equal weight to justification and, in sound dogmatics, inseparable.

These are serious protests, by serious protesters, and my concluding argument must wait for some response. There can be no question that Barth rejects the doctrine of justification by faith alone as it was repristinated and elevated by the Lutheran and Reformed traditions. Its commanding presence within Protestant Liberalism, especially in the elegant dress of faith-experience, only serves to strengthen Barth's rejection. In Barth's *Dogmatics* neither justification nor faith can retain the meaning that they once assumed: only the form of this doctrine, the motion of divine turning toward the creature, the shape of free, divine condescension can remain. Once again, Barth will take up the *loci* of the tradition and see in them the impress of revelation— not in their particular content perhaps, but in their shape alone does Barth find witness to God's self-revelation. Or their doctrinal content he may preserve within another form, one conformed to its Object, and ordered to its End. In the doctrine of justification by faith, Barth stands ready to empty much of its traditional content. Unlike many other Protestant legacies, the justification doctrine does not receive the loving conservation and energetic reworking Barth devoted to the doctrines of predestination or providence. His treatment of its history and its controversies shows Barth seized by a rare irenic spirit, and he seems wearied by the ceaseless efforts of Protestant polemicists to establish justification as *"the* Word of Gospel."[8] In fact, "even a cursory glance at the problem reveals the particular difficulty of the doctrine. The sweet fruit is here found in a shell which is unusually hard and bitter."[9] Hardly congenial stuff to a sturdy Reformed critic like Berkouwer! But Barth's hesitancy before the "problems" of justification, his moderating voice, and his odd reticence should not lead us to a conclusion foreign to Barth's intention. He intends, I think, to strengthen the form the doctrine of justification lays upon dogmatics, to strengthen it by weakening its customary supports.

Consider Barth's opening appeal:

> The task of the doctrine of justification is to demonstrate the right-eousness of God which overrules in the reconciling grace of God, and

---

7. In *Dogmatics,* 4.1:524–27, Barth observes that the center of Calvin's theology rests on doctrines other than justification, and that Luther—read correctly!—holds that the "whole Gospel" joins sanctification to justification as Barth himself does.

8. *Dogmatics,* 4.1:521.

9. Ibid., 518–19.

the grace of God which truly and actually overrules in the righteousness of God. It is the task of finding a reliable answer to the question: What is God for sinful man? and what is sinful man before the God who is for him? The basis of the community and the certainty of faith stands or falls with the answer to this question. The doctrine of justification undertakes to answer the question of this presupposition. Hence its importance and theological necessity.[10]

Characteristically, Barth transforms a question of pious experience into a dogmatic proclamation about God, and God's righteousness over sinners. No longer an investigation into the origin, experience, and saving certainty of faith, the justification doctrine is the examination of God's ways and works with creation and with rebellious creatures. It is a description—to speak with Barth's own boldness—of God's self-justification. God will justify the divine act of election, that election of the Son, and his obedient election of human flesh, by taking the creature's part and by suffering in its place. In the divine will to be with and for the creature, the Creator assumed a risk that the creature, standing on the boundary of creation, would give itself over to Chaos. In the election of the Judge to suffer judgment, God justifies that risk. The divine plan of reconciliation justifies sinners, yes; but more wonderfully, it represents and demonstrates the justification of God's sovereign being, the One who loves in freedom. The history of revelation, the time God has for the creature in covenant, is the enactment of the divine inner life, the drama of divine obedience and confirmation. The narrative of this divine self-affirmation receives doctrinal form in the teaching of justification. More than the salvation of the sinner, more than the forensic righteousness of the believer before God, the justification doctrine concerns the gracious nature and faithfulness of God. For this reason, we might more properly refer to Barth's understanding of this doctrine simply as the divine act of "justification by grace alone."

But to return: Barth's dogmatic presentation of the Jews, and of the "doctrine of Israel" portrays in historical type and event the inner coherence, direction, and legacy of the doctrine of justification by grace alone.

In dogmatic idiom, God's justifying act takes flesh in the people Israel: they are the people elected for rejection. We cannot turn aside the harsh verdict Barth declares. The Jews, elected for covenant with its King, the nation drawn close in "bands of love" before all nations, the recipients of reconciliation and gracious preservation—these Jews are irrevocably elected to wrath.

10. Ibid., 518.

For Barth, the doctrine of election assumes creaturely reality in Israel, and no work of human hands can release, supersede, or deny this election: the promises, covenant, and salvation are of the Jews. The Church deceives itself if it preens its own poor feathers as the successor to Israel, the true and solitary people of the covenant. The community of the Church, called from Jew and Gentile, shows fidelity to its commission by honoring the Jews in its midst, and humbly acknowledging the gracious tenancy of the Gentiles within the house of Israel. But the sweetness of this melody distracts us from its main theme. The Jews are honored within, and indeed outside the Church, because they are the flesh Christ judged, rejected, and condemned. The Messiah, Jesus of Nazareth, came first to the Jews because he came out of them. That Jesus was born a Jew means that Christians for all time honor the Jews as the stiff-necked, disobedient sinners for whom Christ died. Barth, too, raises up Israel as a light to the nations, but it is a light that pitilessly exposes the Jews as "vessels of wrath" through whose disbelief the Gentiles are spared.

Barth's dogmatic summary of the history of Israel, after all, may be expressed briefly, and relentlessly, by the motif of refusal: the Jews are the people who refuse their election; they are those who refuse their Messiah; they refuse their life and mercy in the Church. The long, dark history of Christian anti-Judaism can be distilled in Barth's type of the Jew—those obdurate, arrogant disbelievers. That Barth condemns anti-Semitism, that he exposes "race theories" and "race purity" for the cruel sham they are, that he "discovered Judaism for Christian theology" cannot obscure the medieval caricature that Barth evokes. The joyless ghetto, the blindfolded Synagogue, the lifeless artifact hastening toward an empty future: Barth will give voice to the some of the bitter denunciations of Luther's old age.

But Barth does not rest content with such medieval tropes. Eerily, he borrows from those he despises, the anti-Semites of the New Romanticism. In the *Epistle to the Romans* through the late *Dogmatics,* Barth evokes the cruel caricatures that corrupt European high culture: the Jews as rootless cosmopolitan, as smooth and contemptible bourgeois, as persistent volk that succeed beyond expectation or desire. The Jews of the *Römerbrief* are those who in their human possibility do for themselves, who thrive in self-satisfied and energetic moral earnestness. They are the religious people, par excellence, the sleek inheritors of social progress and noble sentiment. Against them, and against all who take shelter in them, the wrath of God breaks out, the fire of the No-God that consumes all human righteousness.

Barth has been accused of denying Jews any historical reality or particularity, treating them merely as the instruments of his larger purpose, the denunciation of culture-Protestantism. Indeed, the favorable interpretation of Barth laid out in the first part of this chapter builds its argument on just this accusation. And we cannot say this interpretation misses its mark; Barth, after all, had his teachers in mind, the generation of academic Liberals before the First World War, who nurtured him, and led him astray. But it is mistaking emphasis for argument, I think, to conclude that Barth did not also have living and historical Jews in mind. In fact, the criticism that can be raised against Barth lies in the opposite direction: not too little but too much historical particularity, too close an alignment drawn between the Jews of pauline communities and the Jews of modern Europe. Consider the "modern translations" Barth proposes: for the Law, Religion; for Jews, the Church; for works righteousness, bourgeois enlightenment. These biblical categories can be translated into modern content, in part because Jews—as their cultured despisers understood them—serve as a bridge between that time and ours. Christian teachings of contempt, both medieval and modern, invited such comparisons, and Barth implicitly—I do not think consciously—put these associations to work.

Through long centuries, the Jews have been faultless bourgeois, elegantly disobedient; Protestant Liberals have entered their ranks as the Judaizers of the modern Church. As Jews flatter themselves in European high culture, so they called Abraham their father long ago, and those who evoke religious experience as their possession merely repeat the Jews' disobedience. The Jews are the ancient and living ideals of the religious spirit, the antitype in whom the culture-Protestants are their type and replication. That Barth's critics discovered in him the threat of Marcionism, and that Barth felt the sting, pays tribute to the importance and weakness of historical continuity in the theology of *Romans*. Barth vigorously defended himself against the charge, though as I have argued, with only measured success, but his intention remains clear—to "wrestle with the whole material until the walls which separate [the present] century from the first become transparent." A major part of "the whole material" is the Jews, possessed of and by the Law, erupting time and again with "God-sickness," yet preserving and embodying the revelation of wrath. They are elected in our time and in the past to show the righteousness of God's judgment, spoken of by the prophets but rejected by this people called to love the Law.

Both early and late, then, Barth inscribes the people of the Jews with the image of those elected for rejection. They live out the twofold reality of grace: the condemnation of the righteous and the justification of the ungodly. God is free in grace; the Jews, to whom the promises came, cannot lay claim to them. God is righteous in grace; all that is not-God, all that rebels, all that loves its own life will perish. The justification that lives by faith alone lies on the far side of judgment and death. We cannot lay too strong a stress on this dogmatic proclamation: Barth's recapitulation of the history, significance, and future of the Jews lays out the depth of suffering and rejection that God exacts on those who "pass away" before divine grace. All flesh—Barth insists on this point—must take the form of those passing, turning, dying away before God's wrath; no one stands before God's judgment seat blameless. No one—but the Jews are those elected to this form, and in them, all flesh is baptized into death. That, after all, is the reality Barth calls the "riddle of Jewish existence": they are consumed by the fire of God's justice, they are the alien "no-people" of world history, oppressed and exiled, yet like the burning bush not consumed. They persist, they thrive, they show all signs of their election, even bringing into modern history the echoes of the ancient nation of Israel. Indeed, they must persist. The Jews live and flourish as the embodiment of that which must pass away, of the sinful righteousness God condemns and redeems.

From all nations, and for all time, the Jews are elected for this history of divine self-justification. To be elected means to be called to pass away, because in the counsel of divine election, God wills in Christ to die for sinful flesh. God elects to justify the divine risk of creation by taking on the rejection, the exile, the suffering death of sin, meeting human disobedience with obedience, injustice with justice, pride with humility, rebellion with grace and mercy. The Judge will be judged in our place. That this gracious exchange must take place in human time and place, that a history of covenant enacts this work of divine election demonstrates God's will to be with and take the part of the creature. The divine work of reconciliation could have taken place without human history and covenant; God is sovereign in grace. But the Bible witnesses to God's fidelity to creation, to God's turning towards it, sustaining it, again and again forgiving, using, and guiding it toward divine ends. In Christ, God elects Israel as the instantiation and representation of this sovereign work of justification and reconciliation.

This majestic act of divine condescension and justification takes place apart from merit: Israel demonstrates in its long history the virulent power of pride and self-reliance. It will be its own god and judge, taking for itself idols of its own making and tributes to its own achievements. Again and again, it hears the voice of Nothingness—Ye shall be as gods—and hands itself over to disobedience and chaos. Breaking the commandments, murdering the prophets, rejecting its Messiah: Barth brings this biblical litany to bear on the divine work of grace apart from merit. *This* particular flesh, this rebellious people, this covenant nation slave to sin—*this* disobedient creature Christ takes for his own. The journey of the Son of Man into the far country is the journey into this Israel and unto this people. Christians recognize in Jews the Church's Messiah because in them they see the truth that applies to all: the depth to which God must condescend to rescue, and the suffering Christ must endure to redeem.

But Barth's dogmatic interpretation of Israel is bolder still. The hearts of the Jews, like Pharaoh's, are hardened; in their disobedience and sin, they serve God's will. They are elected—Barth does not pull back—for rejection. In this, the Jews are far from blameless. Indeed, God's wrath against them is just and justified. But human history is ordered and directed by God's providence toward a divine end: good will be brought out of evil. Through this people of disobedience, the world will be reconciled in Christ to God. The dual nature of God's predestinating act of election shows its stern logic here. To justify the work of creation, God has determined to take the judgment for sin upon himself. In Christ, God will suffer the rejection, death, and horror that awaits the creature across the frontier of creation. Nothingness will become God's terrible instrument in this work, and the irrational destruction of evil will burn with God's wrath. In Judas, all Israel finds its head and representative. In him, they will act their part, their final, terrible work of rejection. In God's plan, they will, in Judas, hand over their Messiah to the Gentiles; and it is evil work that they do. God intends to take this evil upon himself, to be judged for what the covenant people do, but they must do it. The history of the Jews is the story of preparation for *this* act, and it is *this* betrayal that makes their flesh the sinful flesh Christ elects to assume. This is what Barth means by the "mystery of the Jews," and we must see his meaning, shorn of all sentiment and pious good will. The Jews are the "potter's clay"; they are determined for rejection, to suffer and to pass away. They cannot complain of this terrible work, this election for refusal, because God in Christ will take on their judgment, and in the final act of grace, redeem them and all flesh apart from merit. They exist so that God can reconcile the world in just this way, to die to sin in Christ and to rise to new life, justifying God's own being of love and freedom. To speak of election is to speak of Israel, and in Barth's relentless logic we can only say: it is a terrible thing to fall into the hands of the living God.

We must ask whether this must be so, whether Christian dogmatics must speak of Jews and of Israel in just this way. For Barth, the answer appears to be a clear yes. Despite Marquardt's best efforts, I think, we must say that Barth's own reaction is fitting: while impressive and accurate in its own right, Marquardt's reconstruction of Barth's *Israellehre* is oddly unrecognizable, and does not show its maker's hand. The *Church Dogmatics* is irreconcilably anti-Judaic—though not anti-Semitic—because the actualism of Barth's theology demands it. The victorious Christ lives: that is Barth's biblical expression of the crisis of Revelation, joining in unbroken line the early impress of the Blumhardts and the late, dogmatic exposition of the resurrection. All creation, all human history is caught up in this "moment" of resurrection, this mighty act of God when Jesus obeys the will of the Father, turning from death, and receiving life. Every historical period, from this time of revelation forward, is witness to this sovereign, divine motion of turning, of passing away, and rising up to life. *Now* is Christ risen, Barth stresses, *now* is the time between the times, when the old is gathered up and hastens towards its completion. In this time left to us, we creatures are "on the way," pilgrims drawn from "here to there." We are caught up in this act of turning over, still flesh, still sinful, still enslaved to death, but rising, waking, following this way to resurrection in Christ. The vigorous dynamism in Barth's thought, his masterful actualism breathes life into doctrine, and animates every theological creature with lively purpose. It is one of Barth's great gifts to theology, and alone makes the *Dogmatics* a living word to the Church. But it is not a free gift. The cost to Christian understanding and interpretation of Judaism is high, far higher than students like Marquardt wish to acknowledge. The past, after all—the history of world-occurrence and of revelation—can never be fully left behind. All is gathered up in this act of Christ, repeated, preserved, made new in each time and place. God's justifying work of grace, the beginning and end of all God's ways and works, is the event that dominates our time, the time God has for us. The Church must hear time and again the judgment that breaks out over sinful flesh; it must find itself over and over dying to this rebellion. Looking to Christ, it must see the victory over evil that will be poured out and tasted in the last days. But it can only see these acts of death and victory by turning toward the God of the Bible, the King of Israel. The great revelation of grace takes place in Israel and for its sake, and it will not cease or leave the appointed place. For all human time, the Jews must live out their election to be this flesh, condemned and passing away. Whether within or outside the Church, Jews are permanent sentinels, witnessing to judgment, and they cannot leave their post. The Church needs this witness, Barth writes, and the Jews will give it, whether in the "gruesome relic of the Synagogue" or the community of the Church. They are disobedient flesh—as all human beings are—but they are marked for this work, a mark of Cain, and in oppression and exile, they will be sustained to show forth this mark to the nations. Of course, Barth does not teach that Jews are lost souls, unredeemed and unredeemable: All flesh is reconciled in Christ. But they cannot be released from the work they were called, gathered, and are still appointed to do: to embody the rebellion that enlists every creature, and to exhibit the Jew that claimed victory over the rebellion, reconciling the world apart from merit, in the fullness of grace. That, Barth teaches, is the terrible majesty of grace, the living, twofold form of election, the inner meaning and coherence of the fact that Jesus was born a Jew. The motion, direction, and purpose of all creation, to journey from judgment to mercy, from rebellion to obedience, from wrath to sovereign grace, is typified, prefigured, and enacted in the history of the Jews. They are the covenant people of the King of Israel, "closed up in disobedience," "hardened in disbelief," that God may have grace on all.

Thus far, Barth. But we must ask whether the Christian form of every theology, the pattern of sin and gracious redemption, does not entail an anti-Judaism of this kind. The recent efforts to recircumscribe the Christian drama, making of "two covenants" only one, binding Christianity up into Judaism, appear to offer an escape from this unwanted conclusion.[11] But Christian theology, I think, will have a more difficult and painful time extricating itself from this pattern than these solutions seem to suggest. Brevard Childs has drawn our attention to the canonical shaping of the Christian Bible, and the irrepressible Christian stamp tradition has applied to the common scriptures, making of the Hebrew Bible the Christian Old Testament.[12] Childs vividly draws together this tradition: the pattern of promise and fulfillment; the prophetic warning of judgment on Israel's sins; the history of exile and destruction the Deuteronomist records in Christian eyes; the faithful remnant of Israel restored in the Church; and the Christological interpretation of the Law and prophets. This overarching form, joining together the two testaments, poses more stubborn obstacles than the anti-Judaism of the New. The most ready "teachings of contempt" spring from the

11. For arguments in support of "one covenant in two forms," see A. Roy Eckardt, *Elder and Younger Brothers* (New York: Charles Scribner's Sons, 1967), and van Buren's "Christ in Context," vol. 3 of *A Theology of the Jewish-Christian Reality*. In chapter 6.2, van Buren writes: "It seems best to say that there is the one eternal covenant between God and the Jewish people, that Jesus is portrayed by the Apostolic Writings as standing within that covenant, and that His Church is invited to hold onto him as its way into discovering the gift of the love of God and the claim upon them to love all whom God loves—a gift and claim that are certainly expressed for Israel in the covenant but which for the church find its formulation in Jesus' summary of (itself a quotation from) the Torah (147). But van Buren does not hold the line entirely; other, covenantal language can be used for the Church as well: "The calling of Jesus was, of course, fully in the line of and coherent with the calling of Abraham and the calling of Israel. But it was unlike any other calling in that its response opened the new chapter in the history of the covenant that came to be called the Church" (228).

12. Brevard Childs, "The Hebrew Scriptures and the Christian Bible," in *Introduction to the Old Testament as Scripture* (Philadelphia: Fortress Press, 1979), chap. 44, pp. 659–71.

New Testament—the "crime" of "Christ-killing"; the "externality" and "legalism" of the pharisees; and the terrible divine verdict pronounced in the destruction of Jerusalem and the Temple. These "teachings" have been addressed, and in part redressed, in the remarkable document of Vatican II, *Nostra Aetate*. In my judgment, the recognition that Jesus "came to his own," made disciples, enemies, and reformers of Jews like himself—a point indelibly made by Barth—can mitigate and perhaps resolve the unmistakable criticism of Jews within the New Testament. But the canonical work of Christian theology, the traditional mandate to reconcile and incorporate the Old and New Testament, presents a complex of benefits and burdens that will not be easily put down. Friedrich Marquardt has claimed that the final "open wound" in the one people of God is the dispute over the interpretation of the Old Testament.[13] This debate breaks open from time to time, and is indeed a painful one. But I think the controversy runs deeper.

What are Christians, and Christian theology, to do about the biblical witness to Israel, the somber and majestic foreshadowing between the Testaments, and the emergence of rabbinic Judaism, the Church's contemporary in the first years of the common era? Does Christian theology concern itself with Jews and Judaism, with Israel and its prophets and judges, and with the God Barth calls the King of Israel? What does it mean for theology that Jesus was born a Jew, and that Judaism "receives him not"? Two narrowing barriers hem in Christian thought on either side. A form of Liberalism leans in from one side to assign to Jews and Judaism the form of a religion, and set it free from Christian concern—and Christians from obligation or homage. A crude and vigorous anti-Judaism leans in from the other side to dismiss this "chosen people" as the disobedient disbelievers they have been since the days of Aaron and the golden calf. It is just this two-sided attitude of deference and contempt in Christian doctrine that I have called the "obsession" of Christian theology with Judaism. The ambivalence of this attention, its giving and taking away, its recognition at a cost marks this question as a love troubled by intimacy and odd forgetfulness. Shall Christian theology remember its origin, and can it honor this living past?

As one committed to the tradition and complexity of Christian theology, I cannot envision a ready escape from this irresistible, critical and honorable obsession with Judaism. As an admirer of Barth, one who has learned time and again of the patience, precision, and beauty of dogmatic work, I acknowledge the inner coherence and rigorous logic of this traditional, Christian response. I have been led to see that theology must assert its dogmatic

13. Marquardt, *Die Entdeckung des Judentums,* 359–60.

claims, obey its truths with tough-minded readiness, and walk in this path until better instructed. Those who have tasted the bittersweet fruit of Barth's theological passion cannot rest easy with anything less. But some doors, I am convinced, are closed. The stern majesty of Barth's position cannot remain untouched. Christian theology, better instructed by the sharp reality of our time and place, must turn away from some positions and some claims permanently.

The teachings of contempt; the crude mythologies of race and *Volk;* the more genteel savageries of secret envy and attack upon the bourgeois, the civilized, the urban, those familiar code-words for Jews; the cheap and ready critique from the Left: these doors, some standing open in Barth, must close. This much can be said, and while it is critical for theology to expressly say these things, they are close at hand, and easily said. The labor of a Christian theological response to Judaism, the work that Paul van Buren and others have undertaken, remains the difficult task ahead. The detailed effort to take Barth's dogmatic interpretation of Israel seriously, however, may yield some good fruit along the way.

In my judgment, a positive Christian theology of Judaism must begin by acknowledging the irreconcilable and ineradicable differences that lie between Christianity and Judaism. These must not be bemoaned or tragically borne, but simply and directly acknowledged and accepted. Christianity and Judaism—and Christian theology should not shrink before that term, Judaism—these two communities of faith face each other as different systems, different ways of life and thought, with separate rituals and ideals, separate historical forces and realities at work. They share a common set of texts, though sharply divided in interpretation, canonical form and order, and use within religious teaching and authority. They share, too, a common history of interaction; of engagement, controversy, and withdrawal; of persecution and suffering; of Christian pogroms and Jewish survival and exile. But these events that tie Christianity and Judaism together, events at times of deep Christian shame, should not blind theology to the permanent division between these two traditions.

The reality and memory of the past separates Christian and Jewish experience, and theology that takes the "Holocaust" as a datum for Christian thought runs the risk of subsuming Judaism once again under the categories of Christian doctrine and experience. In the same way, though of course in differing world views, the generous effort to combine Christianity and Judaism under the accommodating rubrics of two "types of faith" or two "types of peoples" endangers the conflicting, competing and independent realities of these two traditions. Or again, the Christian confidence that

Judaism and Christianity form a single covenant, one engrafted in the other, or one through Christ received into the other diminishes the sharp disagreements and polemics that lie at the heart of these two realities. Christian theology must acknowledge and accept these differences, rather than attempt to wish them away either in pious sentimentality or dogmatic certainty. Barth's ready admission that he "did not have time" for the study of Judaic thought merely confirms the suspicion that Christians do not wish to understand the integrity and difference of Judaism apart from Christian interpretation, nor do they consider it necessary. That door—the door of willful ignorance and confident self-satisfaction—must close. If Christian theology is to develop a doctrine of Judaism, it must know its object, in its resemblance to Christianity, but also in its ineradicable difference.

From the perspective of an outsider in fact, an observer or scholar, Judaism and Christianity would be most congenially understood as two separate religions, and should be spoken of in that way. They are not "Abrahamic monotheisms" or "traditions of the ancient near-East"; rabbinic Judaism and Christianity are religious systems, integrated and coherent under their own principles, and should be accorded that quiet dignity.

But to the insider, the participant in Christian life and thought, theology might speak of Christianity and Judaism as "doublets," two identities separate yet mirroring each other, reflecting the rich biblical idiom of Barth's dogmatic exegesis. Theology must not say that Judaism alone is a doublet of Christianity, or that Judaism merely prefigures or anticipates Christianity, its fulfillment and perfection. Judaism *and* Christianity are doublets; they reflect and distort each other, both preserving and transforming the other. Both stand before the other, seeing in its double itself—a shock of recognition— and another, a stranger and infidel. The names Christianity and Judaism share, the place names, the figures, the events of Israel, broadcast as Michael Wyschogrod so hauntingly evokes across the country, on rural backroads, on all-night Christian radio:[14] these common points of biblical speech and tradition make doublets of these two religions. But doublets are not identities; they are not sublated, united, or reduced to one reality.

As doublets, Christianity and Judaism retain their separate identities; like the doublets of the Bible, these two traditions lead separate lives and pursue their private ends. But more: the biblical doublets have historical particularity and concreteness. They are doublets because of, not despite, their discontinuities. The Christian study and appropriation of Judaic life and thought does

14. Wyschogrod, "Why Was and Is the Theology of Karl Barth of Interest to a Jewish Theologian?" in *Footnotes to a Theology,* 96–97.

not necessarily entail a "second source" for theology, apart from and beside the Bible. Barth's somber warning can be heeded, I think, while allowing and in fact mandating a theological recognition of an independent Judaism. Because Judaism and Christianity are doublets, their differences as well as their commonalities rise up out of the life and authority of scripture. They are both responses to this one book, and the failure to accept this fact will lead Christian theology to repeat, in unbroken and offensive chorus, the medieval and dogmatic Christian caricatures of Judaism as Barth did. But this obedience to a "second word" of Scripture does not require a sentimental truce on either side.

Christian theology must recognize in Judaism an order and an organization of biblical idiom and response that evokes but competes with its own. As a doublet of Judaism, Christianity, too, must recognize in its own language and life, a reflection of Judaism that differs and conflicts with its own claims and practice. From the position of insider, the location Barth calls the position of faith, Christianity and Judaism will speak of the other with recognition but with criticism and rebuke, as well. The charges of paganism, of corrupted monotheism, of sentimentality about neighbor love—these rebukes lodged at Christianity from the inner identity of Judaism must be allowed their voice, and their truth tested and controverted. So too, the Christian claims to the Old Testament, the evocation of the Messiah in the Law and the Prophets, the insistence on original sin and salvation apart from merit—these criticisms lodged at Judaism must be recognized as internal and, I think, inherent to the Christian position, and their truth, too, must be weighed and brought to trial. These doublets of identity and difference must speak their own language, and walk in their own ways, each confirming that the One God has time and space for us, each created realities that in the divine plan reflect the complex, rich, and inexhaustible Reality that pours out life and spirit on all flesh.

In the *Israellehre* of Karl Barth, in the mastery, power, and elegant description of the one community of God in Christ, Christian theology can look forward and back, taking up into its doctrinal thought the weight, significance, and gracious condescension of its Messiah, Jesus, born a Jew, and straining ahead to grasp the mystery of the two forms of Israel and the Church, each called and created by God, each determined for its own task, and each waiting in its own place for that one day when God will be all in all.

BIBLIOGRAPHY

Auerbach, Erich. *Mimesis: The Representation of Reality in Western Literature*. Translated by Willard R. Trask. Princeton: Princeton University Press, 1953.

Barth, Karl. *Ad Limina Apostolorum*. Translated by K. R. Crim. Richmond, Va.: John Knox Press, 1968.

———. *Briefe, 1961–1968*. Vol. 5 of Gesamtausgabe. Edited by J. Fangemeier and H. Stoevesant. Zurich: Theologischer Verlag, 1975.

———. *Final Testimonies*. Edited by E. Busch. Translated by G. W. Bromiley. Grand Rapids, Mich.: William Eerdmans, 1977.

———. *Den Gefangenen Befreiung: Predigten, 1954–1959*. Zurich: Theologischer Verlag, 1975.

———. *The German Church Conflict*. Vol 1. of *Ecumenical Studies in History*. Translated by P.T.A. Parker. Richmond, Va.: John Knox Press, 1965.

———. *Gesammelte Vorträge*. Vol 2, *Die Theologie und die Kirche*. Vol. 3, *Theologische Fragen und Antworten*. Zurich: Evangelischer Verlag Zöllikon, 1957.

———. *God in Action*. Translated by Elmer G. Homrighausen and Thomas Keenan. Introduction by Elmer G. Homrighausen. Manhasset, N.Y.: Round Table Press, 1963.

———. *Der Götze Wackelt: Zeitkritische Aufsätze, Reden, und Briefe von 1930 bis 1960*. Edited by K. Kupisch. Berlin: Käthe Vogt Verlag, 1961. Translated by R. G. Smith as *Against the Stream: Shorter Post-War Writings, 1946–1952*. New York: Philosophical Library, 1954.

———. *Jesus und das Volk*. Zurich: Evangelischer Verlag Zöllikon, 1944.

———. "Die Judenfrage und ihre christliche Beantwortung." *Judaica* 6 (1952): 67–72.

———. *Kirchliche Dogmatik*. Zurich: Evangelischer Verlag Zöllikon, 1932–70. Translated under the editorial oversight of G. W. Bromiley and T. F. Torrance as *The Church Dogmatics*. Edinburgh: T. and T. Clark, 1936–69.

——. *Die Menschlichkeit Gottes*. Theologische Studien 48. Zurich: Evangelischer Verlag, 1956. Translated by John Newton Thomas as *The Humanity of God*. Atlanta: John Knox Press, 1960.

——. *Natural Theology*. Translated by Peter Fraenkel. London: Geoffrey Bles, Centenary Press, 1946.

——. *Die protestantische Theologie im 19. Jahrhundert. Ihre Vorgeschichte und ihre Geschichte*. Second edition. Zurich: Evangelischer Verlag Zöllikon, 1972. Published in English as *Protestant Theology in the Nineteenth Century. Its Background and History*. London: S.C.M. Press, 1972.

——. *Der Römerbrief*. Erste Fassung, 1919. Edited by Hermann Schmidt. Reprinted as vol. 2 of *Gesamtausgabe*. Zurich: Theologischer Verlag, 1985.

——. *Der Römerbrief, 1922*. Edited by Hermann Schmidt. Zurich: Theologischer Verlag, 1940. Translated by Edwyn C. Hoskyns as *The Epistle to the Romans*. London: Oxford University Press, 1933.

——. *Texte zur Barmer Erklärung*. Zurich: Theologischer Verlag, 1984.

——. "La Théologie, le Monde et la Vie: Entretien à la Télévision avec Georges Casalis." *Reforme*, 30 May 1964.

——. *The Theology of Schleiermacher: Lectures at Göttingen, Winter Semester of 1923/24*. Edited by D. Ritschl. Translated by G. W. Bromiley. Grand Rapids, Mich.: William Eerdmans, 1977.

——. *Das Wort Gottes und die Theologie*. Munich: Christian Kaiser Verlag, 1924. Translated by D. Horton as *The Word of God and the Word of Man*. New York: Harper & Row, 1957.

——. *Zum Kirchenkampf*. Munich: Christian Kaiser Verlag, 1956.

——, Jean Daniélou, and Reinhold Niebuhr. *Amsterdamer Fragen und Antworten*. Special issue of *Theologische Existenz—NF 15*. Munich: Christian Kaiser Verlag, 1949.

——, and Gerhard Kittel. *Ein theologischer Briefwechsel*. Stuttgart: Verlag von W. Kohlhammer, 1934.

Barth, Markus. *Ephesians*. Vols. 34 and 34a in the Anchor Bible Series. New York: Doubleday Anchor, 1974.

Berkouwer, G. C. *The Triumph of Grace in the Theology of Karl Barth*. Grand Rapids, Mich.: William Eerdmans, 1977.

Bock, Paul. *Signs of the Kingdom: A Ragaz Reader*. Grand Rapids, Mich.: William Eerdmans, 1984.

Borowitz, Eugene. "Anti-Semitism and the Christologies of Barth, Berkouwer, and Pannenberg." *Dialogue* 16 (Winter 1977): 38–41.

——. *Contemporary Christologies: A Jewish Response*. New York: Paulist Press, 1980.

Bouillard, Henri. *Karl Barth: Parole de Dieu et Existence Humaine*. Aubier: Editions Montaigne, 1957.

Bouwsma, William J. *John Calvin: A Sixteenth-Century Portrait*. New York: Oxford University Press, 1988.

Bromiley, G. W. *An Introduction to the Theology of Karl Barth*. Grand Rapids, Mich.: William Eerdmans, 1984.

Browarzik, Ulrich. *Glauben und Denken: Dogmatische Forschung zwischen der Transzendentaltheologie Karl Rahners und der Offenbarungstheologie Karl Barths*. Berlin: Verlag Walter de Gruyter, 1970.

Buber, Martin. "Das Judentum und die Juden." In *Reden über das Judentum*. Berlin: Schocken Verlag, 1932.

Buess, Eduard. *Zur Prädestinationslehre Karl Barths.* Zurich: Evangelischer Verlag, 1955.

Busch, Eberhard. *Karl Barth: His Life from Letters and Autobiographical Texts.* Translated by J. Bowden. Philadelphia: Fortress Press, 1976.

————, J. Fangemeier, and M. Geiger, eds. *Parrhesia: Karl Barth zum achtzigsten Geburtstag.* Zurich: Evangelischer Verlag, 1966.

Calvin, John. *Institutes of the Christian Religion.* Edited by J. T. McNeil. Translated by F. L. Battles. Philadelphia: Westminster Press, 1960.

Casalis, George. *Portrait of Karl Barth.* Translated by Robert McAfee Brown. Garden City, N.Y.: Doubleday, 1963.

Childs, Brevard. *Introduction to the Old Testament as Scripture.* Philadelphia: Fortress Press, 1979.

Cochrane, Arthur. *The Church's Confession under Hitler.* Philadelphia: Westminster Press, 1962.

Cohen, Hermann. *Der Begriff der Religion im System der Philosophie.* Giessen: Alfred Töpelmann, 1915.

————. *Religion der Vernunft aus den Quellen des Judentums.* Second edition. Frankfurt am Main: J. Kauffmann, 1929. Edited and translated by S. Kaplan as *Religion of Reason out of the Sources of Judaism.* New York: Felix Ungar, 1972.

Collingwood, R. G. *The Idea of History.* London: Oxford University Press, 1956.

Croner, Helga. *Stepping Stones to Jewish-Christian Relations: An Unabridged Collection of Christian Documents.* New York: Paulist Press, 1977.

Dantine, W., and K. Luthi, eds. *Theologie zwischen Gestern und Morgen: Interpretationen und Anfragen zum Werk Karl Barths.* Munich: Christian Kaiser Verlag, 1968.

Davies, W. D. *Paul and Rabbinic Judaism: Some Rabbinic Elements in Pauline Theology.* Philadelphia: Fortress Press, 1980.

Dawidowicz, Lucy. *The War against the Jews, 1933–1945.* New York: Holt, Rinehart, and Winston, 1975.

Dibelius, Otto. *Die Verantwortung der Kirche.* Berlin: Kranzverlag, 1931.

Dietrich, Wendell S. *Cohen and Troeltsch: Ethical Monotheistic Religion and Theory of Culture.* Chico, Calif.: Scholars Press, 1986.

Dowey, Edward. *"John Calvin." Journal of the American Academy of Religion* 57, no. 4 (Winter 1989): 845–48.

Duke, J. O., and R. R. Streetman, eds. *Barth and Schleiermacher: Beyond the Impasse?* Philadelphia: Fortress Press, 1988.

Eckardt, A. Roy. *Elder and Younger Brothers.* New York: Charles Scribner's Sons, 1967.

Elert, Werner. *Law and Gospels.* Philadelphia: Fortress Press, 1967.

"Erklärung zur zagorsker Verlautbarung der christlichen Friedenskonferenz." *Junge Kirche* 28 (1967): 504–5.

Fisher, Simon. *Revelatory Positivism? Barth's Earliest Theology and the Marburg School.* London: Oxford University Press, 1988.

Flannery, Austin P., ed. *Documents of Vatican II.* Grand Rapids, Mich.: William Eerdmans, 1984.

Fleischner, Eva. *Judaism in German Christian Theology since 1945: Christianity and Israel Considered in Terms of Mission.* ATLA Monograph Series, no. 8. Metuchen, N.J.: Scarecrow Press, 1975.

Ford, David. *Barth and God's Story: Biblical Narrative and the Theological Method of Karl Barth in the Church Dogmatics.* Frankfurt: Verlag Peter Lang, 1981.

Franz Rosenzweig zum 25. Dezember 1926: Glückwünsche zum 40. Geburtstag. Reprint. New York: Leo Baeck Institute, 1987.

Frei, Hans. "The Doctrine of Revelation in the Thought of Karl Barth, 1909 to 1922: The Nature of Barth's Break with Liberalism." Ph.D. dissertation, Yale University, 1956.

———. *The Eclipse of Biblical Narrative.* New Haven: Yale University Press, 1974.

Frey, Rudolf, E. Wolf, and Christian von Kirschbaum. *Antwort: Karl Barth zum siebzigsten Geburtstag am 10. Mai 1956.* Zurich: Evangelischer Verlag, 1956.

Gay, Peter. *Weimar Culture: The Outsider as Insider.* New York: Harper & Row, 1968.

Geiger, Abraham. *Judaism and Its History.* Lanham, Md.: University Press of America, 1985.

Geis, Robert Raphael, and Hans-Joachim Kraus. *Versuche des Verstehens. Dokumente jüdisch-christlicher Begegnungen aus den Jahren 1918–1933.* Vol. 33 of *Systematische Theologie.* Munich: Christian Kaiser Verlag, 1966.

Glatzer, Nahum. *Franz Rosenzweig: His Life and Thought.* New York: Schocken Books, 1961.

Gollwitzer, Helmut. *Vietnam, Israel, und die Christenheit.* Munich: Christian Kaiser Verlag, 1967.

———, Rolf Rendtorff, and Nathan P. Levinson. *Thema: Juden-Christen-Israel.* Stuttgart: Radius Verlag, 1978.

"Guidelines on Religious Relations with the Jews." Vatican Commission for Religious Relations with the Jews, 1975.

Gunton, Colin E. *Becoming and Being: The Doctrine of God in Charles Hartshorne and Karl Barth.* London: Oxford University Press, 1978.

Harnack, Adolf. *History of Dogma.* 1900. Reprint. New York: Dover Publications, 1961.

Hausmann, W. J. *Barth's Doctrine of Election.* New York: Philosophical Library, 1969.

Hegel, Georg Wilhelm Friedrich. *Lectures on the Philosophy of Religion.* Edited and translated by Peter Hodgson, R. F. Brown, and J. M. Steward, and assisted by H. S. Harris. Berkeley and Los Angeles: University of California Press, 1988.

Heyer, R. *Jewish-Christian Relations.* New York: Paulist Press, 1974.

Hunsinger, George, ed. and trans. *Karl Barth and Radical Politics.* Philadelphia: Westminster Press, 1976.

"Introduction to Theology: Questions to and Discussions with Dr. Karl Barth." *Criterion* 1963, no. 1 (Winter): 3–11, 18–24.

Isaac, Jules. *The Teachings of Contempt: Christian Roots of Anti-Semitism.* New York: Holt, Rinehart, and Winston, 1964.

"Der israelisch-arabische Konflikt." *Junge Kirche* 28 (1967): 453–54.

Jenson, R. W. *Alpha and Omega: A Study in the Theology of Karl Barth.* Nashville, Tenn.: Thomas Nelson and Sons, 1963.

———. *God after God: The God of the Future and the God of the Past Seen in the Theology of Karl Barth.* Indianapolis: Bobbs-Merrill, 1969.

Juden-Christen-Judenchristen: Ein Ruf an die Christenheit. Herausgegeben vom Schweizerischen Evangelischen Hilfswerk für die Bekennende Kirche in Deutschland. Zurich: Verlag der Evangelischen Buchhandlung Zöllikon, 1939.

Jülicher, Adolf. *The Beginnings of Dialectical Theology.* Edited by James Robinson. Translated by K. R. Crim and L. DeGrazia. Richmond, Va.: John Knox Press, 1968.

Jüngel, Eberhard. *Barth Studien.* Zurich: Benziger Verlag, 1982.

———. *Gottes Sein ist im Werden.* Tubingen: J.C.B. Mohr, Paul Siebeck, 1986. Trans-

lated by Horton Harris as *God's Being Is in Becoming*. Grand Rapids, Mich.:
William Eerdmans, 1976.

———. *Karl Barth: A Theological Legacy*. Translated by G. E. Paul. Philadelphia:
Westminster Press, 1986.

Kant, Immanuel. *Religion within the Limits of Reason Alone*. 1793. Translated by
Theodore M. Greene and Hoyt H. Hudson. New York: Harper & Row, 1960.

"Karl Barth: A Memorial Symposium." *Reflection* 66, no. 4 (May 1969): 3–12.

Karl Barth–Rudolf Bultmann Letters, 1922–1966. Edited by Bernd Jaspert. Translated
by G. W. Bromiley. Grand Rapids, Mich.: William Eerdmans, 1981.

Karl Barth's Table Talk. Edited by John Godsey. Richmond, Va.: John Knox Press, 1963.

Kelsey, David. *The Uses of Scripture in Recent Theology*. Philadelphia: Fortress Press,
1975.

Kierkegaard, Søren. *Philosophical Fragments*. Translated and edited by H. Hong and
E. Hong. Princeton: Princeton University Press, 1985.

Klappert, Bertolt. *Israel und die Kirche: Erwägungen zur Israellehre Karl Barths*.
Munich: Christian Kaiser Verlag, 1980.

Klein, Charlotte. *Anti-Judaism in Christian Theology*. Philadelphia: Fortress Press,
1978.

Kluback, William. *Hermann Cohen: The Challenge of a Religion of Reason*. Chico,
Calif.: Scholars Press, 1984.

Kraft, R. A., and G.W.E. Nickelsburg, eds. *Early Judaism and Its Modern Interpreters*.
Philadelphia: Fortress Press, 1986.

Kulka, O. D., and P. R. Mendes-Flohr, eds. *Judaism and Christianity under the Impact
of National Socialism*. Jerusalem: The Historical Society of Israel and the
Zalman Shazar Center for Jewish History, 1987.

Küng, Hans. "Karl Barth and the Postmodern Paradigm." *The Princeton Seminary
Bulletin*, n.s., 11, no. 1 (1988): 8–31.

———. *Justification: The Doctrine of Karl Barth and a Catholic Reflection*. Translated
by Thomas Collins, Edmund E. Tolk, and David Granskou. Nashville, Tenn.:
Thomas Nelson and Sons, 1964.

Lampe, G.W.H., and K. J. Woollcombe. *Essays on Typology*. London: S.C.M. Press, 1957.

Lindbeck, George. "Barth and Textuality." *Theology Today* 43 (1986): 361–76.

Lindemann, W. *Barth und die Schriftauslegung*. Translated by Herbert Reich. Ham-
burg: Evangelischer Verlag, 1973.

D. Martin Luthers Werke. Kritische Gesamtausgabe. Weimar: Herman Böhlau,
1883– . Edited by Jaroslav Pelikan and translated by W. I. Brandt as *Luther's
Works*. St. Louis: Concordia Publishing House, 1962.

Mackintosh, H. R. *Types of Modern Theology*. New York: Charles Scribner's Sons, 1967.

Marquardt, Friedrich W. *Bedeutung der Landverheissung für die Christen*. Munich:
Christian Kaiser Verlag, 1964.

———. "Christentum und Zionismus." *Evangelische Theologie* 28 (1968): 629–60.

———. *Die Entdeckung des Judentums für die christliche Theologie: Israel im Denken
Karl Barths*. Munich: Christian Kaiser Verlag, 1967.

———. *Die Gegenwart des Auferstandenen bei seinem Volk Israel*. Munich: Christian
Kaiser Verlag, 1983.

———. *Die Juden im Römerbrief*. Zurich: Theologischer Verlag, 1971.

———. *Theologie und Sozialismus: Das Beispiel Karl Barths*. Munich: Christian Kaiser
Verlag, 1972.

Marshall, Bruce. *Christology in Conflict: The Identity of the Savior in Rahner and
Barth*. Oxford: Basil Blackwell, 1987.

McGarry, Michael B., CSP. *Christology after Auschwitz*. New York: Paulist Press, 1977.

Meynell, Hugo. *Grace versus Nature: Studies in Karl Barth's Church Dogmatics*. London: Sheed and Ward, 1965.

Mosse, George L. *The Crisis of German Ideology: Intellectual Origins of the Third Reich*. New York: Grosset and Dunlap, The Universal Library, 1964.

Mosse, Werner. *Entscheidungsjahr 1932: Zur Judenfrage in der Endphase der Weimarer Republik*. Ein Sammelband. Tübingen: J. C. B. Mohr, Paul Siebeck, 1965.

Mussner, Franz. *Tractate on the Jews: The Significance of Judaism for Christian Faith*. Translated by L. Swidler. Philadelphia: Fortress Press, 1984.

Niemöller, Martin. *Wort und Tat im Kirchenkampf*. Munich: Christian Kaiser Verlag, 1969.

"Notes on the Correct Way to Present Jews and Judaism in Preaching and Catechesis in the Roman Catholic Church." Vatican Commission for Religious Relations with the Jews, June 1985.

Nürnberger, K. *Glaube und Religion bei Karl Barth*. Marburg an der Lahn, Inaugural dissertation, 1967.

Obermann, Heiko. *Luther: Between God and the Devil*. New Haven: Yale University Press, 1988.

Oesterreicher, J. *Commentary on the Documents of Vatican 2*. New York: Herder and Herder, 1969.

Ogletree, Thomas W. *Christian Faith and History*. Nashville, Tenn.: Abington Press, 1965.

Parker, T.H.L. *Karl Barth*. Grand Rapids, Mich.: William Eerdmans, 1984.

Pawlikowski, John, OSM. *Christ in the Light of the Christian-Jewish Dialogue*. New York: Paulist Press, 1982.

Peck, Abraham. *Jews and Christians after the Holocaust*. Philadelphia: Fortress Press, 1982.

Petuchowski, Jakob. *Heirs of the Pharisees*. New York: Basic Books, 1970.

Quadt, Anno. *Gott und Mensch: Zur Theologie Karl Barths in ökumenischer Sicht*. Munich: Verlag Ferdinand Schöningh, 1976.

Ramsey, Paul, ed. *Faith and Ethics: The Theology of H. Richard Neibuhr*. New York: Harper and Brothers, 1957.

Rendtorff, Trutz. *Israel und sein Land*. Munich: Christian Kaiser Verlag, 1975.

Roberts, R. H. "The Ideal and the Real in the Theology of Karl Barth." In S. Sykes and J. D. Holmes, eds., *New Studies in Theology*. London: Duckworth Press, 1980.

Rosenstock-Huessy, Eugen. *Judaism Despite Christianity*. Tuscaloosa: University of Alabama Press, 1969.

Rosenzweig, Franz. *The Star of Redemption*. Translated by W. Hallo. Notre Dame: University of Notre Dame Press, 1985.

Ruether, Rosemary. *Faith and Fratricide: The Theological Roots of Anti-Semitism*. New York: Seabury Press, 1974.

Rumschiedt, Hans-Martin, ed. *Footnotes to a Theology: The Karl Barth Colloquium of 1972. Canadian Corporation for Studies in Religion, 1972*.

———. *Karl Barth in Review: Posthumous Works Reviewed and Assessed*. Pittsburgh: Pickwick Press, 1981.

———, ed. and trans. *Revelation and Theology: An Analysis of the Barth-Harnack Correspondence of 1923*. Cambridge: Cambridge University Press, 1972.

Ruschke, Werner. *Entstehung und Ausführung der Diastentheologie in Karl Barths zweiten "Römerbrief."* Neukirchen-Vluy: Neukirchener Verlag, 1987.

Sanders, E. P. *Paul and Palestinian Judaism*. Philadelphia: Fortress Press, 1977.

Schoeps, Hans-Joachim. *Jewish Christianity.* Translated by D. Haves. Philadelphia: Fortress Press, 1964.

Schulz, Hans-Jürgen. *Juden, Christen, Deutsche.* Stuttgart: Kreuz Verlag, 1961.

Schürer, Emil. *Geschichte des jüdischen Volkes im Zeitalter Jesus Christi.* 1885. Revised and edited by G. Vermes, F. Miller, and M. Black as *The History of the Jewish People in the Age of Jesus Christ.* Edinburgh: T. and T. Clark, 1979.

Smart, James, ed. *Revolutionary Theology in the Making: Barth-Thurneysen Correspondence, 1914–1922.* Richmond, Va.: John Knox Press, 1968.

Stendahl, Krister. "The Apostle Paul and the Introspective Conscience of the West." *Harvard Theological Review* 56 (1963): 199–215.

Sykes, S. W. *Karl Barth: Studies of His Theological Method.* Oxford: Clarendon Press, 1979.

Tal, Uriel. *Christians and Jews in Germany: Religion, Politics, and Ideology in the Second Reich, 1870–1914.* Translated by Noah Jonathan Jacobs. Ithaca: Cornell University Press, 1975.

van Buren, Paul. *A Theology of the Jewish Christian Reality.* Three Volumes. Vol. 1, *Discerning the Way.* Vol. 2, *A Christian Theology of the People Israel.* Vol. 3, *Christ in Context.* San Francisco: Harper & Row, 1980–88.

von Balthasar, Hans Urs. *Karl Barth: Darstellung und Deutung seiner Theologie.* Cologne: Hegner Verlag, 1951.

von Brück, Michael. *Möglichkeiten und Grenzen einer Theologie der Religionen.* Berlin: Evangelische Verlagsanstalt, 1979.

Wagner, Falk, W. Sparn, and F. W. Graf. *Die Realisierung der Freiheit.* Edited by Trutz Rendtorff. Gütersloh: Gütersloher Verlagshaus Gerd Mohn, 1975.

Wallace, Mark. "The World of the Text: Theological Hermeneutics in the Thought of Karl Barth and Paul Riceour." *Union Seminary Quarterly* 41, no. 1 (1986): 1–15.

Wolf, E., and A. Lempp, eds. *Theologische Aufsätze: Karl Barth zum 50. Geburtstag.* Munich: Christian Kaiser Verlag, 1936.

Wyschogrod, Michael. "The Law, Jews and Gentiles—A Jewish Perspective." *Lutheran Quarterly* 24, no. 4 (November 1969): 405–15.

INDEX